John James Lias

The doctrinal system of St. John:

Considered as evidence for the date of his gospel

John James Lias

The doctrinal system of St. John:
Considered as evidence for the date of his gospel

ISBN/EAN: 9783337714284

Printed in Europe, USA, Canada, Australia, Japan

Cover: Foto ©ninafisch / pixelio.de

More available books at **www.hansebooks.com**

THE

DOCTRINAL SYSTEM

OF

ST. JOHN,

CONSIDERED AS EVIDENCE FOR THE DATE OF HIS GOSPEL.

BY THE

REV. J. J. LIAS, M.A.,

PROFESSOR OF MODERN LITERATURE AND LECTURER IN HEBREW AT ST. DAVID'S COLLEGE, LAMPETER;

AND SOMETIME SCHOLAR OF EMMANUEL COLLEGE, CAMBRIDGE.

"For all the doctrinal matter characteristic of St. John (and on this argument the greatest stress should be laid) some parallels at least can be found in the Synoptical Gospels and Epistles." — THOLUCK, *Commentary on St. John, Introduction.*

LONDON: GEORGE BELL AND SONS, YORK STREET, COVENT GARDEN.

1875.

LONDON:
PRINTED BY WILLIAM CLOWES AND SONS
STAMFORD STREET AND CHARING CROSS.

PREFACE.

THE inquiry contained in the following pages has been carried on slowly and with difficulty in the intervals of leisure afforded by a life devoted to other studies. It originated in a remark made some years ago to a friend whose reputation stands high as a scholar and as a preacher, that St. John's Gospel was the necessary bridge over the chasm which separates the theology of the Synoptic Gospels from that of the Epistles, and that if its genuineness be denied, it becomes impossible to account for the origin of the doctrines taught by St. Peter and St. Paul, and received by the universal Church. The encouragement I received from my friend induced me to examine the subject more in detail, and the result is now before the public.

When I had advanced some way in the investigation I had proposed myself, Mr. Sanday's book appeared; when it was almost concluded, and when little remained to be done but to put its results into shape, the Boyle Lectures of Mr. Stanley Leathes were given to the world. As the subject of the former book appeared to be the same as my own, I took it up with some fear that my labour might have been in vain, and my conclusions anticipated by another. I was relieved to find that, notwithstanding the similarity of subject, the treatment was so different that Mr. Sanday's able Essay had only one or two points of contact with my own. It is, however, some time since I saw his Essay, and I may possibly have touched a little more on common ground when I came to say a few words on the Jewish element in St. John's Gospel. I have judged it best to avoid reading the treatise of Mr. Leathes, feeling that, as I had gone so far, I might as well publish what I had written, since if I did not happen to go over the same ground as Mr. Leathes, this essay would not be superfluous, while if I did, I should only be confirming his arguments by an independent testimony.

In the endeavour to make what I have written useful to intelligent readers who are not well acquainted with foreign languages, I have translated most of the passages from the Fathers; while in German I have availed myself of the excellent translations published by Messrs. Clark and Co., the more readily, in that I did not happen to have ready access to the originals. I should also add that I have frequently adopted a literal rendering of the Greek Testament, when it seemed to make clearer the bearing of the passage cited in my argument.

I ought to add that the method I have here adopted was first suggested to me by Dr. Liddon's Bampton Lectures. He applies to the one particular doctrine of the Divinity of Christ the comparative mode of treatment, which I have extended to all the leading doctrines of Christianity. As I read those Lectures, it appeared to me that their method was capable of such extension, though I should most probably never have attempted it myself, but for the encouragement to which I have alluded.

I have judged it best to assume the genuineness of St. Paul's Epistles. To have entered into a discussion of the theories of the Tübingen school on this subject would have been beside my point, and would have added much to the bulk and little to the interest of this essay. But I cannot place much reliance on criticism whose results change day by day like the images in a kaleidoscope, and whose only claim to attention is that its last phase is confidently presented to the public by the periodical press of the hour as "the conclusions at which modern criticism has arrived."

I fear that in a work written at such uncertain intervals of time, and corrected in ill-health and under much stress of other work, many repetitions will be found. I can but ask the indulgent reader to excuse them.

It only remains to express a hope that what I have written may not, like many crude though well-intended efforts, serve to injure the cause it was meant to advance, but, on the contrary, may help to remove the doubts which have been so widely disseminated, and sometimes so keenly felt, concerning the authenticity of the most important book, as I venture to think, in the Sacred Canon.

CONTENTS.

INTRODUCTION.

Ancient and modern ideas concerning the origin of St. John's Gospel—Its purpose as stated by the author—Reasons for doubting its authenticity—Difference between the Synoptists and St. John in their mode of presenting Christ to their readers—Epistle-writers, with the exception of St. James, identical with St. John in their conceptions—Synoptists, with one exception, the companions and pupils of St. Peter and St. Paul—No evidence in ecclesiastical history of any disagreement among the original teachers of Christianity in their doctrine concerning Christ—The only countenance to such an opinion to be found in criticism—Object of the present treatise to ascertain whether criticism lends any real countenance to it 1-15

PART I.

THE DOCTRINAL SYSTEM OF ST. JOHN COMPARED WITH THAT OF THE OTHER WRITERS OF THE NEW TESTAMENT.

CHAPTER I.

THE NATURE AND ATTRIBUTES OF GOD.

Speedy declension from the Apostolic model, whether shared by the author of the fourth Gospel or not—His doctrine of God—Fundamental principle, *God is Spirit*—Truth—Life—Light—Love—Beyond the reach of our intellects—The Author of all Being—Significant absence of any philosophy of the Infinite—Personality of God—Plurality of Persons—Ultimate union of humanity with God excluding pantheistic conceptions—Doctrine of the Synoptists—Absence of some of these fundamental conceptions supplied in Acts—St. Stephen's doctrine of the nature of God identical with that of St. John—Coincidence of phraseology between St. John and the two remarkable passages St. Matt. xi. 27 and St. Luke x. 22 — General agreement between the Evangelists in their teaching concerning God—Doctrine of the Epistles—God is Spirit—Above the reach of human language—Truth—Light—Life—Love—His Unity—Plurality of Persons — Avoid pantheism—Combine simplicity with mysterious depth in precisely the same manner as St. John—Complete harmony between all the New Testament writers on this head 16-32

CHAPTER II.

DOCTRINE OF THE LOGOS AND THE PERSON OF CHRIST.

Origin of St. John's doctrine of the Logos—Opinions of Tholuck—Neander—Dorner—St. Paul not less guilty than St. John of appropriating "Philonian" expressions—These "Philonian" expressions older than Philo—Peculiar suitability of the word Logos to express the Christian doctrine of the Person of Christ—Correspondence of Old Testament expressions with those of St. John regarding the Logos—Foreshadowings in the writings of the other Apostles of St. John's supposed peculiar use of the word Logos—St. John's doctrine of the Person of Christ—His Divinity—Derived from that of the Father—Yet equal with Him, and possessing a distinct personality—And perfect man—Doctrine of St. John's Epistle—Of the Apocalypse—Identical with that of the fourth Gospel—Synoptic Gospels—Their humanitarianism less emphatic than that of St. John—Tacit assumption of Divine authority by Jesus Christ—Supernatural power residing in Him—Portents attending His birth—Application of Old Testament passages to Him in which the Incommunicable Name is found—If not a formal, yet a virtual assertion of His Godhead—Doctrine of the Acts—Disputed passage in Acts xx. 28—Other passages—Doctrine of St. Peter

Contents.

and St. James—Absence of any attempt of the latter to combat St. Paul, after whom he wrote—Identity of the conceptions of the former with those of St. John—Doctrine of St. Paul—Assertion of the same paradox—The highest attributes of Divinity combined with those of humanity—Singular agreement on a question of much complexity 33–64

CHAPTER III.

DOCTRINE OF THE INCARNATION.

Feeble hold of modern theology on the Incarnation—Anthropology of St. John—σάρξ and πνεῦμα—Salvation of σάρξ through πνεῦμα, effected by Jesus Christ—Similar doctrine of the Epistle—Agency of the Spirit—Laws of the higher life—Birth—Nourishment—The Sacraments—Condition on man's part, faith—Supposed tendency of St. Paul to base his system on faith, St. John on love—God's and man's part in the work of salvation—Faith—Love—The Church, the company of believers—Summary of St. John's doctrine—The Synoptists—Their Anthropology—St. John's doctrine of the life from above implied—Faith—The Sacraments—The Church—The Acts—Gospel the revelation of Life—Office of the Spirit—The Sacraments—Faith—St. John's theory of the Church exemplified in the Acts—St. Paul—From whom did he derive his system?—Nature of the system—Communication of life and light to lost humanity—Justification by *imparted* as well as *imputed* righteousness—Regeneration—Agency of the Spirit — The Sacraments — Faith — Love—The Church—Summary of his teaching—St. James, St. Peter, and St. Jude—St. James's doctrine of Regeneration, the engrafted Word, of the possibility of working righteousness—His Epistle either identical with the other New Testament writings, or opposed to Christianity altogether—St. Peter: his Anthropology—Christ our Life—The Sacraments — Faith—Love—The Church—Singular reference by him to St. John xxi.—Remarkable agreement of the doctrine of the fourth Gospel with the rest of the New Testament 65–134

CHAPTER IV.

THE DOCTRINE OF PROPITIATION.

Teaching of the fourth Gospel concerning sin—Propitiation —Use of the word ἱλασμός in the Epistle—The Synoptists —St. Paul—Epistle to the Hebrews, the formal treatise on Sacrificial Atonement—Significance of the silence of St. James on the doctrine of Propitiation 135-142

CHAPTER V.

THE NATURE AND OFFICE OF THE HOLY SPIRIT.

Personality of the Holy Ghost—His threefold office, expressed by the term Paraclete—St. John's teaching the germ of all we find elsewhere—Agreement of St. John's Epistle and the Apocalypse—Meaning of the "seven spirits" in the latter—Synoptic doctrine—St. Paul's an expansion of the teaching of the four Gospels—St. Peter and St. Jude— —Epistle to the Hebrews explains why Christ must depart before the Comforter could be sent—Promise of the Holy Ghost, referred to in the Acts and elsewhere, only recorded by St. John—Holy Ghost in the after-history of the Church "convinces men of sin, of righteousness, and of judgment" 143-158

CHAPTER VI.

THE DOCTRINE OF THE RESURRECTION AND THE FINAL JUDGMENT.

St. John's doctrine of the Resurrection and of future retribution—Its point of view different from that of the Apocalypse—The Acts confirm the hypothesis that the teaching of St. John's Gospel is the doctrine preached by Christ— St. Paul's agreement yet more thorough—St. James— St. Peter—Conclusion 159-170

Contents.

PART II.

THE PRIORITY OF THE DOCTRINAL SYSTEM OF THE FOURTH GOSPEL.

CHAPTER I.

ST. JOHN AND THE THEOLOGY OF THE SECOND CENTURY.

St. John, if writing in the second century, must display acquaintance with its literature, and especially with the writings of St. Paul—Whether his Gospel contains traces of acquaintance with Valentinus or Basilides—The Prologue contradicts the leading Gnostic doctrines—St. John's doctrine of the Being of God at variance with Gnostic conceptions—The same the case with his view of the Trinity, the Incarnation, the Atonement, and the Resurrection—St. John's conceptions concerning the world, the devil, angels, &c., irreconcilable with the Gnostic systems—Grounds on which the allegations have been made—St. John's supposed use of Gnostic terms—The terms not Gnostic, but Jewish—The fourth Gospel and Montanism —Montanism not a perversion of St. John's Gospel, but of other Scriptures—The term Paraclete a proof of the priority of the fourth Gospel—If the fourth Gospel be a second-century forgery, who forged it? 171–201

CHAPTER II.

ST. JOHN AND THE APOCRYPHAL GOSPELS AND ACTS.

The Apocryphal Gospels avoid doctrine—Simply history blended with legend—Gospels of the Infancy—Gospels of the Passion—Apocryphal Acts 202–207

CHAPTER III.

THE FOURTH GOSPEL AND THE EPISTLES.

Prologue of St. John bears evidence of a later date—The contrary the case with the discourses—Absence of theological terms in them—Such terms of constant occurrence in the Epistles—Nothing in St. John's discourses which could have been spoken save in the infancy of Christianity—The doctrinal matter of St. John always more elementary in form than in the Epistles—Examples—Doctrine of the being of God—Incarnation—Propitiation—Office of the Spirit—Antagonism between the Spirit and the Flesh—Lesser doctrines of the Gospel—Slavery and Freedom—Sanctification — Election — Grace — Peace—Truth—Two-fold conception of the κόσμος—Jewish tendencies of the fourth Gospel—Spiritualizing interpretation of the Old Testament—Conversion of the Gentiles—Undesigned coincidence—Theory of Christian worship 208–248

CONCLUSION.

Result of the inquiry—Discordance between the Gospels much exaggerated—Close connection between their writers and those of the Epistles—Originality of thought and expression in St. John's Gospel—Absence of Gnostic ideas—Of Pauline or Petrine ideas or expressions—Pauline and Petrine language unauthorized by Christ if the fourth Gospel be spurious—Language of discourses in St. John's Gospel the original language of the Founder of a religion, not the later inventions of a disciple—Bridges over the chasm otherwise existing between the Christ of history and the Christ of theology—The development theory of Christ's Divinity, acknowledged to have no historical, shown to have also no critical basis—St. John's Gospel the necessary link between the Scriptures, the absence of which reduces the history of Christianity to chaos 249–256

APPENDIX.

	PAGE
I. On Grace	257–260
II. On Justification	261–263
III. On the traces of Johannean Theology in the Second Century	264–271
IV. On the connection between St. John's Gospel and the Old Testament	272–284
V. On the Last Supper	285, 286
VI. Supplementary Observations	287, 288

THE

DOCTRINAL SYSTEM OF ST. JOHN.

members of the Alexandrian school of theology, a man of extensive learning and high intellectual gifts, and a critic of no mean capacity. He flourished scarcely a century after the Apostolic era, and he had access to many sources of information which have since been lost. For nearly eighteen hundred years this account of the origin of the fourth Gospel has been believed. An hypothesis, however, has lately been put forth, with great confidence and much plausibility, that Clement was mistaken; that he had been imposed upon by a forgery not fifty years old at the date at which he wrote, and that,

ERRATA.

Page 11, last line (note), *for* " their," *read* " his."
,, 12, first line (note), *for* " he," *read* " Marcion."
,, 81, line 15, *for* " his," *read* " St. John's."
,, 138, ,, 2, *for* "by effusion," *read* " by *the* effusion."
,, 142, ,, 18, *for* "in the Gospels," *read* " in the first three Gospels."
,, ,, ,, 19, *for* " Epistles," *read* " fourth."
,, 169, ,, 7, *omit* " than."
,, ,, ,, 8, *omit* " that."
,, 235, *dele* note.

THE

DOCTRINAL SYSTEM OF ST. JOHN.

INTRODUCTION.

A WRITER at the beginning of the third century gives the following account of the origin of the Gospel which goes by the name of St. John. The Apostle, he tells us, perceiving that the three Gospels previously published confined themselves chiefly to the deeds done in the Body by the Lord Jesus Christ, and urged by his friends to place on record the higher spiritual teaching of his Master, composed the Gospel which is now attributed to him. This statement is made by Clement of Alexandria, one of the most distinguished members of the Alexandrian school of theology, a man of extensive learning and high intellectual gifts, and a critic of no mean capacity. He flourished scarcely a century after the Apostolic era, and he had access to many sources of information which have since been lost. For nearly eighteen hundred years this account of the origin of the fourth Gospel has been believed. An hypothesis, however, has lately been put forth, with great confidence and much plausibility, that Clement was mistaken; that he had been imposed upon by a forgery not fifty years old at the date at which he wrote, and that,

B

whatever be the literary value of the Gospel which goes by the name of St. John, and whatever its use as bearing witness to the prevalent tone of theological feeling in the middle of the second century, it is absolutely worthless as an authentic tradition of the sayings and doings of Jesus Christ. The object of these pages is to examine this alleged forgery, to compare its theological system with that of other writings of more generally acknowledged authority,[1] and to inquire whether there is any proof from this point of view of the later origin for which many in our own day so strenuously contend.

We are not left to guess the purpose for which the Gospel in question was written. It is stated in express language by the author: "These things have been written that ye might believe that Jesus is the Son of God, and that, believing, ye might have life through His name."[2] Let us assume for a moment that the ordinary belief about its origin is the true one. Under what circumstances then was the Gospel composed? It is admitted on all hands that, if written by St. John, it

[1] The genuineness of several of St. Paul's Epistles is also vehemently impugned by some critics. In these pages we have assumed the genuineness of them all. But inasmuch as the most important of St. Paul's Epistles are not contested, and as the great bulk of our citations will be made from them, our argument will be little affected by the fact that the canonicity, e.g., of the Pastoral Epistles is disputed by some.

[2] St. John xx. 31. The writer rejects all which does not advance this object. He relates (1) such matter as will manifest the Divine power and authority of Christ and thus lead to the conviction that He is the Son of God, and (2) such as may bear on the communication of a supernatural vitality from Christ to His disciples, and thus might enable them to "have life through His name."—See Hug, 'Einleitung,' sec. 48.

Introduction. 3

was written at the close of his life. The Apostles were all dead but himself. They had left Epistles behind them, professing to be based on the teaching of Christ, but there was a marked difference between the theological principles enunciated in the Epistles, and those contained in the memoirs of Christ which had as yet appeared. These were simple biographies of His human life, with some of His more striking parables and moral exhortations subjoined. But for some reason or other, they said little or nothing of those deeper truths which formed the main feature in the epistolary literature of the Apostolic Church. Much was said of the life and teaching of Jesus Christ while on earth, but only the vaguest hints were preserved (as in Matt. xxviii., and Mark xvi., if the latter be genuine) of the nature of the relations which were to subsist between the Saviour and His disciples after His Ascension. At the same time, error was very prevalent. "Philosophy, falsely so called," was entrapping the votaries of the Cross. As years rolled on the writings of the Apostles assumed a more sombre colouring. St. Paul, St. Peter, and St. Jude vie with one another in the sternness with which they denounce the heresies which threaten the peace of the infant Church.[1] But as yet there was no record

[1] The Epistles of St. Paul's imprisonment are obviously inspired by a feeling of dangers more pressing than any which were apprehended in the earlier years of his ministry. So St. Peter's Second Epistle is far severer in its language than the first. Hug remarks how St. John's Epistle bears witness to the denial of Jesus as the Son of God.— 'Einleitung,' part ii. sec. 49. "That the Gospel of St. John did not owe its origin to any mere impulse to write on the part of the author, but to an historical, practical necessity for its existence in the Church, I think I have shown in opposition to my friend Luthardt."—Ebrard, 'Introduction to St. John's Gospel.'

of the deeper spiritual utterances of Christ, which had formed the basis of Apostolic preaching and teaching. Hitherto they had subsisted in oral tradition only; handed on from one to another as the most sacred deposit of the faith, too sacred to be profaned by common eyes and ears. But now the disciples of St. John appealed to him. Was it well, they said, to leave the Church without a record of that oral teaching which had permeated the Church so widely and borne such admirable fruit. Since error was so dangerous and seductive, might not those profound and touching words of Christ which had sunk so deeply into the Apostle's heart,[1] be soon forgotten or denied if left on the precarious footing of tradition. The Apostle responded to their solicitations. It was *not* well, he declared. The Church must not be left without an authentic record of those living words of Christ which had been the root of his own spiritual life, and of the spiritual life of those to whom he had imparted the Gospel. The strong meat might have been hitherto kept back because there were so many into whose hands it might have fallen who as yet were unable to bear it.[2] But now the pressure of necessity forbade the Apostle to withhold it any longer. He must take in hand the task which no living man but himself could perform; and leave to the world a true report of those mysterious discourses of Christ which were the groundwork of His religion; containing a philosophy, so to speak, of

---

[1] More deeply, perhaps, than into the heart of any of the others. See Hengstenberg, 'Commentary on St. John,' Concluding Observations.

[2] 1 Cor. iii. 1.

Christianity;[1] an exposition of the spiritual truths which underlie its sacraments; a proclamation of the eternal relations between Christ and every believer in His Word.

There is nothing inherently improbable in this explanation of the origin of the fourth Gospel, and, as we have said, it has been universally accepted until within a comparatively recent period. But when that school of criticism arose which has subjected the contents of each book of the New Testament to a far more minute and unsparing analysis than had before been deemed necessary, it was soon discovered that the character of the discourses recorded in the fourth Gospel differed materially from that presented by the discourses contained in the other three.[2] The suggestion was made, doubtfully at first, and then with increasing confidence, that the Gospel was not the composition of the Apostle whose name it bears, but that it must be assigned to another and a later hand. It was the offspring, in fact, of the epoch when the intense and fervent admiration felt by His disciples for Christ had passed into a belief in His Divinity. When once launched upon this track,

[1] "John gives us not merely a history of the external life of Jesus, but in some measure also a philosophy of this history."—Grimm, 'Trustworthiness of the Evangelic Narratives,' p. 66.

[2] Evanson, an Englishman, was the first—if we except an anonymous author about a century earlier—to raise the question in 1792, and was followed by Herder. Nearly thirty years elapsed before Bretschneider revived it in his 'Probabilia,' but he afterwards confessed that he had been wrong. A host of critics have since arisen who have maintained the same thesis with less candour or more resolution. See Reville, 'Revue des Deux Mondes,' 1 Mai, 1866, p. 99, and Liddon, 'Bampton Lectures' (1st Ed.), p. 312, seq. M. Reville has the candour to admit, while assailing the Gospel himself, that former attacks have been successfully repulsed.

the critics grew bolder still. Not only moral and metaphysical, but historical divergences were brought to light, which detracted still more from the credit of the later Gospel.[1] The hand of the forger could be detected alike in what was said and in what was left unsaid.[2] His Christ became an abstract ideal, devoid of reality. The characters introduced upon the scene " lack colouring," are " outside the sphere of real life," and the like.[3] The very fundamental conceptions of Christ's system as presented in this Gospel are so opposed to what we meet elsewhere, that it is quite impossible to acknowledge it as a genuine production of the Apostolic age.[4] It is our purpose to analyse the

[1] St. John mentions three passovers, we are told, while the other Evangelists only speak of one.
[2] The Evangelist " believes that no prophet arose out of Galilee!" — 'Revue des Deux Mondes,' Mai 1866, p. 113. "St. John's name does not once appear!"—*Ib.* p. 106.
[3] According to M. Reville, this is true of the woman of Samaria and of the blind man, in chap. ix.! Strauss also ('Leben Jesu,' part ii. chap. vii. sec. 83) complains that "the interlocutors do not speak in conformity with their position and character." Criticism of this kind carries with it so much evidence of a foregone conclusion that it disposes men rather to the opposite opinion. The absence of St. John's name is, *quoad hoc*, an argument *for* the genuineness of the Gospel. And he who does not perceive the life-like character of the narratives in chaps. iv. and ix. must be devoid of all sense of dramatic reality. Since these words were penned, Canon Westcott has spoken strongly at the Brighton Congress in support of the opinion they express. After observing how entirely we owe our conceptions of the chief friends and enemies of Christ, with the single exception of St. Peter, to the fourth Gospel, he adds "it is barely conceivable that the writer may have been an *unknown Shakespeare*."
[4] M. Reville ('Revue des Deux Mondes,' as above) goes so far as to say that coming to Christ is nowhere in the Synoptists said to be a *sine quâ non*. One is tempted to the belief that Matt. xxviii. 19 must have been absent from his copies of the Gospels, and that he has never happened to light upon Acts iii. 12. He would naturally deny the

doctrinal system of St. John's Gospel, to compare it with that presented on examination by the productions of Apostles and Evangelists whose genuineness is generally admitted, and to ascertain what evidence there is for these assertions.

That there is a marked difference between the discourses of our Lord, as recorded in the three former and in the fourth Gospel, is a position which can hardly be seriously contested. Though the Synoptists claim for Christ the very highest powers and dignities, they do not in express words declare Him to be God. And they say little or nothing of the necessity of a personal and inward union with His Being, of a continual communication of life and strength from Him, doctrines which it would appear to be the main object of the fourth Gospel to disseminate. With the Synoptists Christ is the preacher of righteousness; yet though this righteousness, it is true, is of a more exalted type than any teacher had yet conceived of, Christ is not Himself put forward as the source from which that righteousness proceeds. With the exception of one remarkable passage, to which we shall advert at greater length hereafter, no hint is given of the peculiar intermediate position in which the Son stands between the Father and mankind as the sole channel for the communication of life.[1]

---

genuineness of the last twelve verses of St. Mark's Gospel. But the passage above cited from a work by St. Luke is as strong as any that can be found in St. John. And it should be remembered in the passage cited from St. Matthew (1) that the words rendered "in the name" are εἰς τὸ ὄνομα in the original, and (2) that the name stands in the Scriptures for the person named.

[1] M. Reville, in the above-cited article, p. 120, admits that the

But while admitting to the full the fact of this divergence, we are met at the outset by another fact which does much to diminish the significance of the former. These assertions of the Divinity of Christ, this continual mention of His intimate union with His Father, of His indwelling within the soul of those who come to Him by faith, of Life, Light, Truth, Grace, Arche, Pleroma, which are supposed by some to indicate the later origin of the fourth Gospel,[1] are to be found with equal frequency in the Epistles. They form the groundwork of the teaching of St. Paul and St. Peter, and, though not so completely, of St. James also. The difference between the theological stand-point of the two former Apostles and that of the Synoptists[2] is as irreconcilable as that between them and St. John, while the differences between St. John's Gospel and the Epistles of these two Apostles will be found to be more apparent than real. Nor is this all. Two of the Synoptic Gospels were written by men who were in close and intimate connection with these Apostles. St. Mark is designated by St. Peter as "his son,"[3] and though between St. Mark and St. Paul there was a long estrangement,[4] yet it was entirely of a personal, not of a controversial, nature, and it finally ceased to exist.[5] St. Luke was in the closest and most intimate compa-

---

evangelic cycle would not have been complete in the absence of a biography which essayed to represent the spiritual side of the character of Christ.

[1] See Schenkel, 'Sketch of the Character of Jesus,' and M. Revillo in the above-cited article.

[2] Hengstenberg, in his 'Commentary on St. John,' complains of this ill-sounding title, but submits to it as an inevitable necessity.

[3] 1 Pet. v. 13.   [4] Acts xv. 38.   [5] Col. iv. 10.

nionship with St. Paul for years, and there was the most thorough confidence between them. The cause, then, of the undeniable difference between the theology of the Epistles and that of the Synoptists, cannot be attributed to an hostility on the part of the latter to the views maintained in the former. Nor can we suppose that St. Luke, whose careful scrutiny of all authentic information, oral or written, that came within his reach is avowed as his sole claim to the attention of his readers,[1] would have attached himself to St. Paul if he had been aware of the existence of a party opposed to him, which was more scrupulously careful to adhere to the original principles of the Christian faith. The contents of the Acts of the Apostles are sufficient to refute such a supposition. The form of that treatise is clearly determined by the anxiety St. Luke felt to make it clear that St. Paul was only anxious to keep within the lines marked out for Christ's ministers from the beginning of the Gospel.[2] That there were differences in the Christian body he is willing to admit. But he makes it quite plain what those differences were. They regarded the relations of Christianity to the religion from which it had sprung. They were not the offspring of any radical diversity in the conception of Christianity itself. For while the author of the Acts, in relating occurrences which took place after the dispensation of the Spirit was fully at work, does not fail to drop hints

[1] St. Luke i. 1-3.
[2] This is surely the reason of his commencing with the ministry of St. Peter, of his following the career of that Apostle only as far as the conversion of Cornelius, as also of the introduction of the episode of St. Stephen, where the principles are enunciated which St. Paul followed out to their legitimate conclusion.

occasionally of the deeper teaching of the Apostles,[1] he says not a word of any disagreement between them concerning the person of Christ. Differences on a far less fundamental point had power to rend the Mohammedan body asunder from the very first.[2] It is hardly conceivable, as matter of history, that while a comparatively trifling controversy is recorded concerning the obligation of the Gentiles to keep the Jewish law, not one word should be let fall to indicate that the Apostles were not of one mind about the position occupied by Christ in the scheme of salvation, had such been the case. And as the leaders of the two great parties, St. Peter and St. Paul were clearly agreed upon this point,[3] we require at least some evidence to prove that there were others of the Apostolic band who entered into conflict with their leaders on behalf of the primitive purity of Christian tradition.

There is not one single passage in the Scriptures themselves to warrant the conclusion.[4] And the silence of ecclesiastical history is equally remarkable.

[1] As in the allusion to the Gospel as the words of Life, ch. v. 20; to Christ as the Source of Life, ch. iii. 15; and to Justification by Faith, ch. xiii. 39.

[2] The Sonnites and the Shiites, Gibbon, 'Decline and Fall,' ch. 50. The question whether the Founder of a religion left a Vicar behind Him on earth is surely not more fundamental than whether He be God or man.

[3] See Part I. Chapters ii., iii.

[4] Yet it is confidently maintained by Schwegler, who believes that the original teachers of Christianity were enabled to maintain a semblance of unity, while at the same time rent asunder by fundamental differences. If this be historical fact, it is at least without parallel in the world's history. "Is it likely," asks Tertullian (De Præscr. adv. Hær. 28), "that so many and so great churches should have gone astray into one and the same faith?" "Error in doctrine," he continues, "must of necessity have produced various results."

Introduction. 11

There were many heretics, but there was scarcely one who ventured to assert that Apostolic tradition was in his favour. The Gnostics were humanitarians after their fantastic fashion, but they appealed to no Christian authority on behalf of their creed, and they were energetically opposed by the whole body of doctrinally orthodox Christians, in spite of the divisions among themselves.[1] The Ebionites were humanitarians, but they rejected with equal impartiality St. Peter and St. Paul, the Synoptists and St. John, and contented themselves with a mutilated Gospel of St. Matthew.[2] The school of Theodotus and Artemon made a feeble attempt to represent their doctrines as the original doctrines of the Christian Church, but they supported it by no evidence.[3] And Marcion, who seems to have endeavoured to mediate between Gnosticism and the Church, rejects impartially the Synoptists and St. John, and fixes on a mutilated Gospel of St. Luke, and such portions as he chose to accept of the Epistles of St. Paul.[4] When we remember how

[1] Tertullian, after he had separated from the Church, remained a violent opponent of Gnosticism.
[2] This would seem to be the conclusion at which the generality of inquirers have arrived. Whether there were an Hebrew original of St. Matthew's Gospel or not, it is generally agreed that the Ebionitish Gospel of the Hebrews of which St. Jerome speaks is not that Gospel. See Alford, 'Prolegomena to the Gospels,' chap. ii. sec. ii.; Westcott, 'Introduction to the Study of the Gospels,' p. 225. Iren. 'Contr. Hær.' i. 26, asserts that they accepted the Gospel of St. Matthew, but Eus. 'Eccl. Hist.' iii. 27, calls it the Gospel according to the Hebrews. Hippolytus is silent on the subject.
[3] See the account of the rise of this school in Eusebius, 'Eccl. Hist.' v. 28.
[4] Iren. 'Contr. Hær.' I. xxvii. 2, 4. Irenæus seems more angry with Marcion for daring to mutilate the Scriptures than with other heretics for rejecting them altogether. But it is at least clear from their

jealously Apostolic tradition was guarded,[1] and how eagerly it was sought after in the early Church,[2] this silence of history is not a little surprising. And when we add to this the facts that the early opponents of Christianity, in endeavouring to bring arguments from the divisions among Christians, have been obliged to make the most of the trifling dissensions spoken of in the Acts and in the Epistle to the Galatians,[3] and that the ecclesiastical writers of the second and third centuries, when referring to Apostolic tradition, do so

account that he abandoned many of the distinctive tenets of Gnosticism. Tertullian ('Adv. Marc.' IV. i.-iv.) enters into arguments for the genuineness of the four Gospels, which prove that the early Church was not entirely ignorant of the science of criticism.

[1] The Quarto-Deciman controversy is an evidence of this. It was elevated into importance solely by the fact that both sides pleaded Apostolic tradition. The presbyter, Tertullian tells us, who fabricated the spurious Acts of Paul and Thecla was deposed for so doing. De Baptismo, 16.

[2] Iren. 'Contr. Hær.' III. iv. 1: "If concerning some ordinary question there were a discussion, would it not be our duty to recur to the oldest Churches, and to ascertain from them what is certain and clear in the matter? For, supposing the Apostles had left no Scriptures, would it not be our duty to follow the order of the tradition which they handed down to those to whom they committed the Churches?" So also Tert. 'De Præscr. adv. Hær.' xxxvi.

[3] Marcion (Tert. 'Adv. Marc.' iv. 3), the heretics generally (Tert. 'De Præscr. adv. Hær.' xxiii.), and Porphyry make the most of the trifling disagreement in Gal. ii. I do not remember seeing it noticed that Marcion, who was contemporary with Polycarp, and met him at Rome A.D. 160, is especially charged in the above-cited passage in Tertullian with having endeavoured to undermine the credit of those Gospels which were published as authentic (*propria*) and *under the name of Apostles*. Marcion does not deny their genuineness, be it observed, but asserts that their writers are the "false Apostles" spoken of by St. Paul. M. Reville (p. 115) remarks that "had Marcion had access to the fourth Gospel, he could not have failed to mould it to his views." It would seem from the passage just mentioned that he had seen it, and did not find it so pliable as has been imagined.

Introduction. 13

in entire unconsciousness of any absence of agreement among the Apostles, it must be admitted that history gives no support to the theory of fundamental divergencies in the Apostolic conceptions of Christ and His scheme of salvation. Whatever claim, therefore, the supposition that the humanitarian was the original creed of the disciples, and that it was a later school which pushed its reverence for Christ so far as to assert His Divinity, may have on our acceptance, it must be admitted to rest on critical considerations alone.

To criticism, therefore, let us betake ourselves. We will endeavour to scrutinise minutely the doctrinal system of St. John, and compare it with that of the Synoptists on the one hand, and with that of the Epistle writers on the other. We will compare it also with the systems in existence at the time in which it has been supposed to have originated; and we will thus endeavour to ascertain whether it be indeed the product of a later age, or whether the theory be true that the Synoptists were actuated in their reticence by a desire not to cast pearls before swine—not to make too heavy demands at first upon the faith of their readers, but to induce them first to acquaint themselves with the human character of Christ, confident that if they were once brought into contact with a character at once so pure, so majestic, and so tender, with teaching so far exceeding in moral elevation that of all former times, they could not fail in the end to exclaim with the centurion, "Truly this was the Son of God."

But it must be remembered in common fairness that, in the absence of historical evidence, the internal evidence of the later origin of the fourth Gospel ought to be absolutely unequivocal. It is quite true that a careful scrutiny of documents has often led to the rewriting of history, and that no forgery, however skilful, has been able to bear the test of close investigation. But, on the other hand, the establishment of the fact that a document is forged must not rest upon assumption and conjecture—upon bold assertions and foregone conclusions. No mere general dissimilarity in colouring and tone can be relied on. It must be shown beyond a doubt that reference is made to opinions or facts unknown at the time to which the writing is ascribed. If the fourth Gospel be really written under the influence of Gnostic and Montanistic thought of the second century,[1] we must have not merely vague general assertions of the fact, but specific allegations, supported by quotations of which there can be no doubt. It must be made clear that the Gospel derived its ideas from Basilides and Valentinus, and not they from it. Otherwise, the utmost that the opponents of its genuineness will have a right to say is, that they regard it as suspicious. They can have no right to speak as though their case were proved.

We will proceed, then, to our inquiry. We will ask, first, whether there be that amount of divergence between the fourth Gospel and the other books of the New Testament which has been alleged. Next, we will inquire into the allegation that its writer was indebted for many of his ideas to the Gnostics of the

[1] So says M. Reville, in the above-cited article. Others (as Strauss, Schenkel, &c.) are content with assigning a Gnostic origin to its peculiarities. According to Schwegler, it was invented to mediate between Montanism (which he seems to identify with Ebionitism!) and Paulinism. See Ebrard 'Gospel Hist.' p. 34-36.

Introduction.

second century. We will then proceed to compare the Gospel with those which are confessedly spurious, and then with the acknowledged writings of St. Peter and St. Paul, in order to ascertain which of them contains the more primitive form of Christian theology. The examination must needs be minute; possibly to many it will be wearisome. But let it be remembered that only thus can we arrive at a candid conclusion. The more complete the analysis, the more certain the result. Not until we have thoroughly sifted the contents of the Gospel can we be in a position to judge whether it be a forgery of the second century or the genuine composition of an Apostle of Christ.

PART I.

THE DOCTRINAL SYSTEM OF ST. JOHN COMPARED WITH
THAT OF THE OTHER WRITERS OF THE
NEW TESTAMENT.

CHAPTER I.

THE NATURE AND ATTRIBUTES OF GOD.

Our first subject of inquiry will be the *theology*, properly so called, of the fourth Gospel, that is to say, its doctrine concerning the Being of God. On no subject did the Christian Church so soon decline from the spirit of her first teachers as on this. The tender and loving Father on whose perfections Christ and His Apostles delight to dwell, Who wills that all men shall be saved, Who loves the world so deeply that He gave His only-begotten Son to save it from its corruptions and their inevitable result, becomes in later theology too frequently the fierce and malignant spirit, who is extreme to mark what is done amiss, in whose name revilings, anathemas, and curses are freely showered on all who do not accept not only his revelation of himself, but the interpretation which human intellects have thought fit to put on it. Already, in the second century, we see the first germs of this harder conception of the Deity, which grew into such forms as Novatianism, Donatism, and the stern discipline of the Church herself towards offenders.

The Nature and Attributes of God.

Already they might be discerned in the increasing harshness of the language of divines towards the heretics, and the growing severity towards those who, in a moment of weakness, apostatised from the faith.[1] If the fourth Gospel be tainted with these faults, we shall not be able to deny that it must have been of later date than has been hitherto believed. If, on the other hand, its conceptions of the Divine are as pure and exalted as those to be found in the rest of the New Testament, if there be not even a symptom of the tendency to substitute for the Eternal Jehovah a mere deification of human qualities and passions, we shall as infallibly be led to the conclusion that in this book we have the genuine words of Jesus Christ.

At the outset, then, let us observe that the author of this Gospel puts into the mouth of Christ the important declaration, "God is Spirit."[2] He thus rejects all an-

[1] We can see this in the account of the conduct of the martyrs described in the Epistle of the Churches of Lyons and Vienne as compared with that of the Church a little later, and in the distinction between the sympathetic mode of treatment of adversaries adopted by St. Paul and Jesus Himself, and the absence of it even in so moderate and gentle a writer as Irenæus.

[2] Not necessarily "a spirit," as in our version. We must endeavour, in estimating the meaning of this and other common words in the New Testament, to divest our minds of the conventional sense in which they are too frequently used. The use of the word πνεῦμα, to denote the incorporeal part of man, is of Jewish origin. It dates as far back as the first chapter of the book of Genesis, where Moses describes the Almighty as "breathing into man's nostrils the breath of life," and is not in use among the old Greek philosophers. It means either (1) a life-principle of whatever kind; (2) the Divine life-principle in itself; (3) the Divine life-principle in man. See Cremer, 'Lexicon of the N. T.,' s. v. πνεῦμα. Other lexicographers seem hardly to have distinguished sufficiently between πνεῦμα and ψυχή, that is to say between the Hebrew רוּחַ, or נִשְׁמַת חַיִּים, and נֶפֶשׁ. Cremer rightly distinguishes between "πνεῦμα the Divine life principle,

thropopathical notions of His essence. He repels the notion that His worship, like that of the heathen deities, is to be confined to one place, as though God were nearer at one spot than another. He is Spirit, in spirit He must be worshipped. Christ is also here represented as rejecting the local ideas of the Jews, as treating with indifference the disputes between Jerusalem and Gerizim regarding the question which of the two places were most honoured by the Most High. He would lead them to a higher idea of the Godhead than they had imbibed from God's apparent localisation of Himself in His temple by the presence there of the Shekinah. He enters, however, into no philosophical disquisitions; no dissertation on general principles, no reference to the dogmas of theological or philosophical schools. The majestic declaration stands alone, an authoritative assertion of the nature of God, by His mouth whose mission it was to reveal Him. Next, God is Truth, the abstract, eternal Verity itself. For Jesus in this Gospel repeats again and again that God is true,[1] and teaches that He Himself, the Revealer of the Father, mysteriously united to Him in being, is not only "full of grace and truth,"[2] but, in virtue of His Divine essence, is Himself absolute truth.[3] Again, God is Life, the source of all being, He is the "living Father."[4] He hath "life in Himself," and has imparted this Life to His Son, through Whom it is communicated to all creation.[5] Once more, God is Light, the power which

---

ψυχή the individual life in which the πνεῦμα is manifested, and σῶμα the material organisation vivified by the ψυχή." See Genesis ii. 7.
[1] St. John v. 32; vii. 28; viii. 26. [2] Ib. i. 14.
[3] Ib. xiv. 6.   [4] Ib. vi. 57.   [5] Ib. v. 26; cf. i. 4, 18.

The Nature and Attributes of God. 19

illuminates the whole being of man, physical, intellectual, moral, spiritual. "God is light, and in Him is no darkness at all," we read in the Epistle.[1] And thus it was that His Revealer, the only-begotten Son. acquired the right to declare Himself to be the Light.[2] The Father had "given Him to have life in Himself," and that Life was the Light of men. The eyes of men had long been closed in a sleep which could only end in death. The Light of Life was to dawn on those who accepted the revelation of the Father which came by Jesus Christ.

Again, God is Love. These are the very words of St. John in the Epistle which bears his name,[3] but they are simply the epitome of the teaching of the Gospel. Christ, Who declares Himself again and again to be the representative of the Father, refers continually to His own love.[4] He speaks of the mutual love that exists between Himself and His Father.[5] He intimates that this love is communicated through Him to His disciples.[6] And he seems to speak of the love of God as a principle inherent in His nature,[7] which when implanted in us produces results conformable to His will.[8] The love which He bears to His creatures induces Him to take means for their preservation from the fate which threatens them. Not only does He not condemn them, but His Son comes not from heaven to pronounce judgment, which has already, in the nature of things, been passed, but to provide deliverance. He did not come to judge the world, but to save it.[9] He

---

[1] 1 John i. 5. [2] St. John viii. 12; ix. 5; xii. 35, 46. [3] 1 John iv. 8.
[4] St. John xiii. 1; xiv. 21; xv. 9, 10, 13.   [5] Ib. x. 17.
[6] Ib. iii. 16; xv. 10; xvi. 27; xvii. *passim*.
[7] Ib. v. 42, compared with 1 John ii. 5; iii. 16, 17; iv. 9. [8] 1 John v. 3.
[9] It is remarkable that our authorised version, which renders κρίσις

so loved the world that He gave His only-begotten Son, in order that all who believed in Him should have everlasting Life. And yet, though the Son did not come to judge the world, by a kind of paradox not unfrequently to be met with in every writer of the New Testament, He will judge it nevertheless.[1] The threatenings of vengeance against the ungodly, so prominent in the Old Testament, so solemnly denounced in the Synoptists and the Epistle-writers, so unsparingly applied in the next age of the Church, though mitigated here, are not entirely left out of sight.[2] God is also beyond the range of mortal vision. "No man hath seen God at any time."[3] "Ye have neither heard His voice at any time, nor seen His shape."[4] It needed the Revelation of His only-begotten Son, Who existed in His bosom, to declare Him to the world. Lastly, He is the Father of all; the source of all existence, created or uncreated. From Him His Eternal Son derives His being.[5] He it is from Whom the Spirit of truth is sent. From Him, through the Eternal Son, all other things were called into being.[6] To His eternity

---

by "judgment" in chap. v. 27, should render it "condemnation" in chap. iii. 19, and chap. v. 24; and that it should render κρίνω by "judge" in chap. v. 30, and by "condemn" in chap. iii. 17, 18. Neander remarks that St. Paul "never says that God, being hostile to men, became reconciled to them through Christ, but that they, being enemies to God, became reconciled to Him."—'Planting and Training,' i. 450. St. John's language is different, but it amounts to precisely the same thing.

[1] St. John v. 22, 27. [2] Ib. v. 29. [3] Ib. i. 18; vi. 46.
[4] Ib. v. 37. [5] Ib. v. 26.

[6] δι' αὐτοῦ: through His instrumentality. This by no means excludes the notion of the Father being the ultimate source of Life—a doctrine handed down from the earliest times. See Gen. i. 1. Exod. xx. 11. The term "Father" implies as much.

The Nature and Attributes of God.

we need not refer; it is admitted on all hands. Thus then, to sum up what has been said, God is set before us as Spirit, as Truth, as Light, as Life, as Love. He is described as transcending the limits of our mortal preceptions; and He is moreover the originator of all being. There is no attempt at a philosophy of the Infinite; no allusion to the Absolute—the τὸ ὄν of the Greek and Philonian philosophy; no definitions, no dissertations, no distinctions. Certain fundamental principles are laid down by the aid of which the Divine nature may be apprehended, and no more. But there is one more point, too important to be passed over. God is a Person. He is no mere abstract principle, underlying the world as its soul. We might infer this from the term Father, but we are not left to do so. He who dwells above is capable of love, of care, of tenderness.[1] He gives honour to the Son.[2] He bears witness to,[3] He sends the Son,[4] and the Holy Ghost.[5] He commits His prerogatives into His Son's hands.[6] Jesus speaks of His will,[7] His pleasure,[8] the work which He gave His Son to do.[9] He addresses Him in prayer,[10] and asserts His knowledge of the fact that those prayers are heard.[11] And beside these clear assertions of the personality of the Father, there are not wanting intimations of other Persons, associated with Him in the unity of the Godhead. The Godhead which dwells in Him would seem to be communicated to the Son and to the Holy Ghost.[12]

[1] St. John iii. 16, &c.
[2] Ib. viii. 54.
[3] Ib. viii. 18.
[4] Ib. v. 37.
[5] Ib. xiv. 26.
[6] Ib. v. 22.
[7] Ib. vi. 38.
[8] Ib. viii. 29.
[9] Ib. xvii. 4.
[10] Ib. xi. 41; xii. 27, 28; xiv. 16; xvii.
[11] Ib. xi. 42.
[12] See chapters ii. and v.

This is a point the full consideration of which must be deferred; it will suffice, however, to remark here that any indications of the doctrine of a Trinity are balanced by assertions no less distinct of the unity in the Godhead. "I and My Father are one" says the Son;[1] and the unity is afterwards[2] described to be an unity not of personal existence, but in the possession by each of a Life common to all, coming down from the Father as its source, and in the end enfolding not only the Blessed Trinity Itself, but all who are combined together by the indwelling of the Divine nature. The ultimate result of Christ's work, as declared by Himself in the fourth Gospel, would seem to be a merging all the redeemed into the being of God, not in a pantheistic annihilation of all personality, but by bringing each personal soul, while in full and glad realisation of its own separate consciousness, into a complete union, not only of will and affections, hopes and desires, but of Being also with the Infinite Author of all.[3]

Turn we now to the Synoptists. And let us bear in mind at the outset that, as we have before remarked, it is no proof of the later origin of the fourth Gospel if it be shown that the view of Divinity common to them all is heightened and strengthened by deeper and more mysterious touches in the narrative of St. John. Nothing short of a complete absence of harmony in the conceptions of the Supreme Being would warrant us in coming to so extreme a conclusion. Other circumstances may be sufficient to account for the fact that the outline of the Synoptist conceptions of God is filled in by St. John. The earlier biographies, intended for

[1] St. John x. 30.   [2] Ib. xvii. 11, 21, 22.   [3] Ib. xvii.

simple-minded persons, may have intentionally presented to their readers only the simplest and most childlike ideas of the Almighty Father, while St. John, writing for philosophers, for the Christian Church as a whole, and for the world at large, may have desired to place before them more abstract conceptions of His being. Or the mind of the Apostle may have been so constituted as to enable him to apprehend and to retain more of his Divine Master's teaching than was possible to the other Evangelists. If the main features of the teaching be in all respects substantially the same, no arguments founded on diversity of treatment of minor points can be considered sufficient to disprove the authenticity of the Gospel of St. John.

In dealing with the teaching of the Synoptists about God in the same order which we before followed, we come upon a remarkable confirmation of this view. We find in these Gospels no direct assertion of the spiritual nature of God, no rejection of the localisation of Him to which Jews and Gentiles were alike too much inclined. Yet it is a Synoptist who narrates in a spirit of the fullest sympathy the apology of St. Stephen, which is throughout an attack upon the Jewish tendency to localise the deity, and which culminates in the declaration which roused the passions of his hearers, "God dwelleth not in temples made with hands."[1] It is the same Synoptist who records the repetition in days long subsequent of the same statement in the same words, by one who was driven almost to madness by that very statement when for the first time he heard it.[2] A Synoptist therefore, though not in his Gospel, endorses

[1] Acts vii. 48. [2] Ib. xvii. 24.

the statement that God is Spirit, One who is not only incapable of localisation, but Who "giveth to all life and breath, and all things." Truth, again, does not seem to be spoken of in the Synoptists as an attribute of God, though it is found in every Epistle in the New Testament, and though it is specially noted as one of the characteristics of His Son.[1] The same may be said of Light. These abstract characteristics of God are not introduced by the Synoptists, inasmuch as they are concerned chiefly with the personal relations of God to His people. But He Who came to reveal God[2] is spoken of frequently as the Light.[3] If not in the Gospels, yet certainly in the Acts, we are bid to regard God as our Life. St. Paul is recorded there as having taught that "in Him we live, and move, and have our being." Of His love it is needless that we should speak. Not only is He called "Good,"[4] and mentioned in one Evangelist as the "one chief Good,"[5] but the pages of the Synoptists teem with assertions of His Fatherly care. That in their eyes He is a Person, and that His relation to those whom He has created is that of a Father to His children, we need hardly stop to demonstrate. He is to be addressed in prayer as "Our Father." Such prayer He will never neglect to hear.[6] Without His Fatherly knowledge not an hair of our heads shall perish. Our own care for our children is made the basis of an argument to prove *à fortiori* how

---

[1] St. Matt. xxii. 16; St. Mark xii. 14; St. Luke xx. 21.
[2] St. Matt. xi. 27; St. Luke x. 22.
[3] St. Matt. iv. 16; St. Luke ii. 32.
[4] St. Mark x. 18; St. Luke xviii. 19.
[5] St. Matt. xix. 17, according to the better supported reading.
[6] Compare Matt. vii. 7, xxi. 22, with John xiv. 13, 14.

The Nature and Attributes of God. 25

much more God cares for His. We may safely therefore leave this point, involving as it does the question of the personality of God, to the recollection of every one who has given an hour's study to the Gospels. That the Synoptists speak of Him as the Creator of heaven and earth,[1] while St. John refers this creation to the self-revelation of Himself which was given in the Logos, is a contradiction which may be left to be made the most of by those who ignore such passages as Col. i. 16, "By Him were all things created, that are in heaven, and that are in earth: and He is before all things, and by Him all things consist;" and Heb. i. 2, "By whom also He made the worlds." While the remarkable passage to which allusion has been made[2] in St. Matt. xi. 27, recorded also by St. Luke, is the correlative of that in St. John, "No man hath seen God at any time;" for, it declares, in language more like the usual language of St. John than the passage we have just cited, that "no man knoweth the Father but the Son, and he to whom the Son will reveal Him."

The Synoptic view of the unity of God may be inferred from St. Mark xii. 29, "Hear, O Israel; The Lord our God is one Lord." And beside the various intimations of the doctrine of the Trinity which we must reserve for future consideration, there is perhaps the most emphatic of all at the end of St. Matthew's Gospel, where the disciples of Jesus are commanded to baptize all nations into the *Name* of the Father, and of the Son, and of the Holy Ghost.[3]

In the Epistles, where the deeper doctrines of the faith are brought into fuller prominence than in the

[1] Acts xvii. 24.   [2] Above, p. 7.   [3] Matt. xxviii. 19.

Gospels, we naturally look for fuller manifestations of agreement between them and the work which goes by the name of St. John. Accordingly, when we have to deal with the spiritual and mysterious part of the nature of God, we find St. Paul repeating the language of St. John. "The Lord is the Spirit,"[1] he says, and it is this Spirit-Lord who changes men from glory to glory. The very words of Christ, as recorded by St. John, are repeated by St. Paul in his declaration of the mysteriousness of God's existence, and it is surely not unsafe for us to infer that a tradition of their having been uttered was afloat in the Church, and had reached the Apostle's ears.[2] "Not that any man hath seen the Father,"[3] says Christ, according to St. John. "Whom no man hath seen nor can see," echoes the Apostle.[4] That God is truth the Epistles abundantly testify. Precisely as St. John does, they reaffirm the emphatic statements of the Old Testament on this head, statements which it can hardly be pretended that the Synoptists wished to negative because they did not repeat them.[5] It is one of the chief characteristics of the revelation that it is "the truth,"[6] "the word of

---

[1] 2 Cor. iii. 17, 18. It would seem doubtful whether the Apostle means by ὁ Κύριος to speak of our Lord, or of the Jehovah of the older covenant.

[2] "There is no doubt, for he occasionally alludes to it, that he (St. Paul) had met with a traditionary record of the sayings, actions, and precepts of Christ."—Neand. 'Planting and Training,' book vi. vol. i. p. 415 (Bohn's ed.). Neander gives no references.

[3] St. John vi. 46; cf. i. 18; v. 37.

[4] 1 Tim. vi. 16, also i. 17. Rom. i. 20. Heb. xi. 27.

[5] Yet this is precisely, be it remembered, the argument supposed to be conclusive in regard to St. John!

[6] 2 Thess. ii. 13. Gal. iii. 1. Rom. ii. 8. 2 Cor. iv. 2, &c.

The Nature and Attributes of God. 27

truth."[1] "As God is true," says St. Paul, in a fervid appeal to the Corinthians.[2] Untruth is foreign to His nature.[3] "The truth of God"[4] is another expression which implies the same thing, as also what the Apostle soon after directly asserts, namely, that the judgment of God is according to truth.[5] And one of the results of the revelation contained in the Gospel is to imbue men thoroughly with truth "in the inward parts."[6] Next, God is Light. He "inhabits the unapproachable light."[7] He is the source of all kinds of light.[8] Light is His special possession,[9] and that of all those who are His.[10] That God is Life is not obscurely intimated. The Gentiles are described as "alienated from the life of God."[11] Eternal Life is His gift.[12] He is described as giving Life to His creatures.[13] And all this may be held to be summed up in the title Father, that is to say, source of being, which is universally and continually applied to Him. Nor need we take up much time in proving that He is Love. We might almost infer it from 1 Cor. xiii. But the writings of the other Apostles breathe the spirit of love as strongly as those of St. John. As the result of the revelation of God it meets us everywhere. It is "the love of God" which "is shed abroad in our hearts."[14] From it no power can separate us.[15] His benignity and love toward man were

[1] 2 Cor. vi. 7. Eph. i. 13. James i. 18.   [2] 2 Cor. i. 18.
[3] Tit. i. 2.   [4] Rom. i. 25.   [5] Ib. ii. 2.
[6] Eph. iv. 15, ἀληθεύοντες.   [7] 1 Tim. vi. 16.
[8] πατὴρ τῶν φώτων, James i. 17.
[9] τὸ θαυμαστὸν αὐτοῦ φῶς, 1 Pet. ii. 9.
[10] Eph. v. 8. Col. i. 12. 1 Thess. v. 5.
[11] Eph. iv. 18.   [12] Rom. v. 23; cf. 2 Pet. i. 3. Tit. i. 2.
[13] Tit. iii. 5. James i. 18. 1 Pet. i. 3, 23.
[14] Rom. v. 5; cf. Jude 21.   [15] Rom. viii. 35.

manifested by Jesus Christ.[1] His favour toward them has become a theological commonplace under the well-known word Grace. One of the results of being "strengthened with might by His Spirit in the inner man" is the being "rooted and grounded in love."[2] Surely no more need be said to show that the whole of the Epistles are a commentary upon the text "God is Love." But though the Epistles regard Him as Love, His justice is declared no less plainly. St. John speaks of judgment and condemnation; and the other Apostles speak yet more distinctly on the subject.[3] The personality of God may be inferred both from the title of Father and the attribute of love. It would be a tedious task to multiply references on this point. I therefore pass on to the assertion of the unity of the Godhead. This is so emphatically asserted in one passage by St. Paul that it may serve as a type of all others: "There is one Body, and one Spirit, even as ye are called in one Hope of your calling, one Lord, one Faith, one Baptism, one God and Father of all, who is above all, and through all, and in you all."[4]

[1] Tit. iii. 5.   [2] Eph. iii. 17.
[3] Rom. i. ii.; xiv. 10. 1 and 2 Thess. *passim*. 2 Tim. iv. 1. Heb. x. 27. 2 Pet. ii.; iii. Jude. St. John does not use the word condemnation ($κατάκρισις$), but he implies it in chap. v. 29.

[4] Eph. iv. 4–6. 1 Cor. viii. 6; xii. 6. "Nor does St. Paul, any more than St. John, propound anything when he speaks of Father, Son, and Holy Ghost united, which revolts against sound reason. For equally does John refer all benefits which attach to Christianity to God the Father as the supreme and original Author of all; to Jesus Christ, as the Founder, by the Divine will, of the Christian religion and Church; to the Holy Spirit, that Divine and heavenly power supplied to the believers in Christ, and efficacious in their souls, for the purpose of preserving and strengthening the Divine kingdom."—Grimm, 'De Indole Joanneæ Christologiæ l'aulinæ comparatâ,' part i. cap. ii. sec. 33.

The Nature and Attributes of God.

The consideration of the doctrine of the Trinity will be pursued in detail in subsequent chapters. We pass on to observe that the same doctrine is found penetrating all the Epistles, of the indwelling of God in the souls that He has called into being, knitting them together in the closest union with Himself, so as to make all one, while each at the same time retains his separate personality, to which we have referred in St. John. The fuller consideration of this, too, must be deferred to Chapter II. But we may remark here— and the coincidence is surely worth noticing—that both in St. John and in the Epistles the truth of the pantheistic system is extracted and its fatal error avoided. All those passages which we shall have to consider presently, which refer to the indwelling of Christ in the individual soul, which identify Him with the body in which He dwells, representing it as Himself,[1] or His complement,[2] as well as those which point out the intimate inward union between Father, Son, and Holy Ghost,[3] demand some notice here. For they indicate a by no means simple doctrine of the nature of God— a doctrine mysterious and inexplicable, in which human reason may easily lose itself, as it has often lost itself, in innumerable entanglements.

It is surely no light proof of the deep inward agree-

[1] 1 Cor. xii. 12. "*So also is Christ.*" Compare Gal. ii. 20. Eph. i. 10; ii. 16; iii. 17–19; iv. 12–16; v. 23–32. Col. i. 18, 22; ii. 7, 19; iii. 3. Heb. xii. 10. 2 Pet. i. 4. "There is no difference between Jew and Greek (Gal. iii. 28). There was in all the one life of Christ." —Neand. 'Planting and Training,' vol. i. p. 490.

[2] Eph. i. 23. Some, however, imagine that the word πλήρωμα refers to Christ. Against this, however, Col. i. 24 may be cited.

[3] As for instance 1 Cor. viii. 6. Eph. ii. 18; iii. 16–19. Col. i. 15, 19; ii. 9.

ment between our Gospel and the Epistles that St. Paul,[1] like St. John, contrives to avoid falling into pantheism, while asserting most plainly the union effected between the creature and the Creator by means of Christ and His Spirit, as well as the unity of Christ and the Spirit with the Father. It is attained by virtue of the possession of a Life common to all, and this without the least tendency to annihilate the personality of the individual. "*Through* Christ, in one Spirit, all mankind have access to the Father." God "strengthens us with might by His Spirit" within, and the result is that "Christ dwells in our hearts." "All the fulness of the Godhead dwells in Christ corporeally," and yet all Christians "are filled in Him"—with that fulness surely—"who is the Head of all rule and power." We are "rooted in Him," inseparably conjoined in one body with Him as the Head; and thus, as we grow in perfection, we are advancing to the measure of the stature of Christ's fulness. This extraordinary doctrine, which identifies Christ with His members, and them with the Father, and which is found nowhere in the Synoptists, is, in spite of differences of language and expression such as might be expected when put forward by men of different temperaments, education, mode of apprehending things Divine, precisely the same in substance, whether promulgated by St. Paul or St. John. It has since been imperfectly understood, and, by some, almost lost sight of. The Vulgate translation, like our own, does much to obscure it.[2] But it is worthy of the

---

[1] And St. Peter also. "We are partakers of the Divine Nature." Θείας κοινωνοὶ φύσεως. 2 Pet. i. 3.

[2] Nothing does more to obscure the relation between St. Paul and

The Nature and Attributes of God. 31

utmost attention that here, where there is so much risk of misunderstanding, where the doctrine is so mysterious as to be most easily perverted, there is a most exact agreement between two writers so opposite in many respects as St. Paul and the author of the fourth Gospel, displayed alike in the errors they avoid and in the truths they proclaim. This fact can hardly be without its significance in dealing with the question whether the Gospel be correctly ascribed to St. John.

Thus, then, in our review of the teaching of the New Testament on the Nature of God we find a complete agreement between St. John and St. Paul, and a silence on the part of the Synoptists on some points on which these two writers insist. We could not safely infer that silence implied disapproval, even had we no other data to guide us. It is still less possible when we know that one of the Synoptists ardently embraced the teaching of St. Paul. And we may consider it entirely disproved by the fact, to which we shall presently call attention, that the Synoptists, who are supposed to reflect the Judæo-Christian rather than the Gentile tradition, are silent on precisely those points on which the Jewish Scriptures lay most stress. So far, then, as this point is concerned, we have no evidence that the writer of the Fourth Gospel was at issue with his brethren, still less that he was deeply tinged with Gnostic opinions, and desired to introduce them within the pale of the Christian Church. On the contrary, we have a doctrine of God presented to us exactly corre-

---

St. John than the custom of rendering the preposition ἐν "by" or "through," instead of "in."

sponding to that of the Apostolic age. Where corruption and development were the most rapid, we find our author entirely free from either. So far, then, we have no grounds for concluding that he was a forger of the second century, but, on the contrary, the strongest reasons for supposing him to be what he represents himself, and what for so many centuries he has been supposed to be, an eye-witness of Christ's ministry and an Apostle of His choice.

CHAPTER II.

DOCTRINE OF THE LOGOS AND THE PERSON OF CHRIST.

IT has been a subject of fierce debate from whence St. John derived his doctrine of the Logos. Those who strive to deny the authenticity of his Gospel endeavour to prove that the introduction of this expression into the terminology of Christianity was owing to the wide dissemination of Gnostic ideas, and that it passed over into the Christian Church, together with such phrases as Light, Life, Truth, Fulness (Pleroma), Only Begotten (Monogenes), Archon, Paraclete, and the like. The most moderate of the opponents of the authenticity are content with the assertion that St. John borrowed the phrase from Philo.[1] It is not my intention to enter

[1] "Le quatrième Évangéliste est un disciple Chrétien de Philon." Reville in 'Revue des Deux Mondes,' May 1866, p. 107. M. Reville is not a little at issue with his fellow-countryman M. de Pressensé, who declares emphatically that he "knows not in the history of human thought contradictions more flagrant than exist between their doctrines. . . . . That which is with St. John a capital truth would be to the Jew of Alexandria appalling blasphemy."—'Life of Jesus Christ,' Preliminary Questions. Keim, however, cites Bretschneider, Baur, Baumgarten-Crusius, Lücke, Bleek, Schmidt, and Weiszäcker, on behalf of the Philonic origin of the Johannean Logos. He forgets to note that many more names could be cited on the opposite side, though he is at least consistent in tracing St. Paul's theology to the same source. Mr. J. S. Mill, in his posthumous Essays lately printed, gives it as his opinion that such "poor stuff" as the author's

D

into an examination of Philo's system on this point. This has been lately done so fully and exhaustively by Dr. Liddon in his well-known Bampton Lectures that I need only refer the inquirer to their pages. I may be allowed, however, to cite some authorities. Tholuck has observed, "We discover no necessity for resorting to other sources than the Bible in order to explain the doctrine of the Logos, though it has, to be sure, been customary since Semler to resort to Philo for this purpose."[1] "The whole matter," says Neander,[2] "is narrowed to this, that the Evangelist, from the circle around him, borrowed the term Logos, in order to lead those who busied themselves with speculation on the Logos as the centre of all theophanies, from their religious idealism to a religious realism, to the recognition of that God which was revealed in Christ." He used the term, says Neander again, "because it expressed what he wished to say." But his conceptions of the Logos were very different from those of Philo. "Philo's monotheism," says Dorner, "decisively excludes any duality of Divine persons."[3] The expressions of the Alexandrian writer as regards the Logos are indistinct and inconsistent with themselves.[4] It is, moreover, worthy of remark that, if St. John have appropriated one of the terms used by Philo, St. Paul has

---

attempted philosophy could be manufactured with the utmost ease out of Philo's writings by any one familiar with the literature of the East.

[1] Commentary on St. John, Appendix to 7th edition.
[2] Neander, 'Planting and Training,' i. 402.
[3] 'De Persona Christi,' Introd. p. 27 (Clark's Transl.), cf. Neander, 'Planting and Training,' i. 504.
[4] Liddon, 'Bampton Lectures,' pp. 102, 103.

appropriated another. St. Paul calls Christ the εἰκὼν Θεοῦ, one of the expressions Philo has applied to his Logos.[1] And if Philo calls the Logos the πρωτόγονος Θεοῦ, St. Paul calls Him Whom he styles the εἰκὼν Θεοῦ by the name also of πρωτότοκος πάσης κτίσεως.[2] So that if St. John borrows his doctrines from Philo, it may fairly be contended that St. Paul did the same. Is it not, however, more natural to suppose that they only adopted expressions already in use, in order to convey intelligibly to the world their doctrine of the Person of Christ? The term εἰκὼν Θεοῦ, we must remember, was familiar to the Jews from its occurrence in the book of Wisdom.[3] The term λόγος was equally familiar to them from its use in the Old Testament. This may be more readily understood from the meaning of the word itself. Jesus Christ claimed to be the revelation of the Father.[4] No expression could so thoroughly imply at once His functions as a revealer and His identity of essence as this which we are now considering. The word is the revelation of the thought, and yet at the same time is identical with the thought. It allies itself with material substance, is incarnate, as it were, in order to convey its essence unchanged into the inner being of another.[5] And the Greek

---

[1] Liddon, 'Bampton Lectures,' p. 100. Alford, 'Prolegomena to St. John's Gospel.' [2] Col. i. 15.
[3] I give the passage in the original. "ἀτμὶς γάρ ἐστι τῆς τοῦ Θεοῦ δυνάμεως, καὶ ἀπόρροια τῆς τοῦ παντοκράτορος δόξης εἰλικρινής. . . . . ἀπαύγασμα γάρ ἐστι φωτὸς ἀϊδίου, καὶ ἔσοπτρον ἀκηλίδωτον τῆς τοῦ Θεοῦ ἐνεργείας, καὶ εἰκὼν τῆς ἀγαθότητος αὐτοῦ." This passage had much influence on the expressions the writers of the New Testament applied to Christ.
[4] St. Matt. xi. 27. St. Luke x. 22. St. John i. 18; xiv. 9.
[5] "Just as, when we speak in order that what we carry in our minds should glide into the mind of the hearer by his fleshly ears, the word

word has yet another, and equally applicable meaning.[1] Λόγος is the reason to be rendered of anything which requires explanation, the unfolding of its true nature and meaning to him who knows it not. It was in all respects, therefore, the most suitable word which could be found in the Greek language to express Christ's nature and mission. Consecrated as it had been to such purposes by its use in the Old Testament, familiar as it had become to more modern thought by the learned and acute exegesis of Philo, it was no wonder that St. John, writing at a time when the learned world at large was beginning to inquire curiously concerning Christianity, should adopt it as the expression best adapted to convey his doctrine concerning Christ. There were passages in the Old Testament in which the Word of the Lord had been spoken of prophetically, much as St. John speaks of Him. "By the Word of the Lord were the heavens made, and all the hosts of them by the breath of His mouth."[2] God sent His Word to

---

which we bear in our hearts becomes a sound and is called speech, while yet our thought is not converted into the sound, but remaining perfect in itself takes the form of a voice, whereby it finds its way through the ears without any spot of change, so the Word of God, though unchanged, yet is made flesh, that He may dwell in us."— St. Aug. 'De Doctr. Christ.' i. 13.

[1] See Alford *in loc.* Cremer's Lexicon, s. v. λόγος. The second meaning here assigned to λόγος is not to be found in the New Testament. It may, however, be questioned whether 1 Pet. iii. 15 is wrongly rendered in the Authorised Version.

[2] Ps. xxxiii. 6. Cf. St. John i. 3, 10. The personification is not necessarily contained in the passage, but was deduced from it even before the coming of Christ. See Wisdom vii. 25, as quoted above. We must remember that the word translated "breath" is also often rendered "spirit." And if we can, consistently with orthodoxy, say of Christ Θεὸς ἐκ Θεοῦ, and φῶς ἐκ φωτός, we may surely also sa πνεῦμα ἐκ πνεύματος.

them who were "in darkness and in the shadow of death," "in distress," "fast bound in misery and iron," "afflicted because of their transgression," "and they were healed, saved from their destruction."[1] The Psalmist asks for life "according to Thy Word."[2] Jesus says, "I am come that they might have life."[3] The Word of God is "set for ever in heaven," says the Psalmist.[4] A similar prerogative is claimed by St. John for the Son, who is the Word.[5] The Word is a light to the feet of men.[6] Christ declares Himself to be the Light of the world.[7] Christ is, moreover, the Truth; and the Psalmist declares truth to be, as it were, the chief characteristic of the Word.[8] "My Word," says the prophet Isaiah, "which goeth out from My mouth, shall not return to Me empty, but doeth that in which I have delight, and prospereth in that for which I send it."[9] Must not this passage, coming as it does in the midst of a prophecy which speaks of pardon and deliverance, of support and help, have suggested to the mind of the Evangelist one who came forth from God,[10] who always did what was pleasing to Him,[11] through whom alone forgiveness was to be obtained, and who describes Himself as the living water, which should assuage men's thirst, the food and support of their souls?[12] And

[1] Ps. cvii. 10, 14, 17, 20. "We detect in such passages the first glimmering of St. John's doctrine of the agency of the personal Word." —Perowne on Psalm cvii. Cf. St. John i. 5; iii. 18.
[2] Ps. cxix. 25.   [3] St. John x. 10.   [4] Ps. cxix. 89.
[5] St. John iii. 13.   [6] Ps. cxix. 105.   [7] St. John viii. 12.
[8] ראשׁ־דְּבָרְךָ אֱמֶת. Ps. cxix. 160.
[9] Is. lv. 11.   [10] St. John xvi. 28.
[11] τὰ ἀρεστὰ αὐτῷ. Ib. viii. 29. Cf. a distinct quotation in Ignatius, Ep. to Magnesians, c. 8. "Who in all things did what was pleasing to Him who sent Him."
[12] Cf. Is. lv. 1. "Ho, every one that thirsteth," &c.

when we add to this the well-known fact that the Chaldee Paraphrasts, like Philo, almost personified the Word of God, and transferred to Him in many passages the act of creation, which the original Hebrew assigns to God the Father,[1] we cannot be surprised that St. John should have seen in the word Logos the means of expressing precisely what he wished to convey to mankind as the true doctrine of the Person and nature of Christ.

It may not be desirable to insist on the point, but it is equally undesirable to pass by entirely without notice the fact that there are passages in Holy Scripture which seem to show that St. John's use of the word Logos had at least some foreshadowings in the writings of the other Apostles. It is for those who doubt the authenticity of the fourth Gospel, but who assign the Apocalypse to the Apostle St. John, to explain the significant fact that the name of Him who was "called faithful and true;" on whose "head were many crowns;" who was "clothed in a vesture dipped in blood;" on whose "vesture and on whose thigh was written King of kings and Lord of lords," is declared by "the somewhat narrow-minded and unphilosophical Judæo-Christian"[2] to be the Word of God. It is for them to explain how he became familiar with the terminology of the Alexandrian schools. But passing by this, we have the notion of the Chaldee Paraphrast distinctly reproduced in Heb. xi. 3, and 2 Pet. iii. 5. To the Logos is there ascribed the work of the creation

---

[1] Liddon, 'Bampton Lectures.' Pearson, 'On the Creed,' art. ii. "His only Son, *note.*"

[2] Rev. xix. 11-16. See Davidson, on the Revelation of St. John, in his 'Intr. to N. T.'

Doctrine of the Logos & the Person of Christ. 39

of the world. His work in the regeneration of man's nature is no less clearly asserted by St. James. It was λόγῳ ἀληθείας that the Father begat mankind anew.[1] It is the Logos Himself who is planted within them,[2] or, as some commentators would render, of the same nature with them. We have seen that one of the terms by which Philo denominates his Logos is applied by the Apostle Paul to Christ. We have further to remark how the tendency to personify the Logos seems to have grown in the Epistle to the Hebrews, where God's Word is described as living and energising, and piercing to the very inmost depths of the human heart.[3] There is a yet stronger passage in 2 Cor v. 19, where God is described as existing in Christ, reconciling the world unto Himself, and implanting in us the Word of reconciliation.[4] We may even detect the same phraseology in St. Luke. Those from whom he received the details of his gospel were not only ministers, but eye-witnesses of the Word.[5] And he describes St. Paul as commending his disciples to the Word of God's grace, as well as to Himself; and the grammatical construction seems to imply that it is the Word which is not only able to build them up, but, moreover, to give them their inheritance among the saints.[6] St. Peter, too, would seem to be making his way to a similar personification, when he describes

---

[1] St. James i. 18. Perhaps ἀπεκύησεν should be rendered "brought forth."   [2] λόγος ἔμφυτος. Ib. i. 21.

[3] Heb. iv. 12. Clement of Rome, who paraphrases large portions of this epistle, applies these words to God Himself.

[4] Possibly a Hebraism for the Reconciling Word.

[5] St. Luke i. 2. Cf. 1 John i. 1. ὃ ἐθεασάμεθα . . . περὶ τοῦ λόγου.

[6] Acts xx. 32.

the work of regeneration as being effected through a seed of life, not corruptible, but incorruptible, and explains that seed to be the living and ever-abiding Word of God.[1]

We have therefore some reason for supposing that the expression by which St. John has thought fit to designate the Saviour is not so foreign to the current of thought in the other books of the New Testament as some recent critics would lead us to imagine. We may even assert that, in applying this designation to Christ, he was only falling in with the spirit of traditional and contemporary thought.[2] His fellow-workers had paved the way, perhaps with hesitating steps; the "boldness with fervent zeal" of the Son of Thunder, whose fiery and decided character we are apt to forget when we find him dwelling so exclusively on love, stamped the expression for ever on the theology of the Christian Church.

We next proceed to inquire what were the attributes of the Logos, as taught by St. John; what, in fact, was his doctrine of the Person of Christ. He presents to us a Being having an absolutely unique relation to the Author of all existence. Not only does the Logos issue forth from the fountain of all life; not only is His gaze for ever directed towards the face of the Everlasting Father,[3] but He is Himself actually God. St. John does not, with Philo, represent Him as a

[1] 1 Pet. i. 23. Cf. v. 3, ἀναγεννήσας ἡμᾶς . . . δι' ἀναστάσεως Ἰησοῦ Χριστοῦ ἐκ νεκρῶν. See Liddon, 'Bampton Lectures,' Lect. vi.

[2] The Targum of Jonathan Ben Uzziel is supposed by some to have been written about the time of our Lord. See Kitto, 'Biblical Cyclopædia,' s. v. Targum.

[3] πρὸς τὸν Θεόν. Liddon, 'Bampton Lectures,' Lect. v. p. 342.

δεύτερος Θεός, nor, with the Arians, does he represent Him as a being possessing indeed the name of God, but destitute of the most necessary of His attributes, the possession of His essence. "Θεὸς ἦν ὁ Λόγος," says the Evangelist, and we have the testimony of an unprejudiced witness that the doctrine of the Church is a true interpretation of his words.[1] Existent from all eternity in the bosom of the Father,[2] He yet has a separate personal existence. It is true that this existence is declared by Him to be derived from His Father. He is the only-begotten Son.[3] He acknowledges God to be His Father as well as ours, His God as well as ours.[4] "I came forth from the Father," He says.[5] He represents Himself as sent by the Father.[6] His name, the symbol of His power, His greatness, even of His very existence,[7] must be referred to the Father as having been received from Him.[8] He even admits the priority of the Father in the much controverted words, "My Father is greater than I."[9] And in conformity with this, He ascribes the life inherent in Him, the powers He possesses, the authority He wields,

---

[1] Meyer, cited by Liddon, 'Bampton Lectures.' "John, by omitting the article before Θεός, would signify an essence not inferior to that which God Himself possesses."
[2] St. John i. 18, also ἐν ἀρχῇ chap. i. 1; cf. viii. 58; xvii. 5, 24.
[3] Ib. i. 14, 18; iii. 16, 18.   [4] Ib. xx. 17.   [5] Ib. xvi. 27.
[6] Ib. iv. 34; v. 23, 24, 30, 37, 38; vi. 39, 44, &c.
[7] So the commentators in general explain the word.
[8] ἐν τῷ ὀνόματί σου, ᾧ δέδωκάς μοι, according to the best supported reading in St. John xvii. 11.
[9] Ib. xiv. 28. Some commentators (see Liddon, 'Bampton Lectures,' p. 300) refer these words to the human nature of Christ. The earliest of these is Ignatius, who (Ep. to Magnesians, chap. 13) says that "Christ was subject to the Father *according to the flesh.*"

to His Father as their giver.¹ Yet, in spite of all this, He does not hesitate to place Himself on an equality with the Father.² His language is understood by the Jews to imply such a claim, and He does not dispute their interpretation of it.³ He asserts continually that the Father is in Him, and He in the Father.⁴ While yet on earth, He speaks of Himself as existing in heaven.⁵ Though derived from the Father, His existence is not dependent on the arbitrary will of another; the Father has communicated to Him the prerogative of self-existence.⁶ In Him was life, says the Apostle,⁷ and from Him was life communicated anew to lost mankind.⁸ He is full of grace and truth;⁹ and more than this, He is the Truth itself.¹⁰ He only has seen the Father, and whosoever has seen Him hath seen the Father also.¹¹ It is by these intimate relations with His Father that He possesses the Divine energy which enables Him to control the powers of nature, the laws of disease, and even of life and death. Thus it is that He declares that all power is given to Him,¹²

¹ St. John v. 26, also 19, 20, 22, 27; xvii. 2.
² ὁ ὢν παρὰ τοῦ Θεοῦ.
³ St. John v. 18; x. 33.   ⁴ Ib. x. 38; xiv. 9, 10, 20; xvii. 21, 23.
⁵ Ib. iii. 13.
⁶ Ib. v. 26.   ⁷ St. John i. 4.   ⁸ Chap. iii.   ⁹ St. John i. 14.
¹⁰ Ib. xiv. 6. M. Reville ('Revue des Deux Mondes,' p. 95) remarks that while in the Synoptists Christ is said only to preach the truth, in St. John He is Himself the truth. But St. John also represents Christ as preaching the truth (chap. viii. 40, 45). Either then St. John's Gospel is irreconcilably at variance with itself, and was written by different persons, at different times, or this kind of criticism is not very conclusive.
¹¹ St. John vi. 46; x. 15; xiv. 9.
¹² Ib. iii. 35; xiii. 3; ⁘. 2. Cf. St. Matt. xxviii. 18. The first cited passage perhaps gives the words of the Bapti

Doctrine of the Logos & the Person of Christ. 43

that He quickeneth whom He will.[1] And it is also in consequence of this Divine character that He alone can venture to present Himself to us as an example which His disciples would do well to copy,[2] and to challenge the Jews to find a single blemish in His character,[3] sayings which under all other circumstances would be the height of presumption and folly.

On the other hand, we have the strange paradox set before us, that He who claims for Himself these high prerogatives is nevertheless represented as a human being, possessing His full share of the ordinary weaknesses of humanity.[4] He eats and drinks with His disciples before and after His resurrection.[5] He is tired with a journey;[6] more than once troubled in spirit,[7] and this to an extent which causes Him to shed tears.[8] He enters into the peculiarly human relation of friendship. "The disciple whom Jesus

---

[1] St. John v. 22, 25.   [2] Ib. xiii. 15.   [3] Ib. viii. 46.
[4] "At first Christ presented Himself as a weak mortal, although conscious of possessing a Divine nature and dignity, partaking of all those evils which affect human nature in connection with sin, and as the punishment of sin, so that in His outward appearance he placed Himself entirely on a level with men suffering on account of sin."—Neand. 'Planting and Training,' i. 447 (Bohn's Ed.). "Surely that Mediator between God and man was truly man. as we are men. Who when He fasted was an hungred, when he travelled was thirsty and weary as we are; Who being grieved wept, being in an agony sweat, being scourged bled, and being crucified died."—Pearson, 'On the Creed,' Art. iv. Suffered. Cf. Iren. 'Contr. Hær.' book iii. cap. xxii. 2, which seems to have suggested the above eloquent passage. Cf. also Keim, 'History of Jesus of Nazareth,' p. 150 (Clark's Tr.).
[5] St. John ii. 1 ; xiii. 2 ; xxi. 12.   [6] Ib. iv. 6.
[7] Ib. xi. 33. M. Reville asserts that the Christ of St. John is haunted by "no dark presentiments." Surely he must have forgotten "now is My soul troubled" in St. John xii. 27, and the trouble in spirit recorded in xiii. 21.   [8] Ib. xi. 35.

loved," is an expression which has passed into a proverb. Scarcely less remarkable is the affection He entertained for Martha and Mary and Lazarus.[1] When dying on the Cross, He complains of thirst. Nor does He, even in that hour of supreme solemnity when He is consummating the sacrifice of propitiation upon the Cross, consider Himself free from the claims of filial duty. "Woman, behold thy son," is an exclamation which, uttered at such a moment, places beyond a doubt that the Gospel which sets forth most strongly the Divinity of Christ was also penetrated with the most clear apprehension of His humanity.

The Epistle of St. John, considered by many as little else than a preface to the Gospel,[2] and so obviously by the same hand that the fact needs no demonstration,[3] sets forth the same doctrine concerning Christ. He is the "Word of life."[4] Through Him, it is hinted, is the light in which God dwelleth revealed to man.[5] He manifested to us the life which was with the Father.[6] He is the only-begotten of the Father,[7] to deny whom is to deny the Father.[8] With Him the source of truth, the truth itself, is identified even while it is distinguished.[9] The words "which of you convinceth Me of sin?" have evidently sunk deeply into

---

[1] St. John xi. 5. It is noteworthy how thoroughly St. Luke's portraiture of the sisters of Bethany corresponds to that of St. John.

[2] See Ebrard and Hug on this point.

[3] Dr. Davidson, however, after citing an extraordinary number of parallel passages occurring in the Gospel and Epistle ascribed to St. John, dismisses the argument from them as inconclusive, because in an Epistle of five chapters some of the distinctive doctrines of the Gospel are not introduced.

[4] 1 John i. 1.   [5] Ib. i. 5; ii. 8.   [6] Ib. i. 2.
[7] Ib. iv. 9.   [8] Ib. ii. 22, 23.   [9] Ib. v. 20.

Doctrine of the Logos & the Person of Christ. 45

the Apostle's mind.¹ But notwithstanding this, His true humanity is no less plainly indicated. He is sent by God.² He is "come in the flesh."³ He was looked upon, handled, as a man among men.⁴ So that the view of Christ which is presented to us corresponds in substance, and even in form, with the teaching of the Gospel concerning His Person.

In the Apocalypse the doctrine which is presented to us is substantially the same, though from the nature of the case the form is different. Jesus Christ is now glorified in heaven. But it is no mere apotheosis of humanity that meets us there. Not only is Christ spoken of as the Word of God, but He is the source of all blessing,⁵ the Alpha and Omega, the first and the last,⁶ He who lives unto all eternity, and death and Hades are subject to His power.⁷ To Him, as to His Father, the worship is paid which inferior beings decline;⁸ and He is constantly associated with the Father in His authority and greatness.⁹ His it is to give or to withhold the gifts of which He speaks in His message to the churches. He is King of kings and Lord of lords.¹⁰ Yet His humanity is no less clearly affirmed. He is the first begotten from the dead.¹¹ He overcame and was exalted, even as His followers will be.¹² He is the Lamb as it had been slain, the Lion of the tribe of Judah, the root of David.¹³ He is the man-child of the woman who represents in a figure the identity of the two dispensations, the Church of the

¹ 1 John iii. 5, 7. ² Ib. iv. 14. ³ Ib. iv. 2. ⁴ Ib. i. 2.
⁵ Rev. i. 4, 5. ⁶ Ib. v. 8. ⁷ Ib. vv. 17, 18.
⁸ Ib. v. 8–14; vii. 10. ⁹ Ib. xx. 6; xxi. 22; xxii. 3.
¹⁰ Ib. xvii. 14; xix. 16. ¹¹ Ib. i. 5. ¹² Ib. iii. 21.
¹³ Ib. v. 5, 6; xxii. 16.

law and the Church of the Gospel; and it is thus, as the type of all humanity, that He is caught up to God and to His throne.[1] This is the teaching, be it remarked, of a book which is firmly believed by many to display all the features of Jewish Christianity, and to belong to the period when all attempts at an apotheosis of the Messiah were as yet unknown. It is strange, if this be the case, that it should reflect so accurately the spirit of the Gospel which bears the name of St. John.

We will next review the contents of the Synoptic Gospels. The humanitarian character of these narratives is not denied by any one; it may therefore be sufficient to remark in passing that the character of our Lord's humanity as portrayed in them is precisely identical with its character as depicted by St. John. The same absolute freedom from sin, the same liability to the infirmities as distinguished from the corruptions of our nature, the affection of tears,[2] the capacity for personal and filial affection,[3] appear in the Synoptic Gospels as a matter of course. But let it be observed that these purely human traits of the character of Jesus are more marked in the Gospel which is supposed to be peculiarly the Gospel of an apotheosis, than in the Gospels which are said to negative the idea of a Divinity in Christ. This one fact alone affords a strong argument against the later origin of the Gospel of St. John, against the possibility of its being an attempt to give substance and authority to the teaching of those who had come by degrees to regard Jesus as a Divine Being. But if we examine the Synoptic Gospels care-

[1] Rev. xii. 5.   [2] Luke xix. 41.
[3] Mark x. 21; Luke ii. 51.

fully, we shall see that not only is the Christology of St. John not inconsistent with theirs, but that the truth of St. John's doctrine is the very groundwork of their narrative.[1] While the subordination of Christ to the Father is declared in language which harmonises with that of St. John,[2] His equality, if not expressly asserted, is at least implied.[3] The most cursory examination will show this. He spake as never man spake, and claimed an authority which none but He had ever ventured to assume. An acute writer has lately remarked that there is this essential difference between Christ and every other great teacher who has attracted the attention of mankind. Other teachers directed their hearers to their doctrines, and not to their person: Christ directed His hearers to His Person, and to His doctrines only as emanating from Himself.[4] "He spake with authority and not as the scribes,"[5] we are told. "Heaven and earth shall pass away, but My words shall not pass away," He declared in His first public

[1] "If we try to regard the objective facts from a subjective point of view, we find in St. John only the completion of the Synoptic narratives. Extraordinary and gifted individuals are frequently susceptible of this treatment, and seem different individuals when regarded from different points of view. The Synoptists present the external and national side of the life of Jesus, rather than its deeper side, that in which it must have presented itself to the consciousness of original Christianity." (Grimm on the 'Trustworthiness of the Evangelic Narratives,' p. 66.) The author of 'Ecce Homo' has referred to a singular confirmation of this view in the case of Socrates as portrayed by Plato and Xenophon.

[2] "My Father is greater than I," St. John xiv. 28. "Of that day and that hour knoweth no man, no, not the angels which are in heaven, neither the Son, but the Father," St. Mark xiii. 32.

[3] Liddon, 'Bampton Lectures,' Lect. viii. p. 687, *seq.*

[4] 'Ecce Homo,' chap. ix. p. 94. [5] Matt. vii. 29.

discourse. The whole subject matter of that discourse is characteristic. He does not reason, He does not persuade, He asserts. There is no attempt to search for truth; there is a tacit assumption of an inherent right to proclaim it. So, throughout the three first Gospels, we see Christ directing attention to Himself, in a way which, from a purely humanitarian point of view, would be unwarrantable assumption, if not blasphemy or insanity, and would certainly be fatal to any attempt to set Him up as a perfect human being. "Come unto Me, all ye that are weary and heavy laden, and I will give you rest. Take *My* yoke upon you, and learn of *Me*," is His invitation to His disciples,— words involving a claim which would have seemed to us presumptuous in Socrates, which becomes simply ludicrous in Auguste Comte, but which on the hypothesis of St. John's Gospel, and on it alone, are perfectly intelligible in Jesus Christ. But He is not content with thus directing attention to Himself. In this very first Sermon He indirectly proclaims His own Divinity.[1] By His own inherent authority He puts aside the precepts of the law—that law which, though "ordained by angels at the hand of a mediator," was understood from the first to have come from God. "It was said *to* them of old time .... but I say unto

---

[1] "What prophet ever set himself above the great Legislator, above the law written by the finger of God on Sinai? What prophet ever undertook to ratify the Pentateuch as a whole, to contrast his own higher morality with some of its precepts in detail, to imply even remotely that he was competent to revise that which every Israelite knew to be the handiwork of God? What prophet ever thus implicitly placed himself on a line of equality, not with Moses, not with Abraham, but with the Lord God Himself?"—Liddon, 'Bampton Lectures,' p. 252.

you."¹ " Moses because of the hardness of your hearts suffered you to put away your wives . . . . . but I say unto you." Here we find the distinct claim of an authority coordinate with that of God Himself. And it is in strict keeping with this fact that Jesus demands the unconditional submission of all who come to Him. He is the one Master, Whom all His disciples must own.² He it is Whom His followers are bound, under pain of rejection, to confess in the sight of men.³ He demands an affection beyond what may be given to the nearest and dearest of earthly relatives.⁴ He pronounces Himself to be Lord of the Sabbath and greater than the temple.⁵ He vindicates His claim to forgive sins.⁶ He accepts a homage which is carefully refused not only by His Apostle St. Peter,⁷ but by the angel in the Apocalypse.⁸ No such scruples affect the mind of Jesus when the leper comes before Him, not only asking for relief from his disease, but offering precisely that tribute of worship which inferior beings had declined.⁹ Nor is He content with words. He puts forth powers which prove that those words are no mere extravagant outbreaks of fanaticism. It is not our purpose to attempt in these pages to prove the credibility of the miracles. Whether the Synoptists are credible historians or not is no part of our present inquiry; we are simply endeavouring to ascertain whether they are in harmony with St. John. And we

¹ For the translation "to them," see Alford and Wordsworth. Also Archbishop Trench. 'Authorised Version,' p. 124 (2nd ed.).
² Matt. xxiii. 8. ³ Ib. x. 32. Luke xii. 8.
⁴ Matt. x. 37. ⁵ Ib. xii. 6, 8. ⁶ Mark ii. 5–10.
⁷ Acts x. 26. ⁸ Rev. xix. 10.
⁹ The word προσκυνέω is used in each case.

see that the pages of all the four Evangelists teem with assertions of the extraordinary powers residing in Jesus. The ordinary forces of nature were subject to Him— a fact exemplified not only in His turning water into wine, but in His feeding the five thousand; in His stilling the waves of the sea. The mysterious laws of health and disease were under His control, as cures unnumbered may serve to show; the power of life and death belonged to Him, as is displayed in the cases of Jairus' daughter and the widow's son at Nain,[1] as well as the raising of Lazarus; the strange visitants from the world of spirits owned His authority, as is shown by many a deliverance from demoniacal possession. All these are evidences that it was no mere mortal of whom the Synoptists believed themselves to be writing. And this assertion is borne out by more remarkable facts still. Two of the Evangelists have recorded the various portents which attended our Lord's birth. St. Matthew records the fact of its having been announced beforehand by an angel; of the birth itself being heralded by extraordinary signs in the heavens, and by the still more extraordinary pilgrimage of a band of unknown sages from the far East to offer their gifts before the throne of a mighty King. St. Matthew records, too, the busy part which angels played in the

[1] It is to be remarked that there is a singular, yet undesigned coincidence between the raising of the dead as related in the Synoptists and in St. John. In every instance in Scripture where men are credited with the power of raising the dead there is some declaration of dependence upon a higher power. In every instance where the same power is attributed to Christ, it is dependent upon a virtue inherent in Himself; the possession of the power which St. John represents him as claiming, namely, that of "quickening whom He will," chap. v. 21.

Doctrine of the Logos & the Person of Christ. 51

early part of the career of Jesus. It is impossible to draw the conclusion from his narrative that he saw nothing supernatural, nothing Divine, in the being of Him whose early years he chronicles in such terms. And if we turn to St. Luke, we find a still clearer assertion of the supernatural character of the Person of Christ. His birth is not like that of other men. It was, in fact, a new creation in the womb of a virgin. We are thus naturally prepared for the declaration that His title shall be "Son of the Highest." We are ready to expect such portents as the babe leaping in the womb of Elizabeth, its mother filled by the Holy Ghost with a rapturous joy, and breaking out into exclamations of transport at the honour of a visit from the mother of her Lord—portents which, under any other hypothesis than that of St. John, would be unnatural and absurd. We see why the Baptist himself, at his birth, should be designated as the Prophet of the Highest, and the forerunner of the greater One who was yet to be born. But there are stronger statements still in this early part of the narrative. Not only do St. Matthew and St. Luke ascribe the birth of Christ to the special operation of the Holy Ghost, but the former adds that the child's "name should be called Emmanuel, which being interpreted is, God with us."[1] We cannot admit that in these words there is

---

[1] St. Matt. i. 23. It has been remarked, as an objection to St. John's Gospel, that it contains no allusion to the Incarnation. This fact would surely rather serve to confirm its authenticity. A writer who was writing for a purpose would have eagerly seized on, and heightened to suit his object, the miraculous details in St. Matthew and St. Mark. But he actually raises the objection which naturally suggests itself to his idea of a heaven-descended Logos in chap. vi. 42, and never troubles

only to be discovered an intimation of God's intention to dwell in power among men through the means of the child that was to be born. Doubtless such was the meaning of the prophecy in its more immediate fulfilment in Isaiah's time.[1] But a more complete and literal fulfilment of prophecy is always insisted upon by the Evangelists:[2] and if there be any doubt whether the stricter literal interpretation of this passage is to be insisted on, we find it in the fact that passages in which the incommunicable name Jehovah is used are referred without scruple in the New Testament writers to Jesus Christ. One decisive evidence of this is to be found in the first chapter of St. Mark's Gospel, where, after applying to St. John Baptist the words of Malachi, " Behold, I will send My messenger before Thy face, which shall prepare Thy way before Thee," the Evangelist annexes to this the words of Isaiah, which declare him to be " the voice of one crying in the wilderness, Prepare ye the way of the Lord."[3] One point more

---

himself to refute it. "By combining the two declarations of John, that in Jesus the Eternal Word of God became flesh (chap. i. 14), and that which is born of the flesh is flesh (chap. iii. 6), we cannot escape the inference that a supernatural working of God in the conception of the man Christ Jesus is implied."—Neander, cited in Alford on St. John i. 46.

[1] ' Davison on Prophecy,' Discourse v. part ii., insists on the "double sense" which pervaded the writings of the prophets.

[2] See Matt. xxvii. 35; and the reference of the whole passage to Psalm xxii. Compare St. John xix. 24, 29, 37. Also Matt. xxvi. 31; viii. 17. But the passage commencing " that it might be fulfilled " in St. Matt. xxvii. is very doubtful; probably spurious.

[3] דֶּרֶךְ יְהֹוָה. Cf. St. Luke iii. 4. The Emmanuel of Is. vii. is also surely "the mighty God" of chap. ix. 6, and this prophecy is itself applied to Christ by St. Matt. in chap. iv. 15, 16.

remains to be noticed before we leave the subject of the real inward harmony between the Synoptists and St. John. Jesus Himself gives utterance to some very significant words which we find recorded by two of the Synoptists, which breathe the very spirit of St. John's Gospel, and suggest irresistibly the inference, that if we do not find many other expressions of a like kind in their pages, it was not because they knew of none such, but because such a record was inconsistent with their purpose, or because they knew that in the deep decrees of God the hour for its publication was not yet come. It is to the remarkable passage, which seems as though it had been transferred to their pages from St. John's Gospel, " All things are delivered to Me of My Father, and no man knoweth the Son but the Father, neither knoweth any man the Father save the Son, and he to whom the Son will reveal Him."[1] The same statement as that with which this passage opens is repeated by our Lord after His Resurrection: "All power is given unto Me in heaven and in earth;"[2] but the former passage attests St. John's view that this was no mere grant of heavenly power to Him after His Resurrection,

---

[1] Matt. xi. 27. Luke x. 22. Compare with these words John i. 18; iii. 35; vi. 46; x. 15; xiii. 3; xvii. 2. Had St. Matthew and St. Luke been the writers whose authenticity was in doubt, it would have been useless to have adduced these words as a proof of genuineness. It would have been regarded as an obvious plagiarism from St. John. They are weighty evidence, however, for the fact, that our Lord was in the habit of speaking of Himself in the way St. John represents Him as being in the habit of speaking of Himself—the more weighty because such language occurs but once, either in St. Matthew or St. Luke, and thus was far less likely to attract the attention of a forger.

[2] Matt. xxviii. 18. Compare John iii. 35; xiii. 3.

but was in very truth inherent in Him from the beginning.

We see, then, from a careful review of the Synoptic narratives that they inferentially suggest the two apparently contradictory aspects in which the Person of Christ is regarded in St. John's Gospel. Christ was at once equal to and inferior to the Father. He derived His being from the Father, and yet it resided within Himself. He was the Son of God, and yet He need not scruple to assume the highest titles and prerogatives that belonged to His Father. He kneeled down and prayed to His Father, and yet allowed Himself to be regarded as an object of worship. Is it not clear, then, that whether the doctrine be formally put forth in words by the Synoptists as it is by St. John, or not, they were nevertheless penetrated throughout their narratives with the truth that He of whom they were speaking was God as well as Man? "equal to the Father as touching His Godhead, though inferior to Him as touching His manhood."

Before we enter upon the teaching of the Apostles in their Epistles, let us turn to the narrative in the Acts. And if we find, as unquestionably we shall find, traces of the deeper Christian teaching, we must remember that the writer of this book is the writer of one of the Synoptic Gospels, and we are therefore compelled to admit that, if he does not put forth with the same distinctness in his Gospel the doctrine which he puts forth in the Acts, there can be but one explanation of the fact, namely, that the objects he had in view in the Gospel were inconsistent with such an explicit statement of the doctrines of the faith. The contrast between the doctrinal stand-point of St. Luke's Gospel and that of the Acts, which must be borne in mind throughout the whole of this inquiry, is in itself a sufficient explanation of the differences between St. John and the Synoptists.¹ Let us, then, examine what is the teaching of the Acts of the Apostles on the person of Christ. We may dismiss the famous passage in Acts xx. 28 with the brief remark, that there is strong evidence for the genuineness of the reading Θεοῦ,² that there is every reason why that reading should have been changed into κυρίου by the Arians, while the probability of Θεοῦ being interpolated in the place of κυρίου is rendered improbable by the fact that there are hundreds of other passages in which such an interpolation would have suited the purpose of the orthodox party just as well, and that in not one of them has such substitution ever been attempted. Reasons such as these have induced a candid editor like Alford to restore in his later editions the reading Θεοῦ, which in former editions, from a desire to display perfect fairness, he had admitted to be doubtful.³ Passing over, however, this disputed passage, we have our Lord spoken of by St. Peter as the ἀρχηγὸς τῆς ζωῆς,⁴ an expression which, if it does not rise to the fulness of the expression "in Him was Life,"

¹ See below, part II., where this subject is more fully treated.
² Perhaps the strongest evidence is the way in which Ignatius, writing to the *Ephesians*, uses the expression "blood of God." The passage is found in the Syriac, so its genuineness will hardly be questioned.
³ See Alford's exhaustive note; also Wordsworth *in loc.*
⁴ "Hence comes easily the idea of origination, and so it frequently occurs in Greek writers, especially later ones, of the person from whom anything, whether good or bad, proceeds .... so that it is very nearly

yet at least is equivalent to the words "He gave also to the Son to have life in Himself." But there are statements in the Acts which go further than this. Jesus is Lord of all.[1] It was impossible for Him to be holden of the pains of death.[2] He is received into the heavens until the time of the restitution of all things.[3] If His disciples are able to do any mighty works upon earth, they ascribe to Him, and not to His Father, the power which they possess.[4] Above all, the outpouring of the Holy Spirit, Himself expressly spoken of in the same book as God,[5] is said to be the work of Jesus Christ, and of no other; and He is credited with the power of receiving the spirits of the dying.[6] In the Acts, then, we find powers ascribed to Christ which raise Him far above the level of any created intelligence, and we have the strongest reason to believe that St. Luke, as well as St. John, speaks of Him as God.

The writings of St. Peter and St. James must next come under review. And here, if we find rather less corroboration of the Johannean view of the Lord's Person, we must remember first the extreme brevity of their Epistles, and next the peculiarly practical and undogmatic character of the Epistle of St. James. As in the case of the Synoptic Gospels, we are not entitled to infer from the absence of any strong expressions as

---

= αἴτιος."—Alford on Heb. ii. 10. We can have no right to assume that St. Peter had not this meaning in his words, just because it happens to coincide with the theology of the fourth gospel. It is translated "author" in Heb. xii. 2 in our authorized version.

[1] Acts x. 36. [2] Ib. ii. 24. [3] Ib. iii. 21.
[4] Ib. iii. 16; iv. 10–12. [5] Ib. ii. 33. [6] Ib. vii. 59.

Doctrine of the Logos & the Person of Christ. 57

to Christ's Divinity, that St. James was unacquainted with any doctrine of the kind as a part of the Christian system. The fact is precisely the reverse. St. James' Epistle presupposes a wide circulation and a consequent perversion of the teaching of St. Paul; and it is pretty generally admitted that St. Paul was a firm believer in the Godhead of Christ. St. James' Epistle, too, from the very nature of the errors it is written to combat, bears testimony to an advanced stage of Christian progress; one in which it was possible for the doctrines of the faith to be held as matters of opinion, without exercising their proper influence upon the heart and conduct.[1] We have no right, then, to assume that he was ignorant of, or opposed to, the doctrines then current respecting the Person of our Lord; the only fair inference is that a statement of these doctrines did not enter into his purpose in writing his Epistle. This proposition derives confirmation from the fact which will be startling to many, but is nevertheless true, that our Lord Jesus Christ is only twice mentioned in the course of this epistle. On one of these occasions, however, St. James, though His relative, professes himself His slave, and on the other he places the epithet $\tau\hat{\eta}s$ $\delta\acute{o}\xi\eta s$ after the sacred Name.[2] We may, therefore, venture to dismiss the Epistle of St. James with one remark of Dr. Liddon's on the ex-

---

[1] Alford. Prolegomena to Epistle to St. James.
[2] It seems that many of the commentators have hardly appreciated the force of the construction so common in the Hebrew language, in which one substantive placed in dependence on another is used to supply the place of the adjective. Dean Alford often rejects a rendering in accordance with this principle as a "wretched hendiadys." Yet "glorious Lord" is perhaps the true translation here. See Liddon, 'Bampton Lectures,' p. 434.

pression λόγος ἔμφυτος, which we shall have to consider more fully in another section. "St. James' doctrine of the engrafted word," he says, "is a compendium of the teaching of the first, third, and sixth chapters of St. John's Gospel;" and he might have added of the whole of the Epistles of St. Paul. But such a doctrine can hardly, if there be any reference to Christ—and it is certainly not demonstrated that there is not[1]—regard Him as a mere man. If here we find Christ set forth as the source of our renewed life, we find the doctrine which we have just seen to be that of St. John, and shall hereafter find to be that of St. Paul. And it may be worthy of question how far the sparing use of our Lord's Name in this Epistle, as also its general tone, may be accounted for by the fact that it was not intended to be confined in its use to the Christian Church only, but to be an exhortation to the Jewish nation at large, by whom, as Hegesippus tells us, St. James was held in high respect.[2]

St. Peter's Epistles, if we except the opening words of the second Epistle, which are capable of various renderings,[3] does not assert in express terms the Divinity of Christ, though we may safely affirm that

---

[1] Compare i. 18, where God is said to beget, or bring forth, Christians by His word.

[2] In Euseb. 'Eccl. Hist.' ii. 23. See also Wordsworth, Introduction to Epistle of St. James.

[3] "Undoubtedly, in strict grammatical propriety, both Θεοῦ and Σωτῆρος would be predicates of 'Ιησοῦ Χριστοῦ."—Alford *in loc.* He, however, surrenders this interpretation on account of "considerations which intervene," and refers to his note on Tit. ii. 13, where however his arguments are not conclusive. For σωτήρ is applied equally to the Father and to Christ, while in the epistles of St. Ignatius the expressions which Alford regards as improbable are continually occurring.

Doctrine of the Logos & the Person of Christ. 59

the doctrine underlies them throughout. We cannot therefore insist that the words whose interpretation has been questioned should be translated "our God and Saviour," though there is no objection to a similar passage being rendered "our Lord and Saviour" in ch. iii. 2, where Jesus Christ is unquestionably referred to. But all St. Peter's teaching hangs upon Jesus Christ. Him, having not seen, His disciples love: believing, they rejoice in Him with a joy that is not only unutterable, but glorified.[1] Glory and power are ascribed to Him unto ages of ages.[2] His power is Divine.[3] He manifests this in that He goes up to heaven by His own act, instead of being taken up by another. Angels, authorities, and powers are subject to Him, as there He sits at God's Right Hand.[4] By the knowledge of Him we escape the pollutions of the world.[5] He is without spot or blemish.[6] He did no sin, neither was guile found in His Mouth.[7] He left us an example that we should follow his steps.[8] If we have here no direct assertion of the Godhead of Christ, we have at least nothing inconsistent with such a belief, nothing but what corresponds exactly to many a passage in the writings of St. John and St. Paul, where Christ's Godhead does not happen to be mentioned.[9]

---

[1] 1 Pet. i. 8.   [2] Ib. iv. 11. Cf. 2 Pet. iii. 18.
[3] 2 Pet. i. 3. If the latter part of the sentence refer to the Father, the former must of necessity apply to Christ.
[4] 1 Pet. iii. 22.   [5] 2 Pet. ii. 20.   [6] 1 Pet. i. 19.
[7] Ib. ii. 22. The echo of the words of Christ: "Which of you convinceth Me of sin?" St. John viii. 46.
[8] 1 Pet. ii. 21.
[9] The fact that the Ignatian expression "Jesus Christ our God" is not found in the 2nd Epistle of St. Peter speaks volumes for its genuineness.

60   *The Doctrinal System of St. John.*

We now come to St. Paul himself. Full as his numerous Epistles are of Jesus Christ, the number of passages in which he declares His Divinity are very few.[1] But this doctrine is none the less the groundwork of his whole system. As might naturally be expected, the existence of a various reading in 1 Tim. iii. 16 has led to much controversy on the question whether the words "God was manifest in the flesh" were ever written by St. Paul. We will not presume to enter upon the consideration of a question which has been fully argued by commentators of the highest reputation. But we may venture to observe that whatever the true reading may be, it is probable that it alters the sense less than is generally supposed. To take ὅς as in apposition to τὸ τῆς εὐσεβείας μυστήριον, and to apply the passage thus to Christ, is to make use of an expression entirely foreign to the style of St. Paul, to introduce into his writings an ἅπαξ λεγόμενον of a very startling kind, one which would seem to be little in harmony with the tone of deep reverence with which the Apostle always spoke of the Saviour. The interpretation which has been given by a recent commentator, which would regard ὅς as agreeing with Θεοῦ ζῶντος,[2] appears more in accordance with the parenthetic style of the Apostle, and throws more light on the meaning of a confessedly difficult passage. Whatever may be the reading in Acts xx. 28, the Church is clearly spoken of there as the Church of Christ; therefore it is not absolutely impossible that it may be so

[1] There are whole Epistles of St. Paul, from which, as the Divinity of Christ is nowhere stated, it can only be inferred. This makes the absence of any direct statement in St. Peter's Epistles the less significant.
[2] The Bishop of Lincoln.

spoken of here. Moreover, St. Paul is giving advice to Timothy how to conduct himself in God's habitation, which is also the pillar and foundation of the truth. It is in regard to this observation incidentally introduced, that St. Paul, as his manner is, turns aside to explain how it is that the Church merits this high appellation. The relations of Christ and His Church are, he says, a great mystery, as he had already stated in a former Epistle.[1] But the reason why the Church is the pillar and ground of the truth is because it is the Church of the living God, of Him who, having been manifest in flesh, declared righteous in spirit, seen by angels, and believed on in the world, was now received up to heaven in glory. Through the inhabitation of this Divine Redeemer it is that the Church is able to bear witness to and to support the empire of truth in the world.

But we are not obliged to depend on this passage alone. Christ is the εἰκὼν Θεοῦ,[2] by whom all things in heaven and earth are made.[3] He is the ἀπαύγασμα, the beaming forth of the Father's glory, the revelation of His Light to those who were outside its influence.[4]

[1] Eph. v. 32. It is impossible to avoid noticing the recurrence here of a similar expression on a similar subject. [2] 2 Cor. iv. 4. Col. i. 15.
[3] 1 Cor. viii. 6. Eph. iii. 9, though most of the best MSS. omit ἐν χριστῷ Ἰησοῦ, Col. i. 16. Heb. i. 2, 10; xi. 3. The word in the last passage is ῥῆμα.
[4] Heb. i. 3. I cite the Epistle to the Hebrews among the writings of St. Paul, because the most strenuous opponent of its Pauline authorship will not deny that it represents the Pauline school of thought, and because the more I study it, the more I feel that the points of connection are significant, while the divergencies are no greater than may be expected between a letter written *currente calamo*, and a formal treatise written with deliberation and care. Moreover, if St. Paul did not write it, I fail to see who could have done so.

Far above angels, and principalities, and powers, soars His unapproachable Majesty,[1] insomuch that the Father addresses Him as God.[2] Again, He thought it not robbery to be equal with God,[3] though, as St. John tells us, there were those who did think it such.[4] St. Paul adds that He was "in the form of God;" an expression which is rendered more distinct by the subsequent statement that He took the form of a servant. His unchangeableness is demonstrated by the statement that yesterday, to-day, and for ever He is the same.[5] All things are put under Him, says the Apostle:[6] recalling the declaration in St. John's Gospel[7] that all things were given into the Saviour's hands. He is the Lord from heaven.[8] God was in Him, reconciling the world unto Himself:[9] a passage which seems to throw some light on the interpretation of 1 Tim. iii. 16. But yet His power, His very being was derived. God was His Father as well as ours;[10] nay, even His God as well as ours.[11] Christ was His,[12] and drew His Life from Him as His Head, or source;[13] He was sent by the Father.[14]

[1] Heb. i. 4-7.   [2] Heb. i. 8.
[3] Phil. ii. 6. This seems on the whole the best interpretation of the passage.   [4] St. John v. 18; x. 33.
[5] Heb. xiii. 8.   [6] 1 Cor. xv. 27. Heb. ii. 8.
[7] By the Baptist, in chap. iii. 35; by Christ Himself, in xvii. 2, and by the Apostle, in xiii. 3.
[8] 1 Cor. xv. 47. κύριος is however omitted in many of the best MSS. and versions, though it is found as early as Tertullian. Alford says that Tertullian ascribed its insertion to Marcion, but he does not appear to have done so. His language is not quite clear, but he appears to have read κύριος.—' Adv. Marc.' v. 10.
[9] 2 Cor. v. 19.   [10] Rom. xv. 6, &c.   [11] Eph. i. 17.
[12] 1 Cor. iii. 23. Cf. Rev. xi. 15 and Ps. ii. 2.   [13] 1 Cor. xi. 3.
[14] Gal. iv. 4. It is remarkable that this phrase, so common in St. John, should be confirmed by *one* passage only in St. Paul. Cf. however St. Matt. xxi. 37. St. Mark xii. 4.

Doctrine of the Logos & the Person of Christ. 63

He became to us, from the Father, Wisdom, and Righteousness and Sanctification, and Redemption.[1] He is described as God's Power and God's Wisdom to those who are called.[2] On the other hand, affirmations of His true humanity are not wanting. He is the second man.[3] He "took upon Himself the form of a servant, and was found in fashion as a man."[4] He is "the Man Christ Jesus."[5] He is of the seed of David,[6] of Abraham.[7] In the days of His flesh He offered His supplication with strong crying and tears unto Him who was able to save Him from death."[8] He was "made a little lower than the angels on account of the suffering of death."[9] His death is referred to so frequently as to make reference unnecessary. Thus we see the same paradox with reference to His Nature affirmed by St. Paul and his school as is to be found in St. John.[10] The highest attributes of Divinity are held to be compatible with a kind of subordination, with the assumption of humanity, with humiliation, suffering, and even death.

Now it is necessary to remember that here again, as on the question of the Nature of God, agreement was, à priori, by no means to be expected. The doctrines of

[1] 1 Cor. i. 30.   [2] Ib. i. 24.   [3] Ib. xv. 47.
[4] Phil. ii. 7.   [5] 1 Tim. ii. 5.   [6] 2 Tim. ii. 8.
[7] Gal. iii. 16.   [8] Heb. v. 7.   [9] Ib. ii. 9.

[10] "Paul and John, for the purpose of designating the indwelling Divinity of the Redeemer, employed the idea already formed among the Jewish theologians of a mediating Divine principle of revelation, through which the whole creation is connected with the hidden inconceivable essence of God."—Neander, 'Planting and Training,' i. 504. "Thus, too, the doctrine of the Son of God as the Son of Man, in the sense of John and Paul, was not a mere isolated element accidentally mingled with Christianity, but is closely connected with the whole nature of its doctrine and morals."—Ib. p. 507.

the relation of Christ to the Father, of the two natures united in one Person, are not at all easy to be apprehended. Gnostics, Monarchians, Arians, Nestorians, Eutychians, alike misconceived the teaching of Scripture on this point. Several of the Ante-Nicene fathers, and even the great Origen himself, are charged with making use of loose and inaccurate expressions upon these high mysteries. Marcellus of Ancyra could not defend orthodoxy against the Arians without falling into Sabellianism.[1] But St. Paul and St. John are in exact accord. In spite of all diversities of disposition and of style, they agree in representing Christ to be God, and to be Man; and not only this, but they both hold similar language on the far more subtle question of the relation of Christ as God to His Father.[2] They both believe that the Father is the God of our Lord Jesus Christ,[3] the fount of all being, human, angelic or divine; while at the same time they maintain the essential equality of the Father and the Son. We do not at present inquire which writer represents the earlier form of Christian doctrine. We are content with affirming that, so far as our investigation has yet proceeded, the fourth Gospel, instead of being at variance, is in perfect harmony with the other books of the New Testament, and that this harmony is closest and most remarkable in the case of the Epistles of St. Paul.

[1] Neander, 'History of the Christian Church,' iv. 51; Gibbon, 'Decline and Fall,' iii. 58 (Milman's Ed.).
[2] See above, pp. 22, 29. [3] And so does St. Peter. See 1 Pet. i. 3.

CHAPTER III.

DOCTRINE OF THE INCARNATION.

ONE of the most remarkable characteristics of modern theology is the feeble hold which it has had upon the practical results flowing from the Incarnation of Christ. Most of us can remember the time when the good news of Christmas was explained to consist in this, that Christ came into the world in order that He might die upon the Cross for our sins; and some, like the writer of this Essay in his early youth, may have wondered why the simple initiation of a purpose hereafter to be fulfilled should have been heralded by such rejoicings among the angels above, or celebrated with such tokens of gladness by the Church below. Much of this lack of a due appreciation of the nature and benefits of Christ's Incarnation must be ascribed to the exclusive preaching of the Sacrifice of Propitiation on the Cross[1] by one particular school among us. The effect of this preaching has not been confined to that school, but has been felt among those who, on many points, were most strongly opposed to it. But perhaps we may go further back still. We may doubt whether the absence

[1] I avoid the use of the term Atonement, inasmuch as I conceive it to have been effected by Christ's work as a whole, and not by any one act or part of it.

of a critical study of the New Testament, in the original tongue, among the theologians of the Latin Church, has not led to some indefiniteness in regard to the true doctrine of the Incarnation. Even in St. Augustine himself we may detect the first germs of a disposition to substitute a certain theological conception called grace for the action of the Holy Spirit, and this disposition has been intensified among his successors.[1] Nor did the Reformation do much to correct this tendency. It is only in our own times, when the study of the New Testament in the original has become universal among the clergy, and when a general study of the Greek Fathers has been added to that of the traditional Latin authorities, that a firmer grasp of Christian doctrine has begun to reward the labours of the student. And thus we are escaping from the endless controversies about faith and works, predestination and free-will, nature and grace, justification and its processes, which disturbed our forefathers, into a region which affords a wider range of view—a region where the believer is lost in the contemplation of a fountain not only of pardon but of life, flowing into the heart of every Christian, from the Father as its source, by the Son as its enabling power, through the Spirit as the active and efficient operating cause.

[1] See Appendix I. St. Cyril of Alexandria, as his commentary on St. John when compared with others (e.g. that of St. Chrysostom) shows, has far surpassed his Greek brethren in his hold on the principles of the Incarnation, as they did the Latins. Perhaps in no English divine, till our own time, is the influence of Greek theology on this point more marked than in Bishop Andrewes. It is remarkable, moreover, how little the Pelagian heresy affected the East, and it is not enough to explain this fact, as is frequently done, by the practical nature of the question.

Doctrine of the Incarnation. 67

This doctrine is to be found in all its completeness in St. John. As the course of our inquiry will, however, show us, it is not confined to his pages. It is insisted upon with equal earnestness by St. Paul, and it is expressed or implied with more or less clearness in all the other books of the New Testament. The argument for the genuineness of the fourth Gospel which may thus be adduced derives additional force from the fact that in later times, at least in the West, this doctrine has in some measure been neglected. We proceed to examine the teaching of the New Testament upon this head, remembering that the more complex in detail it appears to be in each separate book, the more powerfully must we be led to seek a common origin for their contents solely in the oral teaching of Jesus Christ. We will commence with St. John's anthropology, as it has been termed. We are not in a position to estimate properly his doctrine of the Incarnation, until we understand his views of the condition of man previous to the Saviour's coming. It happens that St. John is unusually distinct on this point. He frequently describes the condition of man before he possessed the enabling power of the Light of Life. Man was then in darkness.[1] Even when Christ had come man did not always obtain the blessings He came to give.[2] Nay, there were many who preferred darkness to light;[3] in whose hearts there still remained that alienation from all that was good which stirred them up to resist Christ's teaching,[4] and to vex and persecute His followers.[5] This state of mind St. John denotes by the word

[1] St. John i. 5.   [2] Ib. i. 5, 10, 11.   [3] Ib. iii. 19, 20, 21.
[4] Ib. xii. 37, 40.   [5] Ib. xv. 19; xvii. 14, 16.

σάρξ,[1] and it is placed in the sharpest antagonism to that possession of an inner life, breathed into the heart by Divine influence, which is denominated by the word πνεῦμα.[2] From this condition of alienation from God man cannot deliver himself: he needs an intervention from above to rescue him from the empire of darkness.

This was the work the Son of God came to do. If man lay in darkness, Christ came to give him light. If his life was little better than a living death, Christ came to breathe into his nostrils yet again, and more effectually, that breath of God through which man first became a living soul, and through which now he became a quickened spirit.[3] Life and Light are the ever-recurring theme of the Gospel we are now considering. "In Him was life, and the life was the light of men," says the author, of Christ, at the outset. And to establish this innumerable declarations of Christ Himself are cited. He came that men might have Life;[4] He came to give Life to His sheep.[5] He quickeneth whom He will.[6] Nay, He is Himself the Life.[7] Life and Light would seem to be almost interchangeable words in this Gospel. We have just quoted the words of the prologue. Similar declarations are attributed to our Lord in the course of this narrative. "He that followeth Me shall have the light of life,"[8] are His words. He repeats over and over again the expression "I am the light of the world,"[9] and by the connection of this idea with that of Life He would seem

---

[1] St. John iii. 6. Compare viii. 15.   [2] Ib. i. 13; iii. 5.
[3] I have borrowed St. Paul's language to express what is found again and again in St. John's pages.   [4] St. John x. 10.
[5] Ib. x. 28.   [6] Ib. v. 21.   [7] Ib. xi. 25; xiv. 6.
[8] Ib. viii. 12.   [9] Ib. viii. 12; ix. 5; xii. 35, 36, 46.

Doctrine of the Incarnation. 69

to imply something more than mere intellectual illumination, something which entirely changes the current of man's being, just as the sun, when it revisits, after a long absence, the portions of our earth which lie near the poles, causes all organic creation to quicken into activity.

A similar idea seems to be contained in the word πνεῦμα as used in this Gospel. A breath from God, which comes by Jesus Christ,[1] is imparted to man to inspire him with new life. On entering into the kingdom of God he is born anew by this Divine influence from above,[2] and his whole nature as well as relation to God is changed.[3] From σάρξ he becomes πνεῦμα; flesh is revivified by the breath of God, and that reviving influence is compared to that of fresh, living water upon an exhausted frame.[4] This doctrine of the mighty change wrought in man by the Spirit is a first principle of Christ's kingdom, and as such it was revealed to Nicodemus, one of the earliest inquirers concerning the nature of that kingdom. Every one who sought an entrance into it must first of all come under that influence of the Spirit which was called the new generation or birth,[5] a process which is elsewhere declared to have originated not in any human influence whether of natural generation, of the will of the individual himself, or of any other human being, but solely and simply in the will of God.[6] We shall examine more closely the doctrine of this Gospel concerning the Spirit of God in another chapter. Suffice it to say here that He

[1] St. John xv. 26.   [2] Ib. iii. 5.   [3] Ib. iii. 6, 7, 8.
[4] Ib. iv. 14; vii. 38, 39.   [5] Ib. iii. 3.   [6] Ib. i. 13.

is represented as the Personal Being who carries into effect the purposes of God in Jesus Christ.[1] In an inferior degree, again, even the words of Christ, being in a sense the breath of God, are endued with a kind of Divine vitality.[2] And here we come into contact with another statement of the mode in which this Divine vitality becomes operative in the soul. These words, which are Spirit and Life, contain the revelation of the truth that it is the Flesh and Blood, the human nature of Christ, which is the means of giving life to the world.[3] That is to say, humanity in general was to be restored by the humanity of Christ.[4] This was to be inwrought in man by a spiritual communication, analogous in its effects to those of eating and drinking in the natural man. The same truth is taught in another form in ch. xv. Here Christ is the Vine, and His disciples the branches. A constant stream of Life flows from Himself to them, or rather He is identified with them by reason of the mutual possession of a common life which is not really theirs but His. And in that mysterious seventeenth chapter, which however imperfectly apprehended,

[1] St. John xv. 26; xvi. 13.
[2] Ib. vi. 63. Cf. Hengstenberg *in loc.*   [3] Ib. vi. 51-58.
[4] "I wish to impart to you this grace, ministering the full benefit, namely, incorruption; and I grant to you the knowledge of God, my perfect self. This am I: this God desires: this is symphony: this is the harmony of the Father: this is Christ: this the Word of God, the Arm of the Lord, the power of all things, the Will of the Father. . . . I desire to bring you into conformity with the archetype that ye may be like Me. I will anoint you with the ointment of faith, by which ye may cast off corruption, and I show you the naked form of righteousness by which ye may ascend to God." The Saviour is represented as speaking thus in Clem. Alex. 'Cohortatio ad Græcos,' cap. 12.

Doctrine of the Incarnation. 71

has ever been a source of untold comfort to Christians, the mystical union between Christ and His followers is traced to a deeper source still. It takes its rise in the unity of the Godhead itself. There is as close and as personal an union between Christ and the believer who has attained to his perfection as between the Persons in the Sacred Trinity itself. Jesus prays that "all may be One; as Thou, Father, art in Me, and I in Thee, that they also may be one in Us." "I in them, and thou in Me, that they all may be made perfect unto One."

The Epistle of St. John is full of the same teaching. The mutual indwelling of God and man is asserted and reasserted no less explicitly than in the Gospel.[1] Christians "walk in the light," because "the darkness is past, and the true light now shineth."[2] They are born of God, and the result of the completion of that birth is freedom from sin.[3] Eternal Life, which was with the Father, was manifested to the disciples of Christ.[4] The token whereby they may discern the indwelling of God is the possession of His Spirit.[5] If what they have heard from the beginning abide in them, they shall continue not only in the Son, but in the Father.[6] One passage, indeed, may be taken as summing up the Johannean doctrine on this head: "This is the record, that God hath given to us eternal life, and this life is in His Son. He that hath the Son hath life, and he that hath not the Son of God hath not life."[7]

---

[1] 1 John iii. 24; iv. 12, 15, 16.   [2] Ib. i. 7; ii. 8.
[3] Ib. iii. 9; v. 18. The force of the perfect participle would seem to be that given above.
[4] Ib. i. 2.   [5] Ib. iii. 24.   [6] Ib. ii. 24.
[7] Ib. v. 11, 12. Cf. Iren. 'Adv. Hær.,' book iv. 20, 4. "By Him

72   *The Doctrinal System of St. John.*

We have seen that the life inherent in Jesus Christ, God and Man, is, according to the theology of the fourth Gospel, communicated to mankind by the agency of the Divine Spirit. We have next to inquire whether any subsidiary agencies are employed in the work, and if so, what is their nature. We have at the outset of the fourth Gospel an intimation that the communication of Divine life was in some way associated with the employment of a certain external ordinance. Man is not to be born of the Spirit alone, but of water also. It would seem tolerably clear that here we have a reference to the Sacrament of Baptism, which it is admitted on all hands was instituted by Christ. The close connection of the words " water and the Spirit" in the original, to which it is impossible to do justice in a translation, would appear to point to baptism as the ordinary means whereby the gift of the new birth was conveyed. And the manner in which Christ's Passion and Ascension are dwelt upon in connection with this idea[1] would lead us to ascribe the blessing of regeneration, not to this or that portion of the Redeemer's work, but to His career as a whole. By His Life the Father's justice was satisfied by a perfect obedience.[2] By His Death a propitiation was made for the sins of the whole world.[3] By His Resurrection the power of triumphing over death was conveyed.[4] His Ascension was, for some unexplained reason, necessary before the Spirit could

---

was effected a commingling and communion between God and man according to the pleasure of the Father . . . . making us serve Him in holiness and justice all our days, that when man had embraced the Spirit of God, he might walk to the glory of the Father."

[1] St. John iii. 13, 14.   [2] 1 John iii. 5. St. John viii. 29, 46.
[3] 1 John ii. 2; iv. 10.   [4] St. John xi. 25.

Doctrine of the Incarnation. 73

be given.[1] The gift of the Spirit, and the new Life He imparted, was thus the result of Christ's Life on earth, of His Death, Resurrection, and Ascension. It was from these that the Sacrament of Baptism received all its power. This interpretation derives some confirmation from the fact that the Evangelist, immediately after the passage we have been considering, mentions the use of the Sacrament of Baptism by Christ, and we are thus led to the conclusion that in the discourse to Nicodemus Christ is explaining the rudimentary principles of His kingdom, into which, ordinarily speaking, the reception of baptism was at once the token and the means of entrance.

But the Life thus imparted, we are further taught, is governed by the same laws as the natural life of man. It comes to maturity by means of growth, and growth is ministered by nourishment. There is this difference between the two processes. In our natural life we seize on other substances, and convert them by mysterious and inexplicable processes into the means of supporting existence. In the spiritual world, on the contrary, the power which gives Life, and the power which sustains it, is one and the same. It is the Life of Christ which communicates Life to man; and it is the Life of Christ which sustains it. Our life must be in continual dependence upon His, if we are to possess it permanently. Therefore, in another of His discourses Jesus enlarges upon the means of preserving the Life which He has given. He compares His sustaining power to the action of food upon the body. The

[1] St. John xvi. 7. The reason is explained in the Epistle to the Hebrews. See below chap. iv.

soul, He declares, requires bread for its sustenance, and this bread is Himself. He is the living Bread which came down from heaven.[1] The true bread which came down from heaven was not intended, like the manna, to afford a temporary support, but to give a permanent Life to the world.[2] And then He proceeds to connect this doctrine with His humanity, in the assertion that this bread of which He spake was His flesh, which He would give for the Life of the world.[3] Taking flesh and blood as the symbol of His human nature, He announces that a perpetual communication of that flesh and blood to the soul of the Christian was the indispensable condition of the maintenance of the Life he had received from above. No doubt He here would have us understand some reference to the Paschal Lamb, which was not only the deliverance, but the food also of the Jews in the night of their departure from Egypt. And here, moreover, we are again led to connect this spiritual nourishment by Christ of His children with the principal events of His Life upon earth. The whole tenor of the discourse implies a reference to Christ's Death upon the Cross, though it is by no means to be confined to this one point. It is expressly connected with the Resurrection and Ascension of Christ, and with the office of the Holy Spirit, in the 62nd and 63rd verses of this chapter, where Christ answers the objections of His hearers by a mysterious allusion to these events, as yet in the future.[4] We can scarcely, I

---

[1] St. John vi. 51.   [2] Ib. vi. 58.   [3] Ib. vi. 51.
[4] After His manner, it may be observed, as recorded in the Synoptists, "Without a parable spake He not unto them." The manner in which He refers to His Resurrection and Ascension is more compatible

Doctrine of the Incarnation. 75

think, refuse to see in this discourse, so full of dark and hidden sayings, an enunciation of the principles which underlie the institution of the Sacrament of Holy Communion, or to acknowledge, in the words of the institution of that Sacrament at what was regarded by Christ and His Apostles as a Paschal supper,[1] an explanation of the difficulty which repelled so many of His disciples from Him after His discourse at Capernaum.[2]

It would seem, then, that the Life of Christ, imparted to men through the agency of the Holy Spirit, is ordinarily communicated through the medium, as St. John's words seem to indicate, of certain outward signs. But on man's part a certain condition of soul is required, without which he is incapable of receiving the gift which God's mercy has designed for him. This condition of soul is called faith. And here I may take the opportunity of remarking that a view of the distinguishing characteristics of St. Paul and St. John, which has been constantly repeated, even by distinguished Biblical critics and eminent divines, does

---

with the idea that they were still to come, than with the theory that they were past events or else inventions of credulity or inconsiderate zeal, and the discourse invented to square with such inventions.

[1] The difficulty of reconciling the Synoptic narratives, which speak of the Eucharistic meal as the Passover, with St. John's assertion that it was eaten on the day of the Crucifixion, has long perplexed the commentators, and no thoroughly satisfactory solution has yet been offered.

[2] How can this man give us His flesh to eat? St. John vi. 52. The reference to the sacraments in the third and sixth chapters of the Gospel seems to be generally admitted by commentators of the most widely divergent schools, with the curious exception of the ultra-Protestants and the Jesuits.

not seem to possess the slightest foundation in fact. I refer to the idea that the foundation of St. Paul's system is faith, while that of St. John's is love. We hear, on high authority, that the influence of St. Paul on Christian theology is destined henceforth to decline, and that the Christianity of the future will be coloured principally by the teaching of the Apostle of Love.[1] But this distinction between the system of St. Paul and that of St. John disappears before a careful examination. It would appear to be one of those theological commonplaces which men catch up from one another, and repeat without carefully examining the grounds on which they rest. It might with just as much truth be asserted that the keystone of St. John's system was faith, while the main feature of St. Paul's is love. For nowhere can we find more emphatic assertions of the indispensable necessity of faith than in St. John; while, on the other hand, nowhere do we find clearer assertions of the paramount importance of love than in St. Paul.

It is strange that this fact has been so much overlooked. Possibly the peculiarity of our English version, which has rendered ἀγάπη so frequently by charity, may have blinded the eyes even of scholars whose earliest ideas have been tinged by the use of the English Bible. But of the fact itself I think there can be little doubt. It will appear with much greater distinctness when we have concluded the investigation in which we are now engaged.[2] And though perhaps

[1] Mr. Matthew Arnold, 'St. Paul and Protestantism.'
[2] Though it has an affinity with a kind of criticism which has been pressed too far, I may remark that the word ἀγάπη occurs seven times

Doctrine of the Incarnation. 77

we are anticipating a conclusion to which our inquiries will lead us, we cannot fail on this particular point to be struck with the exact identity between Christianity as taught by St. Paul and Christianity as taught by St. John.

That a position of supreme importance is assigned to faith in the Christian scheme as unfolded by St. John there can be little doubt. It is the very starting-point of the Christian life. It is quite unnecessary to multiply references. The assertion meets us on almost every page. God's part in the mystery of salvation is first, however, secured from misapprehension. St. John starts in his Gospel by asserting the whole work to be of God. All salvation comes from Him as its ultimate source. God the Father is declared by God the Word.[1] God the Word it was who gave power to men to become the sons of God by means of the new Life imparted to them.[2] God the Holy Spirit it was through whom that new life was communicated.[3] And it is not till this foundation is thoroughly well laid, the principle clearly asserted which is afterwards expressed in the words "no man can come unto Me, except the Father which hath sent Me draw him,'[4] that St. John introduces Christ's words, declaring man's

---

in St. John's Gospel, seventeen times in his first Epistle, and seventy-three times in those of St. Paul. But the verb ἀγαπάω occurs twenty times in St. John's Gospel, twenty-eight times in his first Epistle, and is only thirty-three times used by St. Paul. I have included the Epistle to the Hebrews, where, however, each of the words in question only occurs twice.

[1] St. John i. 18.   [2] Ib. i. 12, 13.   [3] Ib. iii. 3.
[4] Ib. vi. 44. Also in xvii. 2, 6, 9, 24, Jesus speaks of all His disciples as "given to Him" by the Father.

part in the work of salvation, "He that believeth on Him is not condemned."[1] Henceforth such declarations of the power of faith abound, without stint and almost without qualification. "He that believeth the Son hath everlasting life, and he that believeth not the Son shall not see life, but the wrath of God abideth on him."[2] "This is the work of God, that ye believe on Him whom He hath sent."[3] "He that believeth in Me, though he were dead, yet shall he live, and whosoever liveth and believeth in Me shall never die."[4] "He that believeth on Me, the works that I do he shall do also."[5] "These things are written that ye might believe that Jesus is the Christ, the Son of God, and that believing ye might have life in His Name."[6]

This leading doctrine of faith as the sole avenue through which spiritual power is able to enter the human soul is asserted with equal distinctness in St. John's Epistle. "This is His commandment, that we should believe on the Name of His Son Jesus Christ."[7] "Every spirit that confesseth that Jesus Christ is come of the flesh is of God."[8] The declaration rises in force and depth each time it is repeated, like the sayings of Christ in St. John's Gospel: "Whosoever shall confess that Jesus is the Son of God, God dwelleth in him and he in God;"[9] and finally we are led to regard it as the fundamental principle which lies at the root of all outward confession and of all inward Life: "Whosoever

---

[1] St. John iii. 18. St. John does speak of the power to become the sons of God as given to "those who believe on His name," in i. 12; but it is incidentally, and not by any means emphatically.
[2] Ib. iii. 36; vi. 47.
[3] Ib. vi. 29.
[4] Ib. xi. 25, 26. Also xii. 44; xiv. i. 11.
[5] Ib. xiv. 12.
[6] Ib. xx. 31.
[7] 1 John iii. 23.
[8] Ib. iv. 2.
[9] Ib. iv. 15.

Doctrine of the Incarnation. 79

believeth that Jesus is the Christ is born of God;"[1] and are asked to contemplate its result: "Whatsoever is born of God overcometh the world: and this is the victory that overcometh the world, even our faith. Who is he that overcometh the world but he that believeth that Jesus is the Son of God?"[2]

We observe in this summary of St. John's teaching on the subject of faith, that he attributes to it the same powers which he does to the regenerating principle flowing from Christ Himself, and to the work of the Spirit.[3] We are "born of God" by His will alone: we are "born of the Spirit:" we are "born of God" if we believe in Him. Jesus Christ has "overcome the world." He has "destroyed the works of the devil;" "whatsoever is born of God cannot sin;" yet nevertheless our faith "is the victory that overcometh the world." What conclusion can we come to from this, but that St. John views the work of salvation now from a Divine, now from a human point of view; and that as he views it from one stand-point or the other he attributes the whole work to God alone, or to faith as the only means whereby God can act upon the soul? But while he does not omit to intimate, in the words of Christ Himself, how important a part a certain condition of the human soul has to play in the regeneration of

[1] 1 John v. i. Also verses 9, 10. The repetitions of St. John's Epistle are very far from being vain repetitions.
[2] Ib. v. 4, 5. The same principle is asserted in the Apocalypse, where the unbelieving are classed with the rest of the ungodly, and the sentence of eternal punishment pronounced against them. Rev. xxi. 8.
[3] "The objective on the part of God corresponds to the subjective on the part of man, namely, faith."—Neand. 'Planting and Training,' vol. i. p. 457 [Bohn's Ed.]. "Faith is the reception and vital appropriation of the Divine Revelation," or rather Life.—*Ib.* p. 458.

man, he takes care, as we have seen, to lay it down that the original cause of all is to be found nowhere but in the Will of God,[1] the operating principle of that Love, which is Himself.[2] Faith, then, though subordinate and secondary to the working of God's Spirit, is the one all-important requisite on man's part in order that the regenerating power may act upon his soul. But faith has its laws of working; faith must issue in the communication to the individual of the life of Christ; and this life following the analogy of the natural life, capable of expansion and of growth, depending for its continuance upon external support, must have certain results in its influence on mankind. In point of fact, faith must produce likeness to God—in other words, Love. Love is the very Being of God Himself. When that Being is inwrought into each individual deriving Life from Him, the result must be a vast society, animated as it were by one soul, and breathing the spirit of the universal Love. This result will be seen in measure and degree in this world, though cramped and hindered by the influences still at work in each individual which are opposed to the Gospel of Christ. We should expect to find a theory of a Holy Catholic Church, a society in which faith is the one essential requisite, and love the one abiding principle; a body the members of which are knit to one another and to their Lord by the closest and most inward of ties; a body which assumes a position of antagonism to the principles which sway unregenerate man, and is in continual conflict with those who deny the pretensions

---

[1] St. John vi. 44; xv. 5: "Without Me ye can do nothing."
[2] 1 John iv. 8.

Doctrine of the Incarnation. 81

of Christ to be the Saviour of mankind, or who, while professing to accept Him, reject the fundamental moral and spiritual laws of His kingdom.

The outlines of such a state of things may be clearly seen in the Gospel. Under various types and figures such a society is shadowed forth, while the ties which should bind the members of such a society together, and the feelings which should animate them in their conduct towards each other, are also indicated beforehand by the Saviour. He does not confine Himself to the external relation of His disciples to Himself, though He does occasionally use language incapable of a wider interpretation—language of a kind which, when found in the Synoptists, is regarded as proof positive of an irreconcilable divergence between his views and theirs. He speaks of Himself, for instance, as a Shepherd, and His disciples as sheep,[1] and from that point of view regards His Church as a gathering together of distinct individualities into one society, with no hint at any closer union between Himself and them.[2] But He does not stop there. He prefers to describe His Church as an organic whole, its parts combined in a deep interior unity, the result of the possession by its members of a Life which they all enjoy in common, and which they all derive from Him. The first hint of a closer union is given when Christ is spoken of as the Bridegroom, and they who come to Him as the Bride.[3] But it is amplified by Christ

---
[1] St. John x.   [2] Ib. x. 16.
[3] These words of St. John the Baptist were afterwards expounded by St. Paul (Eph. v.). And the influence they had on St. John's mind is clearly shown by his allusion to them in the Apocalypse, xxi. 2, 9 ; xxii. 17.

82 The Doctrinal System of St. John.

Himself. Thus, as we have seen, He is the Vine; His disciples are the branches.[1] From Him, the source of Life, flows the Life into every portion of His Church. Separation from the Vine is certain death.[2] But if the branches remain in the Vine, an impulse of Life is continually communicated to them, and by this they arrive at their perfection, and bring forth their natural fruit. What that fruit is we need scarcely inquire, although Christ does not specify it. It can be no other than good works. No other result could flow from a participation in the Life of Christ. Their absence could only serve to show that he who had them not had neither part nor lot in Christ. If men are content to submit themselves to the operations of the Divine power within them, the good works will follow as a matter of course. But whether they will do so or not depends on themselves. They may either surrender themselves to the operation of the life-giving principle, or they may resist its operation. This is the force of the exhortations to abide in Christ, which have no meaning except on the supposition of a power to resist the influences of Christ and His Spirit.

Such is the doctrine taught in the parable of the Vine and the branches. But it is not confined to that parable, it also pervades the whole of St. John's writings. It is implied in the declaration that a man needs to be born again. It is enforced in the assertion that he who has received the new birth of the Spirit has henceforth had a new character impressed upon him.[3] It is the pervading idea of the discourse in chapter vi., in which

[1] St. John xv. [2] Ib. xv. 4, 6. [3] Ib. iii. 6.

Doctrine of the Incarnation. 83

Christ proclaims Himself to be the necessary and continual support of all who would receive salvation by His means. In the seventeenth chapter we have it asserted and reasserted that the bond which compacts the people of God together is the possession by each one of them of an inward Life which is not their own, but which proceeds from God. The Life everlasting which they possess is His gift.[1] He prays that they may be made holy in the truth, which is nothing else but the utterance or revelation of the will of God.[2] He goes on to pray for the unity of His disciples,—not for a mere external unity of a visible association, not for a mere agreement in any confession of faith, but an inward unity, the result of the indwelling of the Life of God.[3] This is what the Apostle means by the κοινωνία of which he speaks in his Epistle.[4] The effect of the manifestation of the Life[5] is the association of those who receive it in the possession of this heritage of all Christians; and this heritage is something which we possess in some mysterious way, in common with the Father, and Jesus Christ His Son. The consequences of that possession are manifold. The first and most important of them is holiness. God the Father is asked to sanctify or make holy those whom He has given to the Son.[6] He is asked to preserve them from what

---

[1] Ver. 2.
[2] "Thy word is truth," ver. 17, 19: bearing in mind that our expression "word" does not exhaust the force of the expression λόγος.
[3] Ver. 21, 22, 23. The reading ὅ, instead of οὕς, seems to imply the consolidation of all believers into one visible reality, the Body, in short, of Christ.
[4] 1 John i. 3.   [5] Ib. i. 2.   [6] St. John xvii. 17, 19.

is evil.[1] He is asked to save them from the defiling contact of a world which has no participation in the Life of God.[2] In the necessary antagonism between them and this evil world, a power of strength and victory is given to them.[3] "Be of good cheer, I have overcome the world," says Jesus, and His words would seem to have made a deep impression upon His disciple. He repeats them from time to time in various forms, both in his Epistle and in the Apocalypse. The faith of a Christian is the victory that overcometh the world.[4] It is the pride of a Christian that he has "overcome the wicked one."[5] The spirit of Anti-Christ is overcome by the Christian, because "He that is in him is greater than he that is in the world."[6] All the promises of future glory in the Apocalypse are made to him that overcometh, by virtue of the power conferred by the Divine indwelling.[7] This power, however, it rests with them to employ or not, as they please. No irresistible grace is conveyed to them. They may either come to the light, or refuse to do so.[8] They may either receive Christ, or reject Him.[9] They may either remain with Him, or go away.[10] Nay, even among His closest and most attached followers there may be those who do not cleave to Him aright.[11] But if they will preserve undivided the connection that subsists between them-

---

[1] St. John xvii. 15. Some commentators prefer to render this "the evil one." The context would lead one rather to suppose that what is meant is the evil prevalent in a world which "lieth in darkness."

[2] St. John xvii. 14–16.   [3] Ib. xvi. 33; 1 John iii. 9.
[4] 1 John v. 4.   [5] Ib. ii. 13; v. 4.   [6] Ib. iv. 4.
[7] Rev. ii. 7, 11, 17, 26; iii. 5, 12, 21; xxi. 7.
[8] St. John iii. 20, 21; viii. 12.   [9] Ib. i. 11.
[10] Ib. vi. 67.   [11] Ib. vi. 70.

Doctrine of the Incarnation.

selves and Christ, they are sure of victory in the end,[1] and not only of victory, but reward.[2] The end of the struggle is the victory over death itself. Death has no more than a temporary power over those who are united to Christ.[3] And not only so, but the intermediate state between death and the resurrection is one of life.[4]

The next consequence is that of mutual love. By their mutual love, their union in the life of God, men should recognize Christ's disciples, and Christ Himself as sent by God.[5] Purity and truth were also among the blessings communicated by the Life which resided in them.[6] And they also derived from it the privilege of an entirely different relation to God. They are once more His children, and have a claim on His love.[7] They have henceforth a title to be heard in prayer.[8] Nor is this all. They are to be themselves the medium whereby these blessings are communicated to others. "He that believeth in Me, out of his belly shall flow rivers of living water."[9] Some at least of them are to receive a special mission to the world. In that mission they stand as the representatives of Christ. "He that receiveth whomsoever I send receiveth Me."[10] And again, "As My Father hath sent Me, even so send I you."[11]

---

[1] See passages cited above with reference to overcoming.

[2] Rev. ii. iii. "He united, as we have said, man to God. For if man had not conquered the enemy of man, the enemy was not fairly vanquished."—Iren. 'Adv. Hær.' book iii. 18, 7.

[3] St. John vi. 44, 54.

[4] Ib. xi. 25. Our Lord's promise of life is not confined, in His answer to Martha, to a resurrection at the last day.

[5] St. John xiii. 35; xvii. 21. [6] Ib. xiii. 10; xv. 3.

[7] Ib. xvi. 27. [8] Ib. xiv. 13; xv. 7, 16; xvi. 23-27.

[9] Ib. vii. 37. Compare 1 John i. 2, 3. [10] Ib. xiii. 20.

[11] Ib. xx. 21.

A certain power of discerning the spirits of men, and a certain authority over the external discipline of the Church, was committed to the rulers of His Church. Such, without entering upon the endless controversies suggested by the passage, would seem to be a reasonable inference from the words, " Whose soever sins ye remit, they are remitted unto them, and whose soever sins ye retain, they are retained." These powers resided in the ministers of Christ by virtue of an abiding presence of the Holy Spirit within their hearts, a presence promised and communicated by Jesus Christ Himself.[1] And the peculiar work they were to do among God's people was indicated in the charge given to one among them who was more than once singled out as the representative of his brethren, to be the feeding and shepherding of the lambs and sheep of their Master's flock.[2]

To sum up briefly what has been said of St. John's teaching about the Incarnation and its results, we find its substance to have been this. A Divine influence has been in the world since the Ascension of Jesus Christ, which has effected a thorough change in every one who has received it; a change which not only alters his relations to God, but which has actually communicated to him a new nature—in fact, a new life. This change has been effected by the infusion of the Life of the ascended Lord into the hearts of all who will

[1] St. John xx. 22.
[2] Ib. xxi. 15, 17. Is it fanciful to see here an undesigned coincidence with such passages as St. Matt. xvi. 19; St. Luke xxii. 31, 32 ? Observe ἐξητήσατο ὑμᾶς and ἐδεήθην περὶ σοῦ. The coincidence is all the more remarkable from the entire absence of all prominence given to this fact of the singling out of St. Peter.

Doctrine of the Incarnation. 87

receive it, by the operation of the Holy Spirit. The one necessary requisite on man's part for the reception of this life is faith; a disposition of the soul which it is impossible for man to produce for himself, but which it is intimated that God is in all cases willing to grant to him, though man has the power and consequent responsibility of accepting or rejecting the gift. Certain external signs and means of grace are made use of in the communication of this life from above, namely, the use of water and the use of food. The individuals thus Divinely quickened are gathered into one body, united by the most inward and intimate of ties. The spiritual life imparted to each does not dwell in himself alone, but circulates through the whole body. In this body, moreover, there are certain officers, whose business it is to superintend and direct the streams of imparted life into their various channels, and to assist in promoting the healthy development of the whole.

We will now examine how far this doctrine is agreeable to what we read in the Synoptic Gospels. And here we naturally revert to the history of the Incarnation, and to the prophecies then uttered, in which we should expect to find some indication of the work Jesus Christ was expected to do. We shall not be disappointed. The angel prophesied of Jesus that He should save His people "from their sins,"[1] nor was this the only prophecy concerning Him. In the

---

[1] Matt. i. 21. Cf. Acts iv. 12; v. 31, &c., and St. Luke ii. 30. We may remark that neither in the Synoptists nor in the Acts is there any explanation of the *modus operandi* of salvation by Christ, insomuch that without a fourth Gospel we are absolutely in the dark respecting

inspired songs which the Holy Ghost spake by the mouths of Zacharias and the blessed Virgin herself, we shall find no obscure intimation of what Christ came to do. We are told of men lying "in darkness and the shadow of death,"[1] of a "day-spring from on high,"[2] which came to "give them light."[3] Not only were they to be "delivered from their enemies," an expression which can only be interpreted as referring to the enemies of the soul, but they were to "live in holiness and righteousness before God all their days,"[4] a promise which could hardly have been realized without some change of nature. The "knowledge of salvation," it is true, came "in the remission of sins,"[5] but the salvation itself was something more than this; it was actual safety from "enemies, and all who hated them."[6] And the song of the blessed Virgin herself implies something more than the advent of a mere teacher. A great spiritual revolution is surely foreshadowed in the words, "He hath shewed strength with His arm. He hath put down the mighty from their seats, and exalted them of low degree;" and the expression, "He hath filled the hungry with good things,"[7] does not, at least, exclude the idea of a gift of a new and better nature from above.

Christ and His Apostles, moreover, proclaimed the same truth. The Redeemer affirms that He has come

---

the first principles of the doctrine of Christ. The passage in St. Matthew implies more than forgiveness. It is not only from the consequences of sin but from sin itself that Christ saves men. *How* this is done we only learn from the fourth Gospel and the Epistles.

[1] St. Luke i. 79.   [2] ἀνατολὴ, Ib. i. 78.
[3] Ib. i. 79.   [4] Ib. i. 74, 75.   [5] Ib. i. 77.
[6] Ib. i. 71.   [7] Ib. i. 52, 53.

"to seek and to save that which was lost."¹ He is thus reported in St. Matthew's Gospel, and St. Luke confirms this report by relating three most striking parables in which this doctrine is enforced.² More than once Jesus speaks of the children of Israel as "lost sheep;"³ and St. Luke relates that His Apostle describes his own mission as being intended to "open men's eyes, to turn them from darkness unto light, and from the power of Satan unto God."⁴ Nor, perhaps, shall we be altogether wrong in regarding the Transfiguration as a deeply suggestive part of the Synoptic narratives. It clearly establishes the fact that some hidden power to transform humanity resided in Christ, some virtue inherent in Him which no humanitarian theory is sufficient to exhaust. From this portion of their narratives, alone, we might construct not only the theory of the Resurrection, but the whole scheme of imparted spiritual vitality as taught in the Epistles and St. John.

Although, as we have seen, the Synoptic Gospels embrace nothing beyond the record of our Lord's public teaching, and leave altogether unnoticed those discourses in which He unfolded the inner mysteries of His kingdom, yet in the course of their narrative expressions are casually let drop which imply that such discourses must have been delivered. The remark contained in the Sermon on the Mount, to the effect that unless the righteousness of Christ's disciples ex-

---

¹ St. Matt. xviii. 11; St. Luke xix. 10.
² The parables of the lost sheep, the lost piece of money, and the prodigal son, in St. Luke xv.
³ St. Matt. x. 6; xv. 24.   ⁴ Acts xxvi. 18.

ceeded the righteousness of the Scribes and Pharisees, they should in no case enter the kingdom of heaven,[1] is a saying of this kind. For how were they to know that their righteousness exceeded that of the Scribes and Pharisees? Not by a formal comparison of the merits of the two parties, for this they were expressly forbidden to make in another portion of the same discourse.[2] What test then was there by which they could estimate the relative excellence of the piety of each? It may be said that the standard of the Scribes and Pharisees was external, while that of Christ's disciples was to be internal and real. But this explanation still implies that they were to sit in judgment upon their fellow-men, a course alien from the humility enjoined by the Gospel. But if we believe that Christ is speaking, though as yet obscurely, of an inner righteousness flowing from Himself, of which all who believed in Him were to be partakers, all the apparent inconsistency in the passage is removed, and His disciples may understand His words to refer to a righteousness different not in degree, but in kind, to any which had yet been revealed.[3] This interpretation derives force from the consideration of other passages in the Synoptic Gospels. Thus the seemingly paradoxical declaration that " among them that are born of women there hath not risen a greater than John the Baptist, notwithstanding he that is least in the kingdom of heaven is greater than he,"[4] can only be

---

[1] St. Matt. v. 20.   [2] Ib. vii. 1.

[3] We are expressly informed, let us remember, by the Synoptists, that it was Christ's method to impart His teaching with a certain reserve. See Mark iv. 11. This will fully account for their own.

[4] St. Matt. xi. 11; St. Luke vii. 28.

Doctrine of the Incarnation. 91

satisfactorily explained of that inner righteousness which Christ came down from heaven to impart. So, too, the words kingdom of God, kingdom of heaven, are repeatedly used throughout the Synoptic narratives, but what constitutes a member of that kingdom we are never told. It is contrary to all reason to suppose that no one ever arose who, like Nicodemus, desired to be informed how to enter that kingdom; yet the only account we have of the question being asked, and of the answer given to it, meets us in the narrative of St. John. Similarly we read of exhortations given to "seek the kingdom of God and His righteousness,"[1] but we are never told how the search is to be carried on, nor how success is to be assured. The emphatic assertions in the New Testament of the utter uselessness of attempting to establish one's own righteousness, would make this passage contradict the whole of the Christian Scriptures, unless we interpret it of the righteousness which prophecy tells us "shall look down from heaven."[2] So with the exhortation to "make the tree good and his fruit good,"[3] and the command to "be converted:"[4] the exhortation is given, but man is without power of himself to do what he is commanded. Christ Himself tells us as much when He insists on the difficulty with which a rich man shall enter into the kingdom of heaven, but He reminds us that "the things that are impossible with men are possible with God.[5] But the doctrine that the kingdom of God was to be the result of an inner power transforming the whole character of those who receive it, is not left in

[1] St. Matt. vi. 33.   [2] Ps. lxxxv. 11.   [3] St. Matt. xii. 33.
[4] στραφῆτε, Ib. xviii. 3.   [5] Ib. xix. 26.

the Synoptic Gospels to mere inference. The parable of the sower presents it to us as the fundamental principle of that kingdom in the individual,[1] and the same doctrine is taught in the parable of the leaven concerning the Church in its corporate capacity. Here then we have a view of the kingdom of Christ identical with that of St. John. The same idea is conveyed in St. Luke's Gospel when the disciples are informed that the kingdom of God is within them. The only difference is that St. John informs us of the nature of the inner principle, while the Synoptists do not.[1] But when we come to the requisites on man's part we find all the Evangelists in exact accord. Faith is the one indispensable requisite for all who would come to Christ,[2] and baptism by water the outward means whereby they are made His disciples.[3] This baptism is described prophetically by St. John the Baptist as a baptism with the Holy Ghost,[4] and his words, though they differ in form, are absolutely identical in substance with the language of our Lord to Nicodemus concerning the new birth " of water and the Spirit."[5] The body of Christians thus formed is spoken of by Christ beforehand as "the Church," the collective decision of whose members

---

[1] Perhaps the parables of the ten virgins and the talents point in the same direction, as also the expression, " ye are the salt of the earth," with other similar passages, as St. Mark ix. 50 and St. Luke xiv. 34.
[2] St. Mark i. 15; ix. 23; x. 52; xvi. 16, &c.
[3] St. Matt. xxviii. 19. St. Mark xvi. 16. The importance of baptism may be inferred from St. Matt. iii. 15, where Jesus speaks of it as a necessary portion of the righteousness He came to fulfil.
[4] St. Matt. iii. 11. St. Mark i. 8.
[5] The word παλιγγενεσία, though found in St. Matt. xix. 28, is applied to the final triumph of the Saviour.

ought to settle all differences in the body and preserve its unity.[1] Though God in Christ is not spoken of as the indwelling power in Christians, yet the Holy Spirit, through whose agency the Father and the Son are represented by St. John as living in us, is spoken of in the Synoptists as inhabiting the disciples. God is spoken of as "giving" His Holy Spirit,[2] and the Holy Spirit, they are told, will speak in them in their hour of trial.[3] By His means they are gathered together into one body, beloved by the Father,[4] enjoying a promise that their prayers are accepted before Him,[5] and fed with the spiritual food of His body and blood. The words in the Lord's Prayer convey this truth in no doubtful terms. The ἄρτος ἐπιούσιος, the bread on which we subsist, could hardly be supposed, in a Gospel whose whole object is to depreciate the present world and to elevate that which is to come, to refer to temporal subsistence alone. Christ Himself had rejected such a supposition when He replied to the tempter that "man did not live by bread alone, but by every word that proceedeth out of the mouth of God." But if any difficulty existed in the explanation of these words, it is removed by the institution of the Lord's Supper, in which Christ's Body is spoken of as given for His disciples, and His blood shed for them, and that in some mysterious way they were to be imparted to His disciples through their repeating His acts "in remembrance of Him."[6]

[1] St. Matt. xviii. 17. It can hardly be supposed that St. Matthew would have taken the trouble to record these words, if they related only to a condition of things which was passing away as he wrote.
[2] St. Luke xi. 13.   [3] St. Matt. x. 20.   [4] St. Luke xii. 32.
[5] St. Matt. vii. 7; xviii. 19; xxi. 22. St. Mark xi. 24, &c.
[6] St. Matt. xxvi. 26-28. St. Mark xiv. 22-24. St. Luke xxii. 19, 20.

94   *The Doctrinal System of St. John.*

We proceed to those passages in the Synoptic narratives which relate to the ministry of the Church. These are but few, but those few are extremely important for our purpose. Not only does the Saviour inform His disciples, over and over again, that whosoever received them would receive Him, and whoso received Him, would receive Him that sent Him.[1] He proceeds to announce to His Apostles His determination to impart to them that mysterious power of the keys, in words which, like those of the institution of the Sacrament, have been a stumbling-block and source of division to Christians. Into the controversy as to their precise force and meaning we need not enter. It is sufficient for our present purpose to remark, that though the form of words is different, their substance in each case is precisely the same. Whereas the commission in St. John runs thus: " Whose soever sins ye remit, they are remitted to them, and whose soever sins ye retain, they have been retained;" in St. Matthew, repeated twice over, and on a different and less solemn occasion than that of which St. John speaks, they assume the form, " Whatsoever ye shall bind on earth shall have been bound in heaven, and whatsoever ye shall loose on earth shall have been loosed in heaven."[2] Add to this the fact that, in each case in

---

In the latter passage the reception of the cup is spoken of as " the new covenant in Christ's blood." The words imply more than a bare recognition of the fact that Christ's blood was shed, such as might possibly be inferred from the language of St. Matthew and St. Mark. The inference which may be drawn from the Synoptic account of the institution of the Lord's Supper will be found in part ii., chap. iii.

[1] Matt. x. 40, &c.
[2] Ib. xvi. 19; xviii. 18. The latter passage " is a middle point

Doctrine of the Incarnation. 95

St. Matthew's Gospel, Christ is dwelling on the fundamental principles of His Church, and we can see at once how natural it was that Christ, before His disciples were deprived of His bodily presence, should solemnly republish this peculiar characteristic of His kingdom, and accompany it with a special gift of the Holy Spirit for its due exercise.

We now come to the Acts of the Apostles, in which, though written by a Synoptist, we should naturally expect to find the Church and her doctrines in a more advanced stage of development. We observe, then, that the whole course of the Acts describes the fundamental principle of the Gospel to have been the communication of Life. Christ is called the ἀρχηγὸς τῆς ζωῆς, an expression which is susceptible (as we have seen) of a double meaning.[1] The Gospel is spoken of as Life.[2] It is also "the way;"[3] an expression which occurs in St. John in close connection with "the Life."[4] Though the primary effect of repentance was, as we

---

between" the former and St. John xx. 23 (Alford). But it is singular (1) that St. John should use the present tense in "are remitted" and the perfect in "have been retained," and (2) that St. Matthew should in each case use the neuter to refer to the sins, rather than the masculine as applying to the sinner.

[1] P. 55.
[2] πάντα τὰ ῥήματα τῆς ζωῆς ταύτης, chap. v. 20, an expression which has puzzled those commentators who have failed to understand that the Gospel consisted in the proclamation of life as well as of remission of sins. It is worthy of remark, moreover, that the angel, who knew what the Gospel was, uses this phrase. With the Jews it is "this man," "this doctrine," "this counsel," "this work."
[3] Acts ix. 2; xix. 9, 23; xxiv. 22.
[4] St. John xiv. 6. What is predicated of Christ is also predicated of His Gospel. He is "the way, the truth, and the life." The proclamation of Him is entitled to the same designation.

shall see presently, to dispose the heart to receive remission of sins, yet its ultimate issue was in Life.[1] Those believed who were "disposed towards," "set in order for" (τεταγμένοι) eternal Life.[2] By their faith they were "justified,"[3] a word which we should empty of much of its significance if we explained it simply as being accounted righteous. It bears the signification also, as we shall see more clearly when we come to examine the writings of St. Paul, of a righteousness imparted from on high, but rendered efficacious in man solely by means of faith. Those who believed were also, by that very faith, placed within the range of a power of sanctification.[4] In all these passages there is an allusion to a Divine power revealed through Jesus Christ, able not only to secure forgiveness of sins, but to invest His disciples with new capacities, which should enable them to attain that which man had never attained since the fall, namely, holiness. The stress laid upon the Resurrection of Jesus[5] may also lead us to the same conclusion. The primary point which the recorded utterances of the Apostles use it to attest is the certainty of our resurrection. But if we venture to assign a deeper cause for the prominence given to this doctrine, we shall have advanced nothing contrary to the doctrinal system of the Acts, and shall moreover find abundant warrant for our interpretation in the Epistles both of St. Peter and St. Paul. The Resurrection of Christ

---

[1] Acts xi. 18.   [2] Ib. xiii. 48.   [3] Ib. xiii. 39.
[4] Ib. xx. 32; xxvi. 18. We see in these two passages, as in St. John, sanctification attributed (1) to God's Will, (2) to man's faith.
[5] Ib. i. 22.; ii. 24, 32; iii. 15; iv. 33; xvii. 18, &c.

was a fact on which the whole scheme of the Gospel depended, whether we regard it as a message of reconciliation or as a communication of supernatural Life. The river of death was, as it were, the baptismal flood which cleansed the Body of our Lord from even the bare likeness of sinful flesh, which, as a true descendant of Adam, He had been obliged to put on. As in the case of those who have put Him on by faith, His body was sown a natural body, and was raised a spiritual body. It was this spiritual body, with its enlarged capacities and powers, that He desired to communicate to all who would receive Him. Hence the importance attached to the doctrine of the resurrection in the Acts, and, as we shall see, in the doctrinal system of St. Paul.

When we turn from the source of the spiritual Life of man to its mode of operation, we find ourselves in the midst of a doctrinal system which precisely agrees with that of St. John. A Holy Spirit, promised by God Himself,[1] sent by Jesus Christ,[2] is the power whereby the Apostles of Christ are enabled to do all their works. It is the Holy Ghost who descends upon them at Pentecost;[3] it is He who enables their followers to speak the word with boldness;[4] it is He who resides in the Church, so as to identify Himself, as it were, with the assembly of believers;[5] it is He who inspires Stephen[6] with that faith and courage which make Him so formidable an antagonist to the unbelieving Jews. The Holy Ghost it is who directs the affairs of the Church: He is transmitted to the disciples by means of the ceremony of imposition of hands;[7] and

[1] Acts i. 4; ii. 33.   [2] Ib. ii. 33.   [3] Ib. ii. 4.   [4] Ib. iv. 31.
[5] Ib. v. 3.   [6] Ib. vi. 5.   [7] Ib. viii. 17, 18, 19; xix. 6.

H

His presence in the heart of each believer through the due use of that outward sign is so much a part of the ordinary rules of the Church, that the question is put as a matter of course to the believers at Ephesus, "Have ye received the Holy Ghost since ye believed?" as though some special ordinance existed whereby He was ordinarily pleased to convey Himself to those in whom it was His purpose to dwell.

And whereas the first beginning of the Life of the Spirit was attached by St. John to a particular outward ordinance, we find this outward ordinance held in such reverence by the Apostles, that they never ventured to omit it, even upon the most extraordinary occasions.[1] It formed a part of their most elementary teaching;[2] in fact it was the actual mode of admission into the Church, without which even the believer was not entitled to the privileges of the new order of things established by Jesus Christ.[3] And not only was baptism the mode of admission into the Church, but rightly received it was a baptism of water and the Spirit.[4] Nor was the other sacrament absent from the most rudimentary idea of the Church. The very moment a band of believers had been formed, deriv-

---

[1] Acts ix. 18; x. 47, 48.   [2] Ib. ii. 38; viii. 12, 36.
[3] Ib. xvi. 31-33; xxii. 16.
[4] Ib. ii. 38. Davidson, 'Introduction to the New Testament,' vol. ii. p. 173, regards it as a sign of the non-Pauline authorship of the Pastoral Epistles that baptism is spoken of in connection with regeneration and the renewing of the Holy Ghost. He has overlooked the fact that every writer in the New Testament, with the exception of St. Jude and St. James, has so spoken of it. See St. Matt. iii. 11, 16. St. Mark i. 8. It is hard to see how the statement that baptism saves us by the resurrection of Jesus Christ (1 Pet. iii. 21) can be otherwise explained than of the gift of regeneration. See p. 72.

Doctrine of the Incarnation.

ing their spiritual strength from the Spirit of a risen and ascended Lord, we read how the disciples continued daily in the breaking of bread;[1] and even when the Church had expanded from the little company at Jerusalem into a society which numbered its adherents in every city in the civilised world, we still find that on the first day of the week the disciples met together to break bread.[2]

When we pass from the elementary principle of the Christian life, and the external ordinances whereby that elementary principle was communicated, to the qualifications necessary on man's part for a due reception of the principle, we find the harmony between the writer of the fourth Gospel and the writer of the Acts preserved unbroken. There was but one requisite on the believer's part, and that requisite was faith.[3] They who "gladly received the word were baptized."[4] "When they believed, they were baptized."[5] If the words said to have been uttered to the Æthiopian eunuch are not genuine,[6] they are, after all, only an echo of the proclamation to the Philippian gaoler in answer to the searching inquiry, "What shall I do to be saved?"[7] We have already seen that faith is spoken of by the Apostle Paul as the cause of justification.[8] We also find St. Peter speaking of faith as a means of purification.[9] Not only so, but the keynote of St. Paul's preparatory teaching is declared to be

[1] Acts ii. 42, 46.   [2] Ib. xx. 7.
[3] Faith is here regarded as involving repentance, μετάνοια, change of opinion; that which induced a man to leave the darkness and come to the light. John iii. 20, 21.
[4] Acts ii. 41. Compare St. John i. 12, also Acts xviii. 8, &c.
[5] Acts viii. 12.   [6] Ib. viii. 37.   [7] Ib. xvii. 31.   [8] Ib. xiii. 39.
[9] Ib. xv. 9. There is considerable similarity between this passage and 1 John iii. 3.

repentance toward God, and faith towards our Lord Jesus Christ.[1]

We now come to the result of the Christian life as taught in the pages of the Acts. And it is simply the fulfilment of the prophecy recorded by St. John, "there shall be one flock and one shepherd," limited in its completeness by man's infirmity, as shadowed forth in the fourth Gospel by the words, "Have not I chosen you twelve, and one of you is a devil?"[2] and in the Epistle by the allusion to those who "went forth" from the body of believers, but "were not of" them.[3] Exactly the same picture of God's purpose, thwarted by man's perverseness, is displayed in the historical delineation of the Apostolic Church. Hope, joy, and gladness were its animating principles; love its bond of union. "They that believed were of one heart and one soul,"[4] says the historian, of the Church in her infancy. "They partook of their daily food with gladness,"[5] rejoicing in the salvation which had been proclaimed to them. But soon the spirit of the world invaded the Church, and henceforth the full realization of the ideal was postponed until the time of the restitution of all things, of which the Apostle Peter speaks. Henceforth we hear of "murmurings."[6] We read of dissensions in the Christian body,[7] even of contention among those who were foremost in proclaiming the Gospel message.[8]

Was such a state of things unlooked for? On the contrary, it was distinctly foretold in the Synoptic Gospels. Was it unexpected by the author of the

[1] Acts xx. 21.   [2] St. John vi. 70.   [3] 1 John ii. 19.
[4] Acts iv. 32.   [5] Ib. ii. 46.   [6] Ib. vi.   [7] Ib. xv.   [8] Ib. xv. 39.

Doctrine of the Incarnation. 101

fourth Gospel? It could hardly be so, if, as supposed, he were writing his Gospel about the year 150; and the supposition that his narrative is authentic derives confirmation from the fact that he alone among the Evangelists makes no allusion to it.[1] But it is clear enough that, whenever he may have written, he held such a declension to be not only possible but almost certain. Wherefore the repetition of the commission to bind and loose contained in the other Gospels if no need for its exercise was likely to arise? And it may be well to note that when the Apostle St. Peter acted upon the commission he had received, his language seems to reflect rather the terms of the fourth Gospel than of the first. The remission of sins was the subject of his earliest exhortation. Their retention was the awful feature of the cases of Ananias, Sapphira, and Simon Magus. The powers of the ministers of Christ correspond to the language in which they were announced beforehand in the four Gospels. They spoke in all cases as the representatives of Christ. The Holy Ghost spoke by their mouths.[2] They were overseers of the flock.[3]

[1] Because it did not enter into his purpose, not because he was not aware of it. A later writer would hardly have refrained from putting into the mouth of Christ some prophetic denunciation of existing abuses, which St. Paul, St. Peter, St. James, St. Jude, and St. John himself in his Epistles and Revelation, did not fail to specify and to rebuke. The existence of these denunciations is regarded by many as a proof of the post-Apostolic origin of the Epistles in which they are found. If this argument be valid, the fact of their absence in the fourth Gospel must be taken as affording a presumption of its having been written in the Apostolic age. [2] Acts xiii. 2; xv. 28.

[3] Even the inferior orders of them. The charge in Acts xx. was given to the elders, or, as we should now say, priests. It is hardly necessary to observe that ἐπίσκοπος always in the New Testament signifies the second order of the clergy. It is not so generally allowed that the Apostles represent the first.

It was their task, they were told, in the very words, be it observed, of Christ to St. Peter, in the 21st chapter of the fourth Gospel, to feed ($\pi o\iota\mu a\iota\nu\epsilon\iota\nu$) the flock of Christ. The power of guiding and ruling was exercised by them in the council of Jerusalem. The decrees of that council were sent by the hands of trustworthy commissioners to all the various Christian communities, and it was obviously expected that they would be observed.[1]

Thus the theory of the Church, as set forth by St. John, is fully and frankly accepted by the author of the Acts. If the after-history of the Church has scarcely realised that theory, it is in consequence of a truth set forth by Christ, of the proclamation of which, under any hypothesis, the writer of the fourth Gospel must have been aware. Christ was come to sow good seed in His field, but tares were to spring up among them. It was the work of an enemy. There was no remedy: both must grow together until the harvest.[2] In the Acts of the Apostles, however, we see only the germs of the evil which after-times were to develop into such terrible results. The ideal given us by St. John is almost realised in the earliest record of ecclesiastical history. Christ, the source of life, diffusing His Spirit into the hearts of all who receive Him, and thus constituting a society of which the external signs were the Sacraments and the due subordination to authorized rulers and teachers, while the internal guiding principles were love and joy and brotherly affection, and the one qualification for admission a belief in Jesus Himself—this is the rationale of the Church's

[1] Acts xv. 28; xvi. 4.   [2] St. Matt. xiii. 30.

Doctrine of the Incarnation. 103

existence alike in St. John and in the Acts. It is impossible to imagine a more exact correspondence between theory and fact. Yet we are asked to believe that the theory was framed after man's depravity had made its realisation impossible for at least a century!

Contenting ourselves with calling attention to the identical anthropology of all the four Gospels, and the teaching by inference in the Synoptists of a similar doctrine of the communication of Life from above to that of St. John, we pass on to St. Paul. And here we are absolutely bewildered by the amount of materials before us, arranged according to the workings of a mind which bears the stamp of individuality above that of any other of the writers of the New Testament. If we find that all the varied teaching of St. Paul is reducible to the main principles laid down in St. John's Gospel; that all his reasoning of righteousness, temperance, and judgment to come—all his theories of justification, of grace, of faith, of freedom—all his ideas about the relation of the law to the Gospel, are simply the play of his brilliant intellect upon the surface of the system of doctrine ascribed to Jesus Christ in the very Gospel whose authenticity is so strenuously impugned, we can scarcely avoid the inference that a conclusive answer has been given to its assailants. It can scarcely be seriously urged that the great storehouse from which St. Paul's theology was derived was an invention of later ages. Unwritten tradition these words of Christ most unquestionably were, until some years after St. Paul's death. But if they appeared at that later period, and are yet entirely untinctured by Pauline phrases and turns of thought, we shall be compelled to recognize in them the genuine utterances of Him whom M. Renan is kind enough to recognize as "the true founder of Christianity."[1]

St. Paul, like St. John, starts with the doctrine of the communication of Life to mankind, illuminating those who were formerly in darkness, and serving as a new starting-point of spiritual being. With far more fulness than St. John's Gospel, in many a figure and in many an argument does St. Paul insist on the enlightening and revivifying power which dwells in Christ. We seem to hear the echo of the words, "I am come that they might have Life," "I am the light of the world,"[2] throughout the whole of the Pauline Epistles. The need of the new birth, the entire recommencement of the inner and spiritual life of man, is as fundamental a principle of the Gospel with St. Paul as it is with our Lord, as reported by St. John. In one of the most important passages in perhaps the most important of St. Paul's writings occur the remarkable words, "the gift of God is eternal Life in Jesus Christ our Lord."[3] That this "Life" was "the Light of men," St. Paul takes care to inform us. There is a remarkable passage in the 2nd Epistle to the Corinthians which expands and illustrates the teaching of St. John concerning the Light that shineth in darkness. In this

[1] "Rien n'est plus faux qu'une opinion devenue à la mode de nos jours, et d'après laquelle Paul serait le vrai fondateur du Christianisme. Le vrai fondateur du Christianisme c'est Jésus."—Renan, ' Les Apôtres.' Introduction, p. 4.

[2] St. John x. 10; viii. 12.

[3] Rom. vi. 23. Observe how the force of ἐν is lost in our version (and thus the identity of doctrine between St. Paul and St. John obscured), here as in many other places in St. Paul's Epistles, by translating it "through" as here, or "by" as in other passages.

Doctrine of the Incarnation. 105

passage, as well as in several others that will be cited, we see an exact reproduction of the anthropology of St. John, as well as his doctrine of redemption. "If our Gospel hath been hid," says the apostle, "it hath been hid among those who are perishing; in whom the god of this world blinded the minds (or rather, perhaps, 'mental processes') of the unbelieving, so that the enlightenment of the glorious Gospel of Christ [1] (or the Gospel of the glory of Christ), who is the image of God, should not beam upon them. . . . For God, who bade light shine out of darkness, is He who hath shined in your hearts, to give the enlightenment of the knowledge of the glory of God [2] in the person of Jesus Christ."[3] This doctrine of the Light shining in darkness was no later development of the Apostle's teaching. We find it in the first Epistle he ever wrote. "Ye are sons of light and sons of day," he tells the Thessalonians; "we are not of night or of darkness."[4] Again, to the Ephesians, "Ye were sometime darkness, but now are ye light in the Lord."[5] He speaks to his Colossian

---

[1] It is quite possible, though by no means certain, that the phrase εὐαγγέλιον τῆς δόξης τοῦ Χριστοῦ is a Hebraism.

[2] The sense here requires us to abandon the idea of a Hebrew construction.

[3] "Paul never says that God, being hostile to men, became reconciled to them through Christ, but that they, being the enemies of God, became reconciled to Him."—Neander. 'Planting and Training,' vol. i. p. 450. "In Cor. v. 20, St. Paul does not say amend yourselves in order that ye may be reconciled to God, but rather, let not the grace of reconciliation be in vain for you, because you have not appropriated it."— Ib. p. 452. What could be more minutely agreed than this doctrine and that of St. John in chap. iii., regarding the relation of the light to those who were in darkness?

[4] 1 Thess. v. 5.

[5] Eph. v. 8. Compare chap. i. 18; iii. 9.

disciples about "the portion of the lot of the saints in the light."[1] He reminds Timothy how Jesus Christ brought life and immortality to light by means of the Gospel.[2] In the two striking chapters with which the Epistle to the Romans commences we have a powerful description of the state of degradation and moral blindness[3] into which all men, Jew and Gentile, have fallen, and of their utter inability to raise themselves out of it by their own power. But, like St. John, he is not content to describe the Life that dwells in Christ merely as a means of enlightenment to the darkened soul. He regards it, moreover, as the manifestation of an inward power which effects a new creation of the whole man. Does St. John enlarge on the antagonism between flesh and spirit, and does he describe man in his natural state under the one term and in his regenerate condition under the other,[4] St. Paul appropriates the phraseology,[5] and makes it the groundwork of one of his most striking dissertations.[6] He speaks, it is true, in the fourth chapter of the Epistle to the Romans, as though the gift of righteousness which came by Christ were merely imputed to Christians, as a substitute for their own lack of righteousness; and for many centuries theologians have been content to regard this as the main feature of St. Paul's teaching, instead of, as it is in truth, a subsidiary statement, thrown out by the way in treating of a particular portion of the Old Testament. This doctrine of the imputation of righteous-

---

[1] Col. i. 12. τὴν μερίδα τοῦ κλήρου τῶν ἁγίων ἐν τῷ φωτί.
[2] 2 Tim. i. 10.   [3] "Their foolish heart was darkened." Rom. i. 21.
[4] St. John iii. 6.   [5] Rom. iii. 20; vii. 18. Gal. iii. 3; v. 16–25.
[6] Rom. viii.

Doctrine of the Incarnation. 107

ness is peculiarly St. Paul's own, and it is necessary to the full completeness of the Gospel scheme. But to represent it as the whole system of St. Paul with reference to the righteousness of Christ revealed from heaven, to explain his doctrine of justification as being summed up in this doctrine of imputed righteousness, would be entirely to misrepresent the Apostle. His doctrine of justification is indissolubly bound up with the idea of Christ's indwelling. It therefore includes a doctrine of Christ's imparted, as well as His imputed righteousness. The fact is often overlooked, by reason of theological prepossessions, that the original meaning of δικαιόω is "to make righteous," and in the Septuagint it usually has the meaning of declaring a person to be righteous who is already so.[1] We cannot, therefore, insist upon restricting its meaning to the forensic sense of acquittal, unless the context actually obliges us to do so. But a careful study of St. Paul's writings leads us to precisely the opposite conclusion. Not only in one remarkable passage does the Apostle use the word δικαιόω as a climax after ἁγιάζω,[2] thereby seeming to imply that justification is actually a completion of the work of sanctification; but he gives an interpretation of the work done in us by the righteousness of God which completely negatives the idea of its operation being confined to simple imputation. The end of Christ's "being made sin for us, who knew no sin," is declared in a passage which is a valuable commentary upon the Epistle to the Romans to be, "that we might become the righteousness of God in Him."[3] The com-

[1] See Appendix II.   [2] 1 Cor. vi. 11.
[3] 2 Cor. v. 21.

munication of this righteousness of God to us by means of the Life which comes from Christ is the key-note of the system of St. Paul, as it is declared by St. John to be that of Christ Himself.[1] We have stated the doctrine of St. John to be that Christ came to introduce a power on earth which should change the whole moral and spiritual condition of those who would receive it. Such is also the doctrine of St. Paul. If St. John says that the Logos was "full of grace and truth," and that "of that fulness" all His disciples "had received;" St. Paul says that He came to "fill all things;"[2] that He "filleth all in all;"[3] that the Church is His fulness, or the complement of Himself, because it is filled by Him.[4] That this, and not the imputation of righteousness, is the main doctrine of the Epistle to the Romans, will further appear from the following considerations. In the very outset of the Epistle the Apostle declares it to be power according to the operation of a Spirit of holiness, deriving its activity from the fact of the Resurrection of Christ, which marked Him out as the Son of God.[5] The passage may be obscure, but it is singularly

---

[1] "δικαιοσύνη and ζωὴ were always in his (St. John's) mind correlative ideas."—Neand. 'Planting and Training,' vol. i. p. 416 (Bohn's Ed.). I contend that they were so also in the mind of St. Paul. Neander elsewhere remarks that St. Paul's mode of approaching the subject was affected by his spiritual history. He had once thought that he could become δίκαιος by his own unassisted efforts. He now knew that he could only become so by the operation of a power external to himself. Hence his clear appreciation of the end served by the law.
[2] Eph. iv. 10. 　　　　　　　　　　　　　[3] Ib. i. 23.
[4] Ibid. Compare Col. iii. 11, " Christ is all, and in all."
[5] τοῦ ὁρισθέντος υἱοῦ Θεοῦ ἐν δυνάμει, κατὰ πνεῦμα ἁγιωσύνης, ἐξ ἀναστάσεως νεκρῶν.

Doctrine of the Incarnation. 109

in accordance with the statement, "as many as received Him, to them gave He power to become the sons of God," as also with those which describe the Divine Life within us, as well as the gift of the Holy Spirit, to be the result of the Resurrection and Ascension of Christ.[1] Again, in ver. 16 St. Paul repeats the statement that the Gospel of Christ is a "power of God unto salvation to every one that believeth."[2] And it is such a power "because in it God's righteousness is revealed" (ver. 17).

That righteousness produces an entire change in the condition of the man. Not only is its possessor henceforth "accounted righteous" before God, but he has acquired peace with Him,[3] and rejoices in the hope of the glory of God.[4] For the love of God is not merely manifested to such a man; it is "shed abroad in his heart."[5] He is "reconciled by the death of Christ, but saved by His life."[6] A moral and spiritual change has been wrought by the acceptance of salvation in Christ. Henceforth a man is "dead to sin, and living to God."[7] And this because "the gift of God is eternal life in Christ Jesus our Lord." The antagonism between flesh and spirit, the cause of so much distress to the natural man and to the immature Christian,[8] ceases to exist as soon as the

---

[1] St. John iii. 13; vi. 62; xvi. 7.
[2] The conventional ideas attached to words are a great hindrance to the right understanding of the Apostolic writings. Salvation means safety—and safety as much from sin as from anything else. Cf. St. Matt. i. 21: "Thou shalt call His name JESUS, for He shall save His people *from their sins.*"
[3] Rom. v. 1.
[4] Ib. v. 2. That is surely in the hope of possessing it.
[5] Ib. v. 5. [6] Ib. v. 10. [7] Ib. vi. 11, 13.
[8] The comparison of Rom. vii. with the remark addressed to be-

life of Christ, imparted by the agency of His Spirit,[1] has obtained full dominion in the believer's heart. This change from the flesh to the spirit, this introduction of the Life of Jesus into the soul, is by St. Paul, as well as St. John, denoted by the term regeneration. If St. John tells us in the words of our Lord that it is an essential condition of salvation that a man must be born or begotten again,[2] St. Paul speaks of regeneration and renewing of the Holy Ghost as one and the same thing.[3] He tells us that if any one be in Christ " there is," or " has been," " a new creation: the old things (at his conversion) passed away, behold, everything has become new."[4] This "new creation" is the only thing that availeth anything " in Christ Jesus."[5] The keystone of Gospel teaching, he tells us in another place, is the putting off the old man, which is corrupt according to the deceitful lusts, the being renewed in the spirit of our minds, and the putting on of the new man, which was created after God " in righteousness and true holiness,"[6] or, as the companion Epistle to the Colossians expressed it, " is renewed unto thorough knowledge ($\epsilon\pi\iota\gamma\nu\omega\sigma\iota\varsigma$) after the image of his Creator."[7] Nor are we left in doubt who this new man is. Exhorta-

---

lievers in Gal. v. 17, proves that St. Paul's description in the former chapter must not be entirely confined to the unconverted.

[1] Rom. viii. 9, 10, 14.
[2] St. John iii. 3.
[3] The divines have been accustomed to distinguish between them, but see the significant absence of the article in Tit. iii. 5, as in St. John iii. 5.
[4] 2 Cor. v. 17. "Omnia enim nova aderant. Verbo nove disponente carnalem adventum, ubi cum hominem qui extra Deum abierat, adscriberet Deo."—Irenæus, 'Contr. Hær.' book iii. 10, 2.
[5] Gal. vi. 15.   [6] Eph. iv. 20-25.   [7] Col. iii. 10.

Doctrine of the Incarnation. 111

tions to put on Jesus Christ,[1] assertions that we have put Him on,[2] are sufficient proof that He is the new man thus created by God in the full perfection of man's being. The conclusion of the last cited passage gives us the very words of Christ given by St. John: "Ye are all one in Christ Jesus."[3] Where did St. Paul find such a statement? Where does it appear in the Synoptic narratives? What could it be but an echo borne to his ears by the unwritten traditions of the Christian Church, of the words of that sublime prayer of Jesus to His Father that His disciples might be "one in us?"[4] Nor is this a mere isolated passage in St. Paul. It is as marked a feature in his system as it is of that put forth in the fourth Gospel. The indwelling of Christ is the very heart's core of St. Paul's creed. There is no "new creation," except to him who is "in Christ."[5] "Do ye not understand yourselves," he asks in the same Epistle, "that Jesus Christ is in you, except ye be reprobates?"[6] It is needless to multiply passages. Assertions of the need and of the fact of the indwelling of Christ are to be found in almost every page.[7] I will content myself with two—the passage where St. Paul tells the Colossians that "their life is hid with Christ in God,"[8] and the eloquent description

---

[1] Rom. xiii. 14.
[2] Gal. iii. 27. Compare Eph. ii. 10: "We are His workmanship, created in Christ Jesus unto good works."
[3] Gal. iii. 28.   [4] St. John xvii. 21.   See note 2, p. 26.   [5] 2 Cor. v. 17.
[6] Ib. xiii. 5. ἢ οὐκ ἐπιγινώσκετε ἑαυτοὺς, ὅτι ’Ιησοῦς Χριστὸς ἐν ὑμῖν ἐστιν, εἰ μή τι ἀδόκιμοί ἐστε;
[7] For instance, Eph. ii. 20-22; iii. 17, 19; iv. 6, 13, 15. Col. i. 27, 28; ii. 6, 10, 12, 13. The force of many of these passages has evaporated in our translation.
[8] Col. iii. 3.

of the condition of the Christian in the Epistle to the Galatians: "I have been crucified with Christ; nevertheless I live; yet not I, but Christ liveth in me; and the life that I now live in the flesh I live by the faith of the Son of God, who loved me, and gave Himself for me."[1] Is there no echo again here of a Divine saying not yet recorded, but which floated about the Christian Church, repeated by Apostolic lips, and caught up eagerly by their hearers as the secret of a Christian's hidden strength? Are not these the appropriation by the disciple of the words of the Master, "My flesh, which I will give for the life of the world?"

And if St. John describes the communication of Divine Life under the beautiful figure of a vine and its branches, we find St. Paul clothing the doctrine in figurative language quite as expressive. He comes near the language of the Master in his warning to the Gentile Christians that if they were grafted into the good olive tree in the place of the Jews who had been cut off, and if they were now partaking of its root and fatness in the place of others who were no longer worthy of the privilege, it would be well for them to take heed lest a similar disobedience should insure to them a similar fate.[2] In several passages he represents Christians as the Body of Christ, and Christ Himself as the Head, the source of all Life, nourishment, and support. They are not only members of Himself, but of one another, by reason of the Life which they have in common. And by another figure, to which we shall have to recur again, he represents them as the grains

[1] Gal. ii. 20. [2] Rom. xi. 17-24.

Doctrine of the Incarnation. 113

which individually make up the one loaf, which is Christ. Where do we find teaching similar to this in the Gospels, unless it be in that attributed to St. John?

When we proceed to examine the mode in which this inward Life is communicated, the coincidences between the Evangelist and the Apostle will be found to be quite as numerous and as striking. We gather from the hints in the discourses recorded by St. John that the Third Person in the blessed Trinity was to be the medium of communication to mankind of the Life that dwelt in Christ. St. Paul repeats the statement with far more emphasis and fulness. We have seen how St. Paul regards the power of Christ as being manifested according to the operation of the Spirit of holiness.[1] We have seen how regeneration is intertwined in his mind with renewing of the Holy Ghost.[2] We may further remark in the Epistle to the Thessalonians, to which we turn with peculiar interest as the first record of the epistolary teaching of the great Apostle, the recurrence of the same phrase which we have just noticed at the commencement of the Epistle to the Romans. The Gospel comes to the Thessalonians "not only in word, but in power, and in the Holy Ghost."[3] If we are told in the Epistle to the Romans that "the love of God is shed abroad in our hearts by the Holy Ghost which was given us,"[4] we are afterwards carefully informed that this Spirit, who dwells in us, and in whom we are henceforth privileged to walk,[5] is "the Spirit of Christ."[6] In the Epistles to

[1] Rom. i. 4. [2] Tit. iii. 5. [3] 1 Thess. i. 5.
[4] Rom. v. 5. [5] Ib. viii. 1, 11. [6] Ib. ver. 9.

I

the Galatians and Philippians St. Paul repeats the statement.[1] Moreover, if we are said by Christ's indwelling to be made members of that one Body which is Himself, St. Paul is careful to remind us that this is the work of the Holy Ghost, through whose agency we not only originally enter that one Body, but are continually retained within it.[2] And if Christ be said to dwell in our hearts, it is because " we are strengthened with might by His Spirit in the inner man."[3] We shall have occasion to refer again to the work of the Holy Spirit in our salvation. Under that head we will discuss the many passages in which that work is described. Here it is sufficient to have established the fact that there is a perfect agreement between the Evangelist and the Apostle in the somewhat intricate doctrinal principle which, while it attributes our salvation to the communication to us of Life from Christ, yet points out the Holy Ghost as the agent through whose operation that communication of life is effected.[4]

We now come to the outward means whereby the gift of Life is ordinarily conveyed. We have already seen that the salvation bestowed by Christ is spoken of by St. Paul as a "regeneration and renewing of the Holy Ghost." The connection of this with the baptismal font is all that is necessary to make it correspond

---

[1] Gal. iv. 6, and Phil. i. 19.   [2] 1 Cor. xii. 13.
[3] Eph. iii. 16, 17.
[4] In 1 Cor. vi. 13, ὁ Κύριος is clearly Christ, and he who is joined to Him (ver. 17) is One Spirit. In verses 15, 19, the body is the member of Christ and the temple of the Holy Ghost. See also 1 Cor. vi. 11. 2 Cor. iii. 3 (ἐπιστολὴ Χριστοῦ, ἐγγεγραμμένη οὐ μέλανι, ἀλλὰ πνεύματι Θεοῦ). Also vv. 17, 18. Gal. iii. 5. In Heb. ix. 14, Christ is said to offer Himself to God, διὰ πνεύματος αἰωνίου.

exactly with St. John's expression, "born again of water and the Spirit." And this we find in the use of the word λουτρόν.¹ It was διὰ λουτροῦ παλιγγενεσίας καὶ ἀνακαινώσεως πνεύματος ἁγίου, that Christ, according to St. Paul, was pleased to save His people.² In the waters of baptism, he tells us in another place, Christ was "put on."³ Therein does the Christian become partaker of the death and burial of Christ, and therein is he made partaker of His Resurrection.⁴ That St. Paul was fully imbued with the principles laid down in the discourse to Nicodemus, and that he fully recognised the necessity of a new birth of water and the Spirit as an indispensable preliminary of the work of salvation, will hardly be disputed. Let us see if he recognised a necessity of feeding on the Flesh and Blood of Christ as one of the requisites for the continuance of that work. Turn we to the First Epistle to the Corinthians. Were this Epistle not included in the list of Apostolic writings, and were it not perhaps the very Epistle whose genuineness it was the most hopeless to contest, the opponents of St. John's Gospel might imagine they had detected a shadow of disagreement here. But the Epistle to the Corinthians emphatically endorses the teaching of St. John vi. Not only are the words of institution recorded, but they are brought into complete unison with the doctrine of that

---

¹ This word, usually translated by the disused word "laver," would convey a clearer idea to the modern reader if rendered "font."
² Tit. iii. 5.   ³ Gal. iii. 27.
⁴ Rom. vi. 3, 4. Col. ii. 12. I do not cite the well-known passage in Heb. vi. 2, because the word there is not βάπτισμα, but βαπτισμός, and because it seems extremely probable that no reference to Christian baptism is there intended.

celebrated discourse. The cup is the communion[1] of the Blood, and the bread of the Body of Christ.[2] By partaking of the one bread, Christians are incorporated into the one Body ;[3] that is, of course, the Body of Christ; and when they drank of the cup, they drank into one Spirit.[4] When they partook of that bread and that cup unworthily, they were "guilty of the body and blood of the Lord."[5] And none declined to participate in that mystic feast, for the Apostle says, "we are *all* partakers of that one bread."[6] Can we suppose that Christ had never uttered the words, "Except ye eat the flesh of the Son of Man, and drink His blood, ye have no life in you ;" "the bread of God is that which cometh down from heaven, and giveth life unto the world ;" "I am the Bread of Life ;" and that St. Paul had never heard of them ?[7]

It is scarcely necessary to adduce any arguments to prove that St. Paul held faith to be a requisite on man's part for salvation. The doctrine of justification by faith is so identified with his name that it will be at once conceded to be a fundamental principle with

---

[1] κοινωνία. This word is hard to render into English. Derived from the adjective κοινός, common, it here represents the common share which every Christian had in the Body and Blood of Christ, and perhaps also what we now understand by a *communication* of that Body and Blood.

[2] 1 Cor. x. 16.   [3] Ib. ver. 17.

[4] Ib. xii. 13. It is hardly possible to dissever this expression from the concluding paragraph of chap. xi.

[5] Ib. xi. 27.   [6] Ib. x. 17.

[7] M. Reville, in his above-cited article in the 'Revue des Deux Mondes,' is driven by the difficulty of his case to the remarkable conclusion that the author of the fourth Gospel had access to some authentic traditions of Christ as yet unpublished! It would have been interesting to have learned which portion of the Gospel embodied those traditions, and which the new and spurious matter.

Doctrine of the Incarnation. 117

him. The only caution that is needed has been already given, namely, that faith is a no less fundamental principle with St. John. But faith with St. Paul is no barren acceptance of facts or dogmas. It is the vivid realization of the truths of the unseen world.[1] The Christian sees by it God the Father saving men, and bringing them into obedience to His law, by a Life from above which is given in His Son, and communicated to the heart by the Spirit. This faith is one which must necessarily " work by love."[2] Love is the great end and object of the Christian scheme.[3] It is to be put on in addition to, or above such gifts as kindness, humbleness of mind, meekness, long-suffering, forbearance, for it is the very bond of perfection.[4] The inattentive reader has not the least idea of the way in which St. Paul's Epistles are permeated with this word. Two-thirds of the whole number of times it occurs in the New Testament it is to be found in the Epistles of St. Paul. We shall therefore be ready to expect to find in St. Paul's Epistles, as in St. John's Gospel, a picture of a Divine society, inhabited by Christ and His Spirit, and animated by this Divine principle of love. Such a picture is actually set before us there. It is put forward in theory, as when the Church is described as the " fulness," or " filling up of Christ."[5] It is taught in all those passages which describe Christians

[1] Heb. xi. 1. [2] Gal. v. 6.
[3] 1 Cor. xiii. We seem to be listening to St. John himself when we read in 1 Cor. viii. 3, "if any man love God, the same is known by Him."
[4] Col. iii. 14.
[5] Eph. i. 23. Compare Matt. ix. 16; Mark ii. 21; and observe that the Gnostic idea of the πλήρωμα as the *complement* of something else has more analogy with this passage of St. Paul than with John i. 16.

as being members of Christ; integral parts that is of His Body, identified with Him in the closest manner by the possession of one and the same life. It is inculcated no less intelligibly when He is spoken of as the one loaf, and His disciples as the grains which compose it.[1] In this mystic organism, Christ's Church, the Life flows from one individual to the other. From Christ, the head, the whole body fitly joined together and compacted by that which every joint supplieth, according to the effectual working in the measure of every part, maketh increase of the body unto the edifying of itself in love.[2] St. Paul adopts the very language of Christ as reported in St. John when he speaks of Christians as being grafted into the good olive tree, and partaking of its root and fulness.[3] This communication of Life from one to another issues in two principles, love and holiness. From the beginning Christians are chosen in sanctification of the Spirit, as well as belief in the truth.[4] It is God's will, we are told, from before the foundation of the world, that in Christ a people should be chosen to be "holy and without blame before Him in love."[5] Thus it is that in each Epistle the Apostle addresses the members of the several Churches as "called to be saints" (ἅγιοι), or as actually being such. This holiness is the work of the Spirit, and is the result of the possession of the Life which comes from Christ.[6] But St. Paul, as well as St. John,[7] recognizes the possibility of resistance to the Divine life-principle at every stage of its progress within

---

[1] 1 Cor. x. 17.   [2] Eph. iv. 16. See p. 83.   [3] Rom. xi. 17–24.
[4] 2 Thess. ii. 13.   Compare St. John xvii. 17: "Sanctify them through Thy truth: Thy word is truth."
[5] Eph. i. 4.   [6] Rom. viii., &c.   [7] See p. 84.

Doctrine of the Incarnation. 119

the soul. We are exhorted to work out our own salvation, even though the fact is fully borne in mind that it is God who worketh in us to will and to do of His good pleasure.[1] We are urged not to grieve or to quench the Spirit.[2] We are described as engaged in an endeavour to keep the unity of the Spirit in the bond of peace.[3] Exhortations to fight the good fight of faith,[4] to run as those who mean to win,[5] to keep the deposit,[6] are clear proofs that St. Paul felt that God's work could be resisted by man's obstinacy, and the solemn exhortations in the Epistle to the Hebrews against those who turn back in the Christian course are a proof that he believed in such a thing as a "darkness" which refused to "receive" the Light of God.[7]

Those, however, who received the grace of God in truth were collected into a society, whose unity, as has already been gathered from the fourth Gospel, was "no mere external unity of visible association, nor a mere agreement in any confession of faith,"[8] but an "unity of the Spirit in the bond of peace;" the coming "in[9] the unity of the faith, and of the knowledge of the Son of God, unto a perfect man, unto the measure of the stature of the fulness of Christ,"[10] so that being imbued with truth in love,[11] they might grow up to Christ in all

[1] Phil. ii. 12, 13.　　　　　　[2] Eph. iv. 30. 1 Thess. v. 19.
[3] Eph. iv. 3.　　　[4] 1 Tim. vi. 12.　　　[5] 1 Cor. ix. 24.
[6] 1 Tim. vi. 20. 2 Tim. i. 14.　　[7] St. John i. 5, 11, 12.
[8] See *ante*, p. 83.　　　　　　[9] Or "unto."
[10] Eph. iv. 13. This expression can have no other meaning than that Christ inhabits every man, and that the perfection of each man consists in being identified with Christ. In fact, though the language is extremely different, the doctrine is precisely that of the sixth and seventeenth chapters of St. John.
[11] ἀληθεύοντες ἐν ἀγάπῃ. Eph. iv. 15. Observe the connection of

things. Animated by such a spirit, the Christian need fear none of the enemies of his soul. He is endued with a power whereby he may rise superior to them all. "No weapon that is formed against thee shall prosper," is an echo from the Old Testament which returns to us with augmented force in the New. "Nay, in all these things we are more than conquerors through Him that loveth us."[1] Nothing, how powerful soever it may be, can separate us from the love of God which is in Christ Jesus our Lord. He it is that giveth us the victory in the great and final struggle with sin.[2] In Him it is that triumph is always a certainty for the Christian.[3] And not only triumph, but the reward of victory is his. He who has "fought a good fight, has finished his course, has kept the faith," can look forward with certainty to a crown of righteousness, which the Lord, the righteous Judge, will give to all who love His appearing.[4] Whence did this conviction that God was on our side, and that we need not fear what man, or man's enemy could do unto us, reach the Apostle, unless it derived itself from his knowledge that there was One who had said, "Be of good cheer, I have overcome the world?"

We come, lastly, to the powers of the ministers of Christ. We have seen that Christ, as reported by St. John, describes them as, in a special sense, the representatives of the Most High, and urges that they

---

love and truth as in St. John, *passim*. Is this, or is it not another of those "traditions" of Christ's teaching of which Neander speaks? Compare also Eph. iii. 16, 17.

[1] Rom. viii. 37.   [2] 1 Cor. xv. 57.
[3] 2 Cor. ii. 14. Cf. Eph. iv. 8. Col. ii. 15.
[4] 2 Tim. iv. 8. See *ante*, pp. 84, 85.

Doctrine of the Incarnation. 121

should be received as such. It is precisely in that light that St. Paul would have us regard them. They are not only the ministers of Christ and stewards of the mysteries of God,[1] but they are workers together with Him.[2] Not only did He appoint His Apostles, Prophets, Evangelists, pastors, and teachers for the perfecting of the saints, unto the work of the ministry, unto the edifying of the body of Christ,[3] but St. Paul claims for them the right of being ambassadors for Christ, as though Christ did beseech His people by them; they were to pray them in Christ's stead, to be reconciled to God.[4] If he gives any directions for the well-being of the Church, he does it as possessing an authority delegated to him by Christ.[5] And if Christ communicated to His ministers the awful power of retaining and remitting sins, we find St. Paul not afraid to exercise that power. He "delivers men to Satan for the destruction of the flesh"[6] when they are obstinate in error; he forgives them "in the Person of Christ"[7] when they are penitent with a godly sorrow.[8]

[1] 1 Cor. iv. 1.
[2] Ib. iii. 9. 2 Cor. vi. 1.
[3] Eph. iv. 11, 12.
[4] 2 Cor. v. 20.
[5] 2 Thess. iii. 6, 12. 1 Cor. v. 4.
[6] Ib. v. 5. 1 Tim. i. 20.
[7] ἐν προσώπῳ Χριστοῦ, 2 Cor. ii. 10.
[8] The points of difference between the Apostles hardly come within the scope of this essay, except so far as they serve to illustrate the individuality of the authors of the various books of the New Testament. But St. Paul's vivid sense of the failure of the law to make a man just in God's sight, of its usefulness in bringing men to acknowledge the necessity of a source of righteousness external to themselves, serve to bring into greater relief the absolute identity of his main doctrines with those of the fourth Gospel. In the latter case they are presented in their abstract form as proceeding from the mouth of Jesus Christ; in the former they are accepted because of their entire harmony with the personal experience of the writer.

We may sum up St. Paul's teaching in almost the same words as that of St. John. He regards mankind as lost in darkness, " given over to a reprobate mind,"[1] and as being rescued by the Light and Life that dwells in Christ our Saviour. This Life, breathed into them by the Spirit, and received by them through faith, communicates to them first the blessing of being accounted righteous on account of Him who dwells within them; and afterwards, when His work is fully developed within them, the further blessing of being made "holy and without blame before God in love." The new existence from above, possessed by each Christian in himself, combines the believers into a society, which, by reason of each member of it being inhabited by Christ, and being thus renewed after the image of His humanity, is called the Body of Christ. Of this society faith is the fundamental principle, and love the perfection, and each of these, though required of man, are nevertheless the gift of God.[2] Its outward badges of union, which are also means of grace when rightly used, are the two Sacraments of Baptism and the Lord's Supper; the one the initiation of the believer into the privileges of the Christian Society, the other at once the pledge and the means of his continuation therein. The Life which is granted to each member of this society circulates through the whole, there being the same intimate connection between each member of Christ that there is between the parts of the human body. Nor have all the members of the Christian body the same office. There are some whose business it is to teach, others who are to be taught; some whose

[1] εἰς ἀδόκιμον νοῦν, Rom. i. 28.   [2] Eph. ii. 8; iii. 16.

Doctrine of the Incarnation. 123

privilege it is to rule, others to be ruled;[1] some whose duty it is to feed and minister to the flock, others who are commanded to receive their ministrations; some who are charged with the task of presiding over the discipline of the community, others who are bound to assist in carrying out the sentence of those who are invested with lawful authority in the name of the great Head of the Church. Is there anything here but an exhibition in practice of the principles laid down by our Lord in the Gospel of the disciple whom He loved?[2]

Our examination of the Epistles of St. Peter, St. James, and St. Jude, will be brief. We can hardly expect, within the compass of those short compositions, to find more than a few hints on the subject of our inquiry. But it is important to find out how far those

---

[1] 1 Thess. v. 12. 2 Thess. iii. 6. Heb. xiii. 17.

[2] Both St. John and St. Paul present to us the system formulated by Waterland in his treatise on Justification. The "meritorious cause" is in each declared to be our Lord Jesus Christ; the "efficient and operating cause," the Spirit of God, and "the instrumental rite of its conveyance," baptism. Nor is the "receptive cause," the condition on our side, faith, nor the "final" or "original" cause, the love of God, absent from the mind of either writer. Dr. Keim, however, can venture to say, as if there could be no doubt about the matter: " Christ was exalted [in St. John's Gospel] above the flesh and its lusts, which obscure the perception as well as the will, into the spirit, and spiritual worship, above the ways of darkness into the ways of light. He constrains men to believe in Him, and by faith to attain perfect knowledge, as one who is born again, is full of the Spirit of God, in whom God is abiding and prophesying, though unseen and unheard, telling of the past and of the future, taught of God, and fulfilling the commandments of the Lord, a lover of the brethren, and a child of peace, of joy and love. *Paul, and even the Epistle to the Hebrews, have no analogy to this sphere of ideas.*"—Clark's Tr., p. 190. One is tempted to doubt whether Dr. Keim can have read St. Paul's Epistles. He writes like one whose impressions of an author are obtained at second-hand.

hints tend to confirm, or to weaken our belief in the authenticity of the fourth Gospel. We have already referred to the peculiar character of St. James's Epistle. But the more we insist upon that peculiarity of character, the more striking are any tokens of agreement between St. James and the Gospel of St. John. The key-note of St. John, as we have seen, is the possession of a new and supernatural Life from above, whose characteristics are, first, a revelation of the truth, and, secondly, the infusion of a spirit of love; and so entire is the change wrought in us by the possession of this life that we are said to be born or begotten again. So far, at least, St. James is in accord with him. God is said to have "begotten us," or "brought us forth," by "a word of truth;" and like St. John, he ascribes this regeneration to the will of God.[1] This word is said to have been planted within us,[2] and to be gifted with a power of saving the soul. In another place this word, or perhaps Christ Himself, is spoken of as the "wisdom from above,"[3] and as producing "good fruits," which are "sown in peace." As to the requisite on man's part for receiving this implanted power, it is clear that St. James was well aware of its necessity. He commences his Epistle by assuming its existence as a matter of course, and goes on to represent it as indispensable;[4] and if he takes up a great deal of time in rebutting a false

---

[1] St. James i. 18. St. John i. 13.
[2] St. James i. 21, or "connatural with us." Compare σύμφυτος in Rom. vi. 5.
[3] Ib. iii. 17, 18. He uses the same word ἄνωθεν as St. John in iii. 3. The coincidence is noteworthy. St. James was very probably present at the interview with Nicodemus. Cf. ver. 15, "This is not the wisdom which descendeth from above." [4] Ib. i. 3, 6. Also ii. 1.

Doctrine of the Incarnation. 125

opinion regarding faith which seems to have been current among those he was addressing, it is on behalf of that "faith that worketh by love," which we have seen to have formed so essential a part of the system of St. Paul and St. John. St. James, though he says that a new Life has been imparted to the Christian by the will of God, does not say in so many words that it has enabled men to rise superior to the infirmities of that which they possessed by nature. But it is implied throughout his Epistle. The exhortations to Christian perfection in which he abounds presuppose a power within the Christian to carry them into effect, and absolutely ignore those infirmities of the flesh which might be pleaded as an excuse for failing to do what has been commanded. St. James goes further. He speaks of his readers as having been introduced into, and as about to be judged by a law of liberty.[1] He takes it for granted that they have been called upon to work the righteousness of God;[2] the very phrase which St. Paul so emphatically contrasts with a righteousness of our own.[3] He hints at the possibility of a fulfilment of "the royal law according to the Scripture,"[4] which it is simple matter of fact that no man had been able to do, until Christ came to give men the power.[5] He unhesitatingly asserts that the devil, if resisted, will flee from those he assaults. He speaks of the "grace of God." He acknowledges a power of self-purification in man.[6] He asserts the omnipotence of prayer.[7] All

---

[1] St. James i. 25; ii. 12. [2] Ib. i. 20. Rather, "work out," κατεργάζομαι. [3] Rom. x. 3. [4] St. James ii. 8.
[5] Phil. iv. 13: "I can do all things in Christ who strengtheneth me." [6] St. James iv. 8. [7] Ib. v. 13, et sqq.

these last statements may, it is true, be held to negative any sympathy on St. James's part with the Gospel as taught by St. John and St. Paul. They may even be regarded as indicative of the intention of this Apostle to teach pure Pelagianism. But taken in connection with his doctrine of the engrafted word and the law of liberty, and with his clear assertion that man needs to be saved by the former, they are not a little significant. No Jew—and St. James was a Jew—could have spoken of the Jewish law in such terms. Nor could he have spoken thus of the still more rigorous law laid down by Christ,[1] unless he had known of some power given unto man whereby that law might be fulfilled, and any departure from its provisions atoned for. And if he believed that the mere promulgation of a higher and more searching law by Christ would, of itself, lead men to the fulfilment of that law by their appreciation of its innate excellence, he can only be said to be opposing himself to common sense, and to the whole spirit of Christianity, summed up in the significant words of Christ, "The things that are impossible with men are possible with God."[2] The teaching of St. James then, little as it concerns itself with doctrine, is either capable of being reconciled with the system of St. Paul and St. John, or it is at variance with the facts of history, and with Christianity itself. We must either reject the Epistle of St. James from the Sacred Canon, or admit that he says nothing on the point we are now considering which, rightly understood, is inconsistent either with

[1] St. Matt. v. 48. Liddon, 'Bampton Lectures,' p. 431, remarks that St. James quotes our Lord's words, as recorded by the Synoptists, with remarkable frequency, and the Sermon on the Mount in particular.
[2] St. Luke xviii. 27.

St. Paul's Epistles, or with the words of Christ as handed down to us in the fourth Gospel.

In the writings of St. Peter, and of St. Jude, who may almost be said to repeat St. Peter, we shall find much fuller corroboration of the system of the fourth Evangelist and of St. Paul.[1] St. Peter, like St. John, holds that before the coming of Christ "the whole world lay in wickedness." They had received "a vain conversation by tradition from their fathers."[2] In the time past of their lives they walked in lasciviousness, lusts, excess of wine, and abominable idolatries, working the will of the Gentiles.[3] They had been called out of darkness into God's marvellous light.[4] They have "escaped the corruption that is in the world through lust,"[5] and from " those that live in error."[6] With St. Peter, as with the other Apostles, "that which was born of the flesh was flesh;" "the natural man could not do the things of the Spirit;" for natural brute beasts were destined from their birth to capture and destruction.[7] And if St. Jude does not assert the same truth in the same manner, he gives a very emphatic description of the state of those in whom the power of Christianity does not dwell.

[1] The 2nd Epistle of St. Peter was long among the *antilegomena* in the early Church, and this circumstance has emboldened some to deny its authenticity now. The more I read it the more convinced I am of its genuineness from its simplicity, its absence of later allusions, its entire freedom from later developments of doctrine, from the occurrence of Hebraisms in it, and from its resemblance in style to the first Epistle. And the occurrence of several Pauline expressions in it, from which the first Epistle is free, are strongly confirmatory of the fact which we gather from the Epistle itself, that the writer had just risen from a perusal of the Epistles of St. Paul.

[2] 1 Pet. i. 14, 18.   [3] Ib. iv. 3.   [4] Ib. ii. 9.   [5] 2 Pet. i. 4.
[6] Ib. ii. 18. Also ver. 20.   [7] φυσικά, Ib. ii. 12. See Jude 10.

To such persons there was a dim light in the midst of darkness, even before Christ came—the light of prophecy.[1] But a day was to dawn, and a Light-bearer[2] was to arise in their hearts, which should change their condition, and this was the power and presence of the Lord Jesus Christ, whose Majesty the Apostle had seen with his own eyes.[3] Christianity, we see, is still a power—a power to partake of the Divine Nature.[4] This power, available through the resurrection of Jesus Christ, is once more a regeneration, the begetting of a new nature—the imparting of a new Life—and it takes place by no corruptible seed, but by the Word of a living and everlasting God.[5] Through Him we obtain all things necessary to life and godliness.[6] So far all agrees with what we read in St. Paul and St. John. When we proceed to ask whether St. Peter, like his brethren, recognises any intermediate means by which the blessings of which he has spoken are imparted to mankind, we find him still in perfect accord with the other writers of the New Testament. If we are called to sanctification through the Life that is in Christ, it is "sanctification of the Spirit."[7] If our souls are purified to the obedience of the truth, it is "through the Spirit."[8] The Resurrection Life of Christ thus imparted is connected with the Sacrament of Baptism, "for even

---

[1] 2 Pet. i. 19. Compare St. John i. 45; v. 46.   [2] φωσφόρος.
[3] Ib. i. 16.   [4] Ib. i. 4
[5] 1 Pet. i. 3, 23. Observe that λόγος, in v. 23, becomes ῥῆμα in v. 25.
[6] 2 Pet. i. 3.   [7] 1 Pet. i. 2.
[8] Ib. ver. 22. It is fair to admit, however, that in each of these passages the spirit of the believer may be meant. But St. Peter does at all events acknowledge the operation of a "Spirit of Christ." 1 Pet. i. 11. See below, Chapter v.

Doctrine of the Incarnation. 129

baptism doth now save us by the resurrection of Jesus Christ." And this salvation is not to be confined to a mere remission of sins, but it is intimated that the efficacy of baptism depends upon the infusion of a principle which shall produce that which the candidate for baptism is required to promise, namely, the answer of a good conscience toward God.[1]

There is but one single allusion to the other sacrament, and it is a very distant one. But it conclusively proves that St. Peter regarded the Life conveyed by means of baptism as requiring nourishment in order to bring it to perfection. The new-born babe must earnestly desire the reasonable milk of the Word, to the end that in it, or by it, he may grow.[2] And by this means—by the continual absorption into himself by each member of the Christian covenant of the nourishment designed for him—the body of believers grows into " a spiritual house," where sacrifices acceptable to God are offered up.[3] Christ is the foundation. Upon Him all the members of the Church are built.[4] In Him their actions are all performed.[5] And thus they become the successors of the Jews, " which in time past were not a people, but are now the people of the living God."[6] Henceforth they are the "chosen generation, the royal priesthood, the holy nation, the peculiar people,"[7] whose business it is to set forth the praises of Him who has so called them.

And of this society " faith is the fixed, unswerving

---

[1] 1 Pet. iii. 21. [2] Ib. ii. 2. ἐν here is probably a Hebraism.
[3] Ib. ii. 5. Compare Jude 20. [4] Ib. ii. 7.
[5] Ib. iii. 16. [6] Hosea i. 10.
[7] 1 Pet. ii. 9. Cf. Exod. xix. 6.

130 *The Doctrinal System of St. John.*

root."[1] It is he who "believes in Christ" that "shall not be confounded."[2] Christ is found "precious" to those only who believe.[3] If the Gospel with St. Peter, as with St. Paul, is the power of God unto salvation unto all and upon all, it is through faith that this power is available.[4] If Christ was manifested in the last times, it was for them that believe, that their faith and hope may be in God.[5] This very faith itself was no work of man; it was God's gift, obtained "through the righteousness of God and our Saviour Jesus Christ."[6] To preserve this faith it was necessary for them earnestly to contend[7], for this was the foundation upon which they had to build.[8] This was the channel through which the rest of the Christian graces were to flow, the root from which they must take their beginning.[9] And so was the holy temple, the habitation of God, to be builded.[10] "The house of God, which is the Church of the living God, which is the pillar and ground of the truth,"[11] was, in St. Peter's view as well as that of St. Jude, to be built upon faith as its foundation, and to be permeated with faith as its essential principle. There is the same blending of the Divine and human element that we find elsewhere. Faith, as we have seen, is the gift of God, but its existence is indispensable in man. And the society so interpenetrated with faith as a living principle is bound together into a society whose

---

[1] 'Christian Year.' Hymn for Sexagesima Sunday.   [2] 1 Pet. ii. 6.
[3] Ib. ii. 7. I must regard τιμή as the subjective realization by the believer of the λίθος ἔντιμος in v. 6.
[4] Compare Rom. i. 16; iii. 22, with 1 Pet. i. 5.   [5] 1 Pet. i. 21.
[6] Or, "our God and Saviour." 2 Pet. i. 1.
[7] Jude 3.   [8] Ib. 20.   [9] 2 Pet. i. 5.
[10] Jude 20.   [11] 1 Tim. iii. 15.

Doctrine of the Incarnation. 131

crowning virtue is love. If faith, in 2 Pet. i. 5, 6, is the basis of all Christian virtue, love is its ultimate development. Those who have been "sanctified in God the Father, and preserved in Jesus Christ,"[1] who are "elect according to the foreknowledge of God the Father, through sanctification of the Spirit, unto obedience and sprinkling of the blood of Jesus Christ,"[2] are bid to "see that they love one another with a pure heart fervently;"[3] and that because they had "purified themselves[4] in obeying the truth through the Spirit unto unfeigned love of the brethren." Obedience, purity, holiness, were to be the distinguishing marks of a society of which love was the enduring bond. This fervent, intense, earnest love for one another was to be cultivated above all things;[5] for the sum of the Apostle's teaching was that his disciples should be all " of one mind, sympathising, inspired by brotherly love."[6]

There is but one passage which refers to the outward government of the Church. We may remark, by the way, that it expresses precisely the same views on Church government as are put forth in the other books of the New Testament. But the most important feature in it is the manner in which it breathes the spirit of sayings ascribed to our Lord by St. John. If Christ ever uttered the words recorded by the Evangelist in his twenty-first chapter, we might easily believe that they would ring in St. Peter's ears to his dying day. It is strange that few, if any, have observed the coincidence that in the few words he addresses to the rulers

---

[1] Jude 1.   [2] 1 Pet. i. 2.   [3] Ib. i. 22.
[4] This expression confirms what we have said above of the same expression as used by St. James.   [5] 1 Pet. iv. 8.   [6] Ib. iii. 8.

of the Church he employs the very word he might be expected to have employed if the twenty-first chapter of St. John be a genuine record of the acts and words of Christ. Ποιμαίνε τὰ πρόβατά μου, says the Master to the disciple. Ποιμάνατε τὸ ποίμνιον τοῦ Θεοῦ, says that disciple, when handing on to others the commission he himself has received. The expression is only once used by St. Paul,[1] numerous as are the occasions in which he exhorts the ministers of Christ, or describes their duties; and even on that occasion we may believe his words to be founded on a tradition that Christ had once given such a command to an Apostle. But in the only passage in which we find St. Peter giving advice to presbyters he uses a word which Christ is said to have uttered under circumstances which, had they ever occurred, the Apostle could never have forgotten. Have we not here a striking testimony to the genuineness, not only of the Gospel of St. John, but of the fragment which many of those who defend the Gospel itself are inclined to give up?

There is another utterance recorded in the fourth Gospel, and in it alone, which would seem also to have left a deep impression on the mind of the Apostle. "I am the Good Shepherd," says the Saviour, applying to Himself one of the most beautiful images whereby God is depicted in the Old Testament; and he proceeds, "The Good Shepherd layeth down His life for the sheep." Twice does St. Peter refer to it, and once, be it observed, at the end of a passage in which he has spoken at length, and with feeling, on the Passion of Christ.[2] But the second reference, at the end of the

---

[1] Acts xx. 28.   [2] 1 Pet. ii. 21-25.

passage which treats of the duties of the elders, shows that, deeply as the former saying had taken hold of his imagination, the latter, which handed on the tender relation from the Master to His servants, was yet more deeply graven on his mind.[1] He had good reason to remember the occasion when the "Chief Shepherd" intrusted His erring but repentant follower with the solemn commission, "Feed My sheep."

We have now entered at some length into the examination of the most important principle of the Christian religion as presented to us by the various writers of the New Testament. We have found that there is a remarkable agreement on it among them all, and that though it may appear to have less stress laid upon it by one writer than another, it is very far from being proved that this was because a school of thought existed in the Apostolic Church which acknowledged no such principle. The fact is that the Synoptic Gospels, and the Epistle of St. James, being written for purposes severely practical, make but scant reference to the doctrinal principles upon which their ethical exhortations were necessarily based. They record Christ's precepts, and His example; they commend them to our notice and imitation, but they are silent on the question whence the power to follow them is derived. Yet, though silent as to the source of this power, they clearly acknowledge the power itself, and, as we have seen, they recognize its results as facts of which they have no doubt whatever. A body of which the Holy Ghost is the inspiring soul, faith the condition of life,

[1] 1 Pet. v. 4.

love the abiding fruit, Christ's Body and Blood—a Bread from heaven—the sustaining power; a body which has an organized form, a due principle of subordination—a kingdom of heaven, in fact, of which Christ is the Lord and King, and which witnesses to His power in the midst of a hostile world,[1] is a fact as fully recognized by the Synoptists as by St. John. And when a Synoptist turns aside from his simple narrative of the facts of the life of Jesus to the history of the Church which Jesus founded, we find from hints which he lets drop that he was in full possession of that doctrinal system which is to be found in the fourth Gospel, and in the Epistles of St. Peter and St. Paul—a system which has ever since continued to be the heritage of the universal Church. While, when we turn to the writings of these two Apostles, with whom, let us still bear in mind, two of the Synoptists were in the closest and most affectionate intercourse, we find that their theological conceptions precisely agree with the teaching of Christ which the fourth Gospel presents to our notice. If, therefore, the theological ideas of its author were not borrowed from the writings of St. Peter and St. Paul— which has yet to be proved—there is the strongest presumption that his Gospel is compiled by one who enjoyed the privilege of personal intercourse with Christ Himself.

[1] St. Matt. xiii.

CHAPTER IV.

THE DOCTRINE OF PROPITIATION.

The doctrine of the infusion of a new Life into the believer's heart, and of its triumphal progress there until the whole man is reduced under its power, presupposes, by the very fact of its gradual rather than immediate operation, the existence of a disturbing force—an adverse power which will at least attempt resistance. We come next therefore to the inquiry, whether the fourth Gospel recognizes such a fact as sin, and if so, how is it dealt with? The doctrine of the restoration of human nature through the implanting of a Divine Life, although, as we have seen, it is the central doctrine of our faith, becomes altogether useless to us if that most universal characteristic of human nature, the fact of man's universal transgression of the Divine law, be left untouched. For sin as a disease, the implanting of a Divine Life might be, and no doubt is, a remedy. For sin as an act of disobedience to a Divine Person, the fact of such an implanting is in no sense an atonement. Granted that man could be restored from the effects of his fall by the infusion of a new Life from above, how would this meet the fact that each individual of the race was deeply stained with the commission of deliberate and wilful offences against the Everlasting Ruler of the

136 *The Doctrinal System of St. John.*

universe? How, in fact, to use the vivid language of St. Paul, can God at once be "just, and the justifier of every one who believeth in Him?"[1] Is there any hint that such a difficulty had occurred to St. John? There can be no doubt of it. It would be a simple impertinence to take up the reader's time with the proof that St. John recognized the fact of sin. It is sufficient to inquire how he treats it. There are several significant passages in the Gospel in which the later theology of the Epistles is distinctly foreshadowed. Thus the first historical introduction of Jesus to the reader is in the words of the Baptist, "Behold the Lamb of God, that taketh away the sin of the world."[2] Moreover, the

---

[1] Rom. iii. 26.
[2] St. John i. 29. We might almost infer the identity of the author of the Revelation with that of the Gospel from this one passage. No writer of the New Testament is more impressed by the figure of the Lamb than he who wrote the Revelation. The writer of that book is admitted by many who dispute the genuineness of the Gospel and many other books of the New Testament to be the disciple of the Baptist. But if the fourth Gospel be genuine, he either heard with his own ears, or must immediately after have had reported to him by others, the striking words in which that great teacher first pointed out Jesus to his disciples; for St. John was the partner and friend of St. Andrew, and, as some have thought, his companion on this occasion. Is the continual recurrence of the figure in the Apocalypse no indication of the genuineness of the Gospel? The only other New Testament writer who speaks thus of Christ is St. Peter. The expression does not occur in St. Paul. And if it be urged that ἀμνός is the word in the Gospel, and ἀρνίον in the Apocalypse, we may remember (1) that the only other place where the word ἀρνίον occurs in the New Testament is in the Gospel of St. John; and (2) that it is the figure, rather than the precise word, which is the important point in this case. It has been disputed by commentators to which Lamb under the Jewish law the Baptist must be held to refer. We shall not perhaps be far wrong in embracing every reference which would be likely to occur to the mind of a Jew when listening to such a proclamation. For the different meanings of the word αἴρων, see Hengstenberg *in loc.* Here, again, we

The Doctrine of Propitiation. 137

Son of Man must of necessity (δεῖ) be "lifted up," as the serpent was in the wilderness, and this in order that He may "draw all men unto Him."[1] He "layeth down His life for the sheep," we are told,[2] and the fact is again referred to as a proof of His surpassing love.[3] He is pointed out to us as the Paschal Lamb,[4] whose blood, let us not forget, was to be sprinkled on the doorposts, in order to save the Israelites from destruction.[5] And these prophetic hints of Christ and His forerunner are explained by the other writings attributed to the Evangelist. Christ, who is referred to twenty-six times in the Apocalypse as "the Lamb," is there declared to have "washed us from our sins in His own blood,"[6] and to have "redeemed us by His blood out of every kindred, and tongue, and people, and nation."[7] He is described as a "Lamb as it had been slain," and in His blood all the nations should wash their robes, and make them white.[8] The Epistle, as might be expected, carries the matter further. The effects of Christ's death are formulated into a doctrine. He is the ἱλασμός, the propitiatory offering for the sins of the whole world.[9] He was "manifested to take away sin,"[10] and it is "His blood" that "cleanseth us" from it.[11]

---

may venture to include all those meanings in the scope of this unquestionably pregnant declaration.

[1] St. John iii. 14, 15; Cf. Ib. viii. 28; xii. 32. In the latter passage the expression is explained to refer to the death of Jesus.
[2] St. John x. 11, 15.   [3] Ib. xv. 13.   [4] Ib. xix. 36.
[5] Exod. xii. 13.   [6] Rev. i. 5.   [7] Ib. v. 9.
[8] Ib. v. 6, 12; vii. 14.   [9] 1 John ii. 2; iv. 11.
[10] 1 John iii. 5. Observe here a confirmation of the argument respecting the identity of authorship of the Epistle as well as the Revelation with that of the Gospel. The mind of the writer of the Epistle dwells particularly on the declaration of the Baptist.   [11] Ib. i. 7.

138 The Doctrinal System of St. John.

This cleansing effect of the blood of Christ is moreover symbolised by effusion of blood and water from the Saviour's side mentioned with such emphasis by the Evangelist as having been seen by him at the Crucifixion.[1] That he held the circumstance to have had some symbolical meaning is sufficiently evident from the Gospel itself, but the reference to it in the Epistle[2] removes all possibility of doubt on the point. And if we couple this declaration with that concerning the new birth of water and the Spirit in the discourse to Nicodemus, we can hardly escape from the inference that some allusion was intended to the Sacrament of baptism, as one of the "means whereby" purification by the blood of Christ was conveyed. Yet the words "not by water only, but by water and blood," must surely involve the doctrine of Propitiation to which we have above referred. It is difficult to attach any meaning to them unless we conceive them to imply that no purification could be effectual, but such as was obtained by means of the blood of a Victim, who was offered for the salvation of our souls.[3]

Turn we now to the Synoptists. We shall find them in perfect agreement with the fourth Gospel on this point.

[1] St. John xix. 34. [2] 1 John v. 6.
[3] It has been reserved for the later ages of the Church to systematise, to *humanise* so to speak, this Divine doctrine. The mingled simplicity and mysteriousness of the language of St. John and St. Paul is copied by the earlier Christian writers, with little or no attempt to shape it into formulas. Bishop Patteson, with that rare theological instinct with which he was endowed, has remarked on this. "The doctrine of the Atonement," he writes, "was never in ancient times, I believe, drawn out in the form in which Luther, Calvin, Wesley and others have lately stated it. The fact of the Atonement through the death of Christ was always clearly stated."—'Life of Bishop Patteson,' vol. ii. p. 535.

The Doctrine of Propitiation. 139

All four narratives agree that significant hints were dropped by Christ and those who prophesied of Him, which were expanded by His followers into the theological system we find in the later writings of the New Testament. Remission of sins is the key-note of the Gospel system, as the restoration of fallen humanity is its complete harmony. It was foretold by Zacharias,[1] it was announced by Christ,[2] it was preached to the world with one voice by His Apostles after His Ascension.[3] And that this was to be accomplished by His death we have a distinct declaration in the assertion that He would give His life a ransom ($\lambda \acute{\upsilon} \tau \rho o \nu$ $\dot{\alpha} \nu \tau \acute{\iota}$) for many.[4] The new covenant is instituted in the blood of Christ, which was shed for the remission of sins.[5] And though it is remarkable how little stress is laid by the author of the third Gospel, in his treatise on the Acts of the Apostles, upon the effects of the death of Christ—though it is singular how he, or rather those whose speeches he reports, at once turn away from the thought of the Death of Christ to proclaim "the power of His Resurrection," yet there is one passage in which the sacrificial aspect of that death is plainly, if incidentally, declared. St. Paul speaks of the Church of God[6] as "purchased with His own blood."[7]

But in the Epistles of St. Paul the doctrine of redemption through Christ's blood is most prominently brought out. It is quite unnecessary to cite many passages, when the whole of St. Paul's writings are permeated with the doctrine. But some of the most

[1] St. Luke i. 77.   [2] Ib. iv. 18; v. 20; xxiv. 47, &c.
[3] Acts ii. 38; v. 31, &c.   [4] St. Matt. xx. 28.   [5] Ib. xxvi. 28, &c.
[6] Or, of the Lord. See above, p. 55.   [7] Acts xx. 28.

striking may be selected, in order to show the substantial identity of the teaching of the two Apostles. Jesus is a "propitiatory offering" (ἱλαστήριον) through faith in His blood,[1] and whatever theological difficulties the words ἱλασμός and ἱλαστήριον may suggest, there can be little doubt of the similarity of the ideas they are calculated to convey.[2] So again, "Christ died for us," and we are justified by (or in) His blood.[3] Through His blood we have redemption (ἀπολύτρωσις) and forgiveness of the transgressions,[4] and through it they who sometimes were far off were made nigh.[5] By the death of the Son of God we were reconciled to God.[6] He blotted out the handwriting of ordinances that were against mankind, and took them out of the way by nailing them to His cross.[7] By it [8] He spoiled principalities and powers, and displayed them as captives in His march of triumph.[9] It was "in the body of His flesh, through death," that He "reconciled" mankind to God.[10] But if we seek for a systematic presentation

---

[1] Rom. iii. 25.
[2] ἱλαστήριον is in the LXX. the translation of כַּפֹּרֶת, a Hebrew word which seems to convey the double sense of "cover" and "propitiation." In our English version it is rendered "mercy seat," the symbol, as Philo teaches, of God's mercy—the connecting link between God and man. Suidas, following Hesychius, explains ἱλασμός by "meekness," or "reconciliation," ἱλαστήριον, by "altar." Schleusner regards the former as properly rendered by "expiation," the latter by "expiation," or "expiatory victim." With him agrees Bretschneider. Cremer, following more closely the derivative analogies of the words, renders the former by "expiation"=Heb. כִּפֻּרִים, and the latter by "place of expiation," i.e. mercy-seat, as the visible symbol of Divine forgiveness.
[3] Rom. v. 8, 9. [4] Eph. i. 7. Cf. Col. i. 14.
[5] Eph. ii. 13. [6] Rom. v. 10.
[7] Col. ii. 14. [8] Unless we are to translate ἐν αὐτῷ, "in himself."
[9] Col. ii. 15. [10] Ib. i. 22.

The Doctrine of Propitiation. 141

of this doctrine to our minds we find it in the Epistle to the Hebrews. This is the formal treatise on sacrificial atonement in the New Testament, as the Epistle to the Romans is on justification. Here we have once more the expression ἱλάσκεσθαι used of the work of Christ in His priestly office.[1] And the whole Epistle explains how that propitiatory work was carried on. It was "through death that He destroyed him that had the power of death, that is, the devil."[2] The "priest for ever after the order of Melchizedek"[3] was ordained to offer gifts and sacrifices, as other priests[4] had been. But the sacrifice was the sacrifice of Himself. He "offered Himself without spot to God." By His blood our consciences are purged from dead works to serve the living God.[5] By that blood He entered into the holy place, having found an eternal redemption.[6] He "put away sin by the sacrifice of Himself."[7] By the offering of His Body once for all, we Christians have obtained sanctification.[8] And through His blood an everlasting covenant[9] has been established between God and His people.

The absence of any distinct allusion to the Sacrifice of Christ in the Epistle of St. James confirms the view we have taken of that Epistle above. Unless we are prepared to contend that it represents an earlier form of Christian tradition even than that of the Synoptic Gospels, we cannot deny that the omission in it of all reference to a doctrine so clearly proclaimed by the Synoptists as the Propitiatory offering on the Cross

---

[1] Heb. ii. 17.   [2] Ib. ii. 14.   [3] Ib. v. 6; vi. 20.
[4] Ib. v. 1; viii. 3.   [5] Ib. ix. 14.   [6] Ib. ix. 12.
[7] Ib. ver. 26. Cf. chap. x. 12.   [8] Ib. x. 10.   [9] Ib. xiii. 20.

weakens very much the force of any arguments which may be drawn from the silence of the Epistle on any point whatever. In St. Peter, however, we find the doctrine of redemption through Christ's blood unequivocally set forth. It is by "the precious blood of Christ, as of a Lamb without blemish and without spot," that we are "redeemed (λυτρόω) from the vain conversation handed down from our ancestors."[1] He "bare our sins in His own body on the tree, that we being dead unto sins should live to (or in) righteousness." "By His stripes we are healed."[2] He "suffered for sins, the just for the unjust, that He might bring us to God."[3] And it was to this that we were chosen, namely, unto obedience and the sprinkling of the blood of Jesus Christ.[4]

Surely no more words are needed to demonstrate the substantial identity of the teaching of the Apostles on this point. The detached hints of St. John the Baptist and the Saviour Himself, recorded in the Gospels, are expanded in the Epistles into precisely the same doctrine as that recognized by the Apostles Peter and Paul. It was necessary that the Son of Man should be lifted up[5] in order that He might be the propitiatory Sacrifice for the sins of the whole world. This, and nothing less than this, is the doctrine not of Pauline, or Petrine, or Johannean Christianity, but of the New Testament. Taught by Christ Himself, it has been found singularly adapted to the needs of our fallen humanity. It has been the consolation of His disciples in all ages, and so it will remain until He comes again.

[1] 1 Pet. i. 19. Observe the remarkable coincidence between the language of ver. 20 and that of Rev. xiii. 8. Compare also Eph. i. 4.
[2] 1 Pet. ii. 24.   [3] Ib. iii. 18.   [4] Ib. i. 2.   [5] δεῖ, St. John iii. 14.

CHAPTER V.

THE NATURE AND OFFICE OF THE HOLY SPIRIT.

THE doctrine of St. John concerning the Holy Spirit may be summed up in a few words. Yet in these will be concentrated the essence of the teaching of the rest of Scripture on this head. St. John alone, and the fact has not been unobserved by the assailants of the authenticity of his Gospel, has designated the Holy Spirit by the remarkable title of the Paraclete. But in that term, and in the manner in which it is used, there is a deep and pregnant meaning. The Comforter is a Person. The threefold office implied by His title cannot be fulfilled by any other. He has to exhort and to comfort the people of God, and to be their advocate.[1] He is sent by Christ from the Father.[2] It is from the Father that He proceeds,[2] and the Father Himself is said to send Him. He has a work to do, to convince men of sin, of righteousness, and of judgment.[3] His office is to teach, by declaring what He has heard, by taking of what is Christ's, proclaiming it to Christ's disciples, and thus enhancing the glory of Christ.[4] And this He can do the more readily, in that He

[1] It is scarcely necessary to remind the reader that the word is applied to Christ in 1 John ii. 1, and is there translated "Advocate" in our version.
[2] St. John xv. 26; xvi. 7.   [3] Ib. xvi. 8.   [4] Ib. xvi. 13, 14.

possesses one of the characteristics which Christ has elsewhere declared to be inherent in Himself. He is the Spirit of Truth, and by virtue of this He is enabled to guide the disciples of Christ into all truth, and even to impart to them the gift of prophecy.[1] Through His indwelling the power of remitting and retaining sin was imparted. Whatever may be meant by this commission, and to whomsoever it was communicated, this much is clear, that the commission was a solemn one, and that it was given through the agency of the Holy Ghost.[2] His office, however, was not to commence until after the Ascension of Jesus.[3] But then, we may gather, He was to be the medium of communication between Christ and His people. For Christ came, He says, to give unto His people living water,[4] which should for ever well up within their souls. And it was through His Spirit that this was to be done,[5] by Whom the gift of Divine Life was to be communicated from them to others. " Greater works than these shall ye do, because I go to the Father,"[6] says our Lord. And we can attach no other meaning to His words than that suggested by another passage of the same discourse. If Jesus went to the Father, it was that He might send the Holy Ghost to His disciples.[7] By His influence, and that alone, could they

---

[1] St. John xiv. 17; xvi. 13.   [2] Ib. xx. 22, 23.
[3] Ib. vii. 39 ; xvi. 7. It is impossible to conceive that St. John meant to declare the non-existence of the Spirit before Christ's Ascension in the former of these passages. Such a view would, according to the methods of criticism which are adopted by many, not only prove that St. John was anterior to all the other New Testament writers, but to those of the Old Testament also. See also chap. iii. 34.
[4] St. John iv. 14.   [5] Ib. vii. 38.
[6] Ib. xiv. 12.   [7] Ib. xvi. 7.

The Nature and Office of the Holy Spirit. 145

be enabled to do the yet mightier works than had been done on earth by the very Word of the Father, God from all eternity. Little as there is here concerning the Person and work of the Holy Spirit of God, there is the germ of all that is written elsewhere in the New Testament concerning Him. No doubt can be entertained that His Personality was taught in this Gospel. His Divinity, though not directly expressed, can be inferred from His close connection with the Father and the Son, and from the identity of Their work with His in the redemption of mankind.[1]

St. John's Epistles do little more than echo the language of his Gospel on this head; while the Apocalypse, though it rarely refers to the Holy Spirit, does so in terms which are substantially in agreement with the teaching of the Gospel. Some difficulty has been raised concerning the expressions which seem to imply a belief on the part of the author of the Apocalypse in seven spirits instead of one.[2] But when these expressions are compared with others in the same book, it would seem that there is nothing non-natural in the explanation generally received in the Church, that in these passages the writer has in view the influences of the Holy Spirit, and not His Person. For he is speaking allegorically, and he mentions these seven spirits which he sees in his vision as being before the throne of God,[3] and as being "sent out into all the

---

[1] The absence of any definite declaration of the Divinity of the Holy Ghost ought, according to the received methods of criticism, to be accepted as a proof that the fourth Gospel was written before the Acts and Epistles.

[2] Rev. i. 4; iii. 1; iv. 5; v. 6.   [3] Ib. i. 4; iv. 5.

L

earth."[1] But when he speaks of the message to the Churches, and the invitation to all mankind, he speaks repeatedly of the Spirit as One.[2] Had he conceived of a plurality of persons who were alike entitled to be called spirits of God, he must in these passages have explained to us which of the seven spirits he supposed to be the speaker. The ordinarily received interpretation makes the author of the Apocalypse consistent with the rest of the sacred writers. The interpretation we have been noticing would not only set him at variance with the other writers of the New Testament, but with himself.

As usual with the Synoptists, there is very little definite theological teaching concerning the Spirit of God. He is termed the "Spirit of the Father,"[3] in complete accordance with the statement of St. John that the Paraclete proceeded from the Father. His Personality and Divinity are implied in the statement that whosoever speaketh a word against the Son it shall be forgiven him, but the blasphemy against the Holy Ghost should not be forgiven.[4] From Him was to come the inspiration which should guide the words of Christ's disciples,[5] as well as that which had enabled the prophets of old to foretell the coming and acts of Christ.[6] The Incarnation of Christ was His work.[7] And in the Acts, the only record of the Church under the dispensation of the Spirit, this work of the

---

[1] Rev. v. 6. [2] Ib. ii. iii., *passim*, and xxii. 17.
[3] St. Matt. x. 20.
[4] Ib. xii. 31, 32. St. Mark iii. 28, 29. St. Luke xii. 10.
[5] St. Luke xii. 12. [6] Ib. i. 70. Acts i. 16.
[7] St. Luke i. 35.

Spirit, suggested in the Gospels, is plainly declared. The Holy Ghost descends at Pentecost.[1] He is sent by Christ, and His descent is explained by the fact of Christ's Resurrection and Ascension, according to the principle laid down by Christ in St. John's Gospel.[2] The power from on high, at which St. Luke hints dimly in his Gospel,[3] is explained in the Acts to be that given in the Holy Ghost.[4] Endowed with this Spirit, they were to bear witness to all the world of the Resurrection of Christ.[5] If in the Acts the Holy Ghost is never spoken of as the Paraclete, His work is expressed by the word παράκλησις.[6] He exhorts St. Peter to go with the messengers to Cæsarea.[7] He bids the disciples set apart St. Paul and St. Barnabas for their missionary work.[8] He forbids St. Paul to preach either in Asia Minor or Bithynia.[9] He enables St. Paul and others to anticipate things to come.[10] He superintends the ordination of the presbyters.[11] It was a part of the privileges of every Christian believer that he should have received the Holy Ghost.[12] His personality is clearly enough intimated in the passages to which reference has been made. It only remains to notice that St. Peter expressly declares Him to be God.[13]

St. Paul goes much further than either St. John or

[1] Acts ii.   [2] Ib. ver. 33.   [3] St. Luke xxiv. 49.   [4] Acts i. 8.
[5] St. John xv. 26, 27. Acts i. 22; iii. 15; v. 32; x. 39. Cf. Heb. ii. 4. In chap. v. 32, the very turn of the expression is St. John's. Did he invent it from the passage in the Acts, or does St. Peter quote our Lord's well-remembered words?
[6] Acts ix. 31.   [7] Ib. xi. 12.
[8] Ib. xiii. 2.   [9] Ib. xvi. 7.
[10] Ib. xx. 23; xxi. 11.   [11] Ib. xx. 28.
[12] Ib. viii. 15-17; xix. 2.   [13] Ib. v. 4.

148 *The Doctrinal System of St. John.*

the Synoptists in the prominence he gives to the Holy Spirit in the work of our redemption. Whatever is done by the Father or the Son in us is ascribed to the Holy Ghost as the agent. He is not only the Spirit of God, but the "Spirit of Christ,"[1] as being sent by Christ from the Father. His influence is connected with the Resurrection and Ascension of Christ.[2] It is through Him that Christ has imparted to those who believe on Him; for if we are an "habitation of God," it is "through the Spirit,"[3] and if "Christ dwell in our hearts by faith," so that we attain to the knowledge of His love, it is because we have been "strengthened with might by His Spirit in the inner man."[4] By "the hearing of faith" all believers received the Spirit,[5] who was the earnest of our future inheritance,[6] the seal set by God to the reality of His promises. Nay, even when Christ is said to have "offered Himself without spot to God," it is "through the eternal Spirit" that He is said to have done so.[7] If St. John speaks of the teaching of the Holy Ghost as proceeding from what He heareth,[8] so does St. Paul speak of His teaching as the result of his searching all things, yea, even the deep things of God.[9] If, by the use of the term Paraclete, St. John speaks of Him as the Advocate of the people of God, St. Paul takes care to remind us that He maketh intercession for the saints according to the will of God.[10] If, by that same term,

[1] Rom. viii. 9. Gal. iv. 6. Phil. i. 19.
[2] Eph. iv. 8. Rom. i. 4. [3] Eph. ii. 22. Cf. 1 Cor. iii. 16; vi. 19.
[4] Eph. iii. 16, 17. [5] Gal. iii. 2, 14.
[6] 2 Cor. i. 22; v. 5. Eph. i. 13; iv. 30. [7] Heb. ix. 14.
[8] St. John xvi. 13. [9] 1 Cor. ii. 10–13.
[10] Rom. viii. 26, 27.

The Nature and Office of the Holy Spirit. 149

St. John would have us understand the mission of the Holy Spirit to exhort and to console, St. Paul, who speaks in one place of the consolation of the Holy Ghost, speaks in another of an everlasting consolation (παράκλησις) given by the Father and by His Son Jesus Christ.[1] All the great spiritual works accomplished among mankind are ascribed to the agency of the Holy Spirit. He ministers the various gifts which are allotted to the members of Christ's Church.[2] It is through Him that the quickening of our mortal bodies, promised by Christ in St. John's Gospel, is effected.[3] By Him it is that we are set free from the bondage of corruption, and enabled to fulfil the pure law of Jesus Christ.[4] In obedience to His mandates we display our title to be called the sons of God.[5] By Him we are changed from glory to glory until we reflect the image of Jesus Christ.[6] Our unity with the Father and with His Son Jesus Christ is the "unity of the Spirit."[7] And if Jesus Christ came to make love the abiding principle of our souls through His indwelling, it is through "the Holy Spirit which He hath given us" that this love is "shed abroad."[8] Nor must we forget that, as we have seen above,[9] the initial principle of the Gospel Life is attributed by St. Paul as well as St. John, but by the former with greater minuteness and particularity than the other, to the agency of the Holy Ghost.[10] It would only be wearisome to follow out in

---

[1] 2 Thess. ii. 16, 17. [2] 1 Cor. xii. Cf. Heb. ii. 4.
[3] Rom. viii. 11. [4] Ib. viii. 2. 2 Cor. iii. 17.
[5] Rom. viii. 14. [6] 2 Cor. iii. 18. [7] Eph. iv. 3–6.
[8] Rom. v. 5. [9] Chapter iii.
[10] St. John iii. 5. Tit. iii. 4–7.

detail St. Paul's separate enunciations of his general principle that whatsoever is done by the Father and the Son in the work of our redemption is done through the agency of the Holy Spirit. Life in the Spirit[1] is as distinctly his doctrine as life in Christ. All holy deeds which result from crucifying the flesh as disciples of Christ are attributed to the Spirit's influence.[2] These principles, first clearly laid down in the Epistle to the Galatians, and again expanded and emphasized in the eighth chapter of the Epistle to the Romans, permeate the whole of his writings. From whence did he derive them, if it were not from the words of Christ, well known and fully accepted in the Church, but not committed to writing until years after in the Gospel according to St. John?[3]

We should not expect to find many allusions to the work of the Holy Spirit in the brief Epistles of St. Peter and St. Jude. But what is to be found there is to our point, and far more distinct than anything contained in the longer Epistle to the Hebrews.[4] St. Peter attributes our sanctification to His influence.[5] He asserts that the prophets of old derived their inspiration from the Spirit of Christ, and that it was by His inspiration that the Apostles of Christ were enabled to

---

[1] Gal. v. 25.   [2] Ib. v. 22-24.
[3] St. Paul never expressly affirms the divinity of the Holy Ghost, but in such passages as 1 Cor. iii. 16; vi. 19, 20, he implies it more unmistakeably than any passage of St. John does.
[4] St. James does not mention the Holy Spirit, not, surely, because he was unacquainted with His existence. He could not have read the first verse of the Book of Genesis without hearing of Him.
[5] 1 Pet. i. 2. This, however, may mean the spirit of the believer. But compare St. Peter's own words in Acts ii. 33.

The Nature and Office of the Holy Spirit. 151

proclaim His Gospel.[1] He regards our salvation as due to the Resurrection and Ascension of Christ, thus suggesting, though in no way affirming, the connection of these events with the gift of the Spirit. He speaks of Him as the Spirit of Glory and of God, which rests on those who are enabled to glorify God by suffering.[2] Is it fanciful to imagine that we see in this passage the reflection of those mysterious words, so dark to human apprehension until illuminated by the after-history of the Church, " He shall glorify Me, for He shall take of Mine, and shall show it unto you?"[3] One brief allusion in the short Epistle of St. Jude must conclude this portion of our investigation. The wickedness of the ungodly is explained by the fact that they lead a natural ($\psi v \chi \iota \kappa \acute{o} s$) life, unaffected by the influence of the Spirit of God,[4] in a way which suggests to us the declaration of our Lord to Nicodemus, and the emphatic and reiterated utterances of St. Paul; while the saints of God are recommended to preserve themselves carefully in the love of God, by means of a steady

[1] 1 Pet. i. 11, 12. The allusion to the day of Pentecost here is in keeping with the allusion to the Transfiguration in the second Epistle. St. Peter's mind, unlike that of St. Paul, was pervaded by these memories. The events of the past were ever vividly present to his mind. Compare, too, the similarity in sentiment with the variety in expression in 1 Pet. i. 11 and 2 Pet. i. 21.

[2] 1 Pet. iv. 14, 16.

[3] St. Peter's death, it may be observed, was regarded by St. John as a means of glorifying God, chap. xxi. 19. Also, if the second Epistle of St. Peter be genuine, we derive from the allusion in chap. i. 14 to the saying reported by St. John an additional argument for the genuineness of the Gospel; and even if not, it is clear either that we have here one of M. Reville's "authentic traditions" known only to the author of the Gospel and the Epistle, or that the Gospel was accepted in the Church before St. Peter's second Epistle was composed.

[4] Jude 19.

growth in their most holy faith, and a continual prayer offered up through the indwelling power of the Holy Spirit.[1]

It may be as well, before leaving this subject, to point out some remarkable features of agreement between the doctrine of St. John and that of St. Paul which may have escaped the attention of the reader. They do not lie upon the surface, and for this reason they are the more important to our investigation. The first point is the connection to which attention has already been directed of the Descent of the Holy Ghost with the Ascension of Christ. "If I go not away, the Comforter will not come unto you," says Christ in St. John's Gospel; and not only is the Descent of the Holy Spirit, but the whole work of the Gospel declared by Apostles and Evangelists with one consent to depend upon the Resurrection and Ascension of Jesus Christ.[2] But before we can understand this spiritual necessity; this utter impossibility that the Holy Ghost should descend to carry on the work of salvation until Jesus had ascended into heaven, we must turn to the Epistle to the Hebrews, an Epistle which, as we have seen, makes very little reference to the person or office of the Holy Ghost. There we learn that, since "every high priest is ordained to offer gifts and sacrifices, it is necessary also that Christ should have something to offer."[3] What that something is, we are also told. It was the blood of the Lamb slain from the foundation of

---

[1] Jude 20. Little less than this can be implied by the words ἐν πνεύματι ἁγίῳ προσευχόμενοι.
[2] See Acts ii. 33. Eph. iv. 8. Rom. i. 4. 1 Pet. i. 3.
[3] Heb. viii. 3.

The Nature and Office of the Holy Spirit.

the world,[1] wherewith God is propitiated. It was the "offering up of Himself, once for all,"[2] whereby He "put away sin."[3] As the victim, He was slain, but as High Priest He entered into the Holy Place with the blood of the sacrifice, and appeared in the presence of God for us. Not till then was the atonement made; the sacrifice, though offered, was not till then accepted; but when Christ had once appeared in the presence of God, when He had passed through the veil of His own flesh into the Holy Place not made with hands, the work of redemption was complete, the reconciliation was effected, and the Spirit of God, who had been driven from His habitation among men by their wickedness,[4] could return and make His tabernacle among them. It is only by a comparison of the different books of the New Testament that we arrive at this conclusion. One book states the fact, another gives the reason; but the reason is not connected with the fact, nor the fact with the reason. That the coincidence is remarkable, few

---

[1] Rev. xiii. 8.   [2] Heb. vii. 27.
[3] Ib. ix. 26. The words of Christ in St. John viii. 28 confirm the doctrine advanced in the Epistle to the Hebrews. In themselves they are obscure, but interpreted by the light of the other books of the New Testament, they are full of meaning: " When ye have lifted up the Son of Man, then ye shall know that I am, and I am nothing of Myself, but as my Father hath taught Me, these things I speak."
[4] The descent of the Holy Ghost is the formal repeal of the decree of Gen. vi. 3, in which, according to the more probable translation, God's Spirit is withdrawn from His indwelling in man "*because of their transgression.*" The form (שׁ) of the relative pronoun upon which the translation in our version depends is not found in the Pentateuch. It first appears in the Book of Judges. And the translation καταμείνῃ in the LXX. leads to the supposition that the Greek translators read ילין for ידין. When reconciliation had been made, and not till then, the Holy Ghost returned. This view is adopted by Hengstenberg in his ʽCommentary on St. John.'

will be inclined to deny. But whether the statement of fact preceded the publication of its *rationale*, is a question which must be deferred to another chapter.

Again, St. John certainly speaks with greater emphasis than any other Evangelist of the promise of Christ to send the Holy Spirit. "I will send Him unto you," He says, "from the Father." It is remarkable how distinctly this promise is referred to by the Synoptists. "I send the promise of My Father upon you," He says in St. Luke's Gospel;[1] and yet more emphatically in the Acts, "the promise of the Father, which saith He, ye have heard of Me."[2] When and where had they heard such a promise? There was a hint, it is true, given by St. John Baptist, that He who should come after him "should baptize with the Holy Ghost and with fire."[3] But these were no words of Christ Himself, nor does He, in the Synoptic narratives, say anything amounting to a promise of the Holy Ghost.[4] Yet this "promise" is dwelt upon with the utmost emphasis by Synoptists and the writers of the Epistles. It is hinted at in the narratives of St. Matthew and St. Mark. The Gospel of St. Luke refers to it in significant but not very definite terms. But all ambiguity is removed in the Acts, when the promise of the Father, made by Jesus on some previous occasion, is now declared to be the baptism of the Holy Ghost on the day of Pentecost. Nor are these the only allusions we have

---

[1] ἐπαγγελία, xxiv. 49.   [2] Acts i. 4.   [3] St. Matt. iii. 11.
[4] Unless the exhortation recorded in St. Matt. x. 19, 20, where Christ foretells that His disciples shall receive the aid of the Spirit of their Father to defend themselves when apprehended by the powers that be. But this is a very different thing from the effects of the Descent at Pentecost.

The Nature and Office of the Holy Spirit. 155

to such a promise. St. Peter, in his first sermon, calls the outpouring of the Spirit the promise of the Father.[1] It will not be sufficient to explain this expression of the prophecy of Joel which St. Peter had just cited. "Christ had received of the Father the promise of the Holy Ghost," we are told. Yet, save in the Gospel of St. John, we do not find that Christ had made any such statement. And we may carry our argument yet further. Christ's promise must have been very weighty and solemn before it could have made so deep an impression even upon those who had not seen Him in the flesh. It is not St. Peter only, but St. Paul, who speaks of the Holy Spirit as "promised." He does so emphatically twice—in the Epistle to the Galatians, where he speaks of the "promise of the Spirit" being "received by faith,"[2] and in the Epistle to the Ephesians, where he calls Him, yet more distinctly, "the Holy Spirit of promise."[3] A more remarkable instance could hardly be given of the way in which St. John's Gospel is absolutely necessary to complete the history of Christ's life and sayings. There are many which do not come within the scope of this Essay;[4] but it is impossible to treat of the teaching of

---

[1] Acts ii. 33.   [2] Gal. iii. 14.
[3] Eph. i. 13. A Hebraism, most probably, for the promised Holy Spirit; with more emphasis on the promise, however, than could be given by any other construction.
[4] Such as, for instance, the account of the anointing at Bethany, which in the Synoptists is related in connection with the betrayal. St. John supplies the key to this by stating that the rebuke was addressed to Judas: that of the raising of Lazarus, which supplies a reason for the enthusiastic reception of One who, as far as the Synoptist narratives go, had never been in Jerusalem since the commencement of His ministry: that of the words, "Destroy this temple,"

the New Testament Scriptures with regard to the Holy Ghost without adverting to the fact that He is said again and again in Holy Scripture to have been promised under the Christian dispensation, and that no record of such promise is to be found, save in the pages of the Evangelist St. John.[1]

One more coincidence must be adverted to before we leave this branch of our subject. It is to be found in the harmony between the prophecy ascribed to Christ as regards the work of the Holy Ghost, and the subsequent history of the Christian Church. Of course the prophecy may be attributed to the writer of the Gospel, but it must at least be admitted that such a view would give him credit for great grasp of thought and power of expression. The mysterious character of the passage, however, is surely more reconcileable with the idea of a prophecy on Christ's part, than with that of an epitome of the results of His doctrine, excogitated by a writer of the second century. They are the words of the Master rather than the scholar. The Holy Ghost was to act upon men's convictions. He was to prove to them the existence of sin, of righteousness, and of judgment.[2] One striking instance of the fulfil-

---

recorded only by St. John; but made the basis of one of the chief accusations against our Lord in the Synoptist narratives. So we have an explanation of Judas being able to find our Lord so readily in chap. xviii. 2, and how St. Peter gained entrance into the high priest's palace, in ver. 15. Another piece of confirmatory evidence has just been adduced in this very section, p. 151.

[1] If this be another of the "authentic traditions" to which the author of the fourth Gospel had access, it is singular that it should be found imbedded firmly in a mass of concrete of "obviously later origin," such as chapters xiv.—xvii.

[2] St. John xvi. 8.

ment of this prediction at once occurs to us. Never before had a Roman governor quailed before a prisoner as Felix did, when Paul "reasoned with him of righteousness, of temperance, and of judgment to come." Never, again, had a curious and excited crowd been so pricked to the heart as when Peter's first attempt at preaching drew from his hearers the remarkable words, "Men and brethren, what shall we do?" Whether it were the conviction which worked "godly sorrow unto repentance not to be repented of," or the conviction which only hardened the impenitent heart, this same compunction was again and again the witness to the fact of such a work. As St. Stephen's speech revealed to his hearers the inner hollowness of their creed, they "rushed upon him with one accord, stopping their ears." One at least of that fanatical band could not drive out the recollection of St. Stephen's words, and the conviction of their truth suddenly came home to him when he was trying to conceal his inward misgivings by redoubled rage and fury. The same St. Paul, when he had fully grasped the Christian system, perceived how the revelation of the righteousness of God by Jesus Christ produced the double result of conviction of sin and of the need of a righteousness other than our own.[1] Nor does he forget to give an edge to his preaching, to bring it home to the consciences of men, by constant allusions to the certainty of a coming judgment.[2] He appeals to the witness of their own consciences, informed and enlightened by the Holy Spirit, for the confirmation of what he teaches.[3] In one remarkable

---

[1] Rom. i.—iii.   [2] Ib. ii. 16. 2 Cor. v. 10, &c.
[3] 2 Cor. iv. 2; v. 11.

passage he analyses the work of the Spirit in producing that salutary conviction of infirmity which leads to amendment of life. "For behold this selfsame thing, that ye sorrowed after a godly sort, what carefulness it wrought in you, yea, what clearing of yourselves, yea, what indignation, yea, what fear, yea, what vehement desire, yea, what zeal, yea, what revenge! In all things ye have approved yourselves to be clear in this matter."[1] Surely this is an example of the effect of the Holy Spirit in the heart, by manifestation of the righteousness of an ascended Lord, convincing His disciples of sin and stirring them up to conform themselves to the pattern of His Life. In fact, the whole after-history of the Church is a history of the acts of that "Spirit of truth," arousing men's consciences, and "convincing them of sin, of righteousness and of judgment," being to some "a savour of death unto death," and to others "a savour of life unto life," but to all, whether subduing them to obedience, or rousing them into antagonism, in very deed the voice of God.

[1] 2 Cor. vii. 11.

CHAPTER VI.

THE DOCTRINE OF THE RESURRECTION AND THE FINAL JUDGMENT.

THERE are few points on which St. John's Gospel is more explicit than on that of the resurrection and the final judgment. As we shall see hereafter, the fact that he is so explicit on this head is an argument for the genuineness of his Gospel. At present, however, we will confine ourselves to the doctrines he unfolds. And first, as regards the resurrection. Our Lord, according to St. John, refers both to the fact and its cause. To the fact, in such passages as that in the fifth chapter: "The hour is coming, when they that are in the graves shall hear the voice of the Son of God: and they that hear shall live." "The hour is coming, in the which they that are in the graves shall hear His voice, and shall come forth."[1] "I will raise him up at the last day."[2] "If any man serve Me, let him follow Me; and where I am, there shall My servant be."[3] "I go and prepare a place for you. And if I go and prepare a place for you, I will come again, and receive you unto Myself; that where I am, there shall ye be also."[4] "Father, I will that they also, whom Thou hast given Me, be with Me

[1] St. John v. 26, 28.   [2] Ib. vi. 39, 40, 44, 54.   [3] Ib. xii. 26.
[4] Ib. xiv. 3.

where I am."[1] To the cause, in mysterious language in such passages as these: "I have power to lay down My life, and I have power to take it again."[2] "Except a corn of wheat fall into the ground and die, it abideth alone: but if it die, it bringeth forth much fruit."[3] "I am the Life: no one cometh unto the Father, but by Me."[4] And when the most advanced among His disciples had grasped the truth of a resurrection of the just, He teaches them to connect it with Himself. He is no longer content with the words, "Thy brother shall rise again," but He utters once, and once only, as recorded in the Gospels, the ever-memorable words, the foundation of all the after-teaching of the Apostles, "I am the Resurrection, and the Life: he that believeth on Me, though he were dead, yet shall he live."[5]

On the doctrine of future retribution, too, it is impossible to misunderstand the doctrine of St. John. They who "come forth" from the graves come forth to judgment: "they that have done good unto the resurrection of life, and they that have done evil unto the resurrection of damnation."[6] "He that rejecteth Me, and receiveth not My Words, hath one that judgeth him: the Word which I have spoken, the same shall judge him at the last day."[7] Nor is this all. The Evangelist represents judgment as already passed on mankind, and the only deliverance from that sentence of condemnation is to be found in accepting the salvation proclaimed by Christ. "He that believeth on Him is not condemned: but he that believeth not is condemned already, because he hath not believed on the name of

[1] St. John xvii. 24.   [2] Ib. x. 18.   [3] Ib. xii. 24.   [4] Ib. xiv. 6.
[5] Ib. xi. 25. Cf. vi. 35, 48.   [6] Ib. v. 29.   [7] Ib. xii. 48.

Doctrine of the Resurrection, &c. 161

the only-begotten Son of God."¹ So had taught the Baptist before him. "He that believeth on the Son hath everlasting life: but he that believeth not the Son shall not see life; but the wrath of God abideth on him."² "He that believeth on Me," again says the Saviour, "hath everlasting life, and shall not come into" (or rather, "cometh not unto") "condemnation, but is passed from death unto life."³ A similar doctrine is found in the Epistle. A day of judgment is spoken of wherein we need a boldness derived from God's indwelling,⁴ otherwise we may have reason to be ashamed when He comes.⁵ And when He appears, His disciples will put on His likeness.⁶

It is scarcely necessary to dwell on the teaching of the book of the Revelation. We are all familiar with the awful picture of judgment to come presented to us there, and with the bright visions of glory which were seen by the Apostle, when God should wipe away all tears from the eyes of His people, and when sorrow, and pain, and all the former things should have passed away;⁷ but it is only fair to remark that there is no apparent trace of the theological system of the fourth Evangelist and the majority of the Epistle writers in this book. There is no hint of judgment having been already passed, by reason of the introduction into the world of light through Christ. We read rather of life *with* Christ, than of life *in* Christ: in fact, we have the teaching of the Synoptists, rather

---

¹ St. John iii. 18.
² Ib. ver. 36, if the words are not those of the Evangelist.
³ Ib. v. 24.   ⁴ 1 John iv. 17.   ⁵ Ib. ii. 28.
⁶ Ib. iii. 2.   ⁷ Rev. xxi. 4.

M

162 *The Doctrinal System of St. John.*

than the more esoteric doctrines proclaimed by St. John,[1] St. Peter, and St. Paul. For when we turn to the three former Gospels, though we have the clearest possible intimations of a future judgment,[2] no kind of anticipation of the judgment is even hinted at; nor, though we read over and over again of the resurrection as an integral part of Christ's teaching,[3] do we find it ascribed to any inherent union between the believer and Christ.

The more we are inclined to remark on this distinction between the teaching of the Synoptists and the other writers of the New Testament on this head, the more important become the hints incidentally dropped in the Acts, that such teaching as we find in St. Paul and St. John was of the essence of the Gospel. And such hints we find; not, it is true, in great numbers, but sufficient to show that the doctrine of these latter writers was no innovation upon that of the earlier preachers of the Gospel. Not only is the prophecy of the Lord, that He would come again,[4] repeated in similar, but more emphatic terms by the angel,[5] but we find St. Peter sanctioning the doctrine of an inherent life in Christ, in the declaration that "it was not possible that He should be holden of death."[6] And when he proceeds to call Him the "Author of Life,"[7] he is but repeating the words of our Lord to Martha. We

---

[1] Exception, however, may be made of passages such as Rev. ii. 7, 17; xxi. 6; xxii. 17. It is also noticeable how these passages presuppose such discourses of Christ as are to be found in the fourth and sixth chapters of the Gospel.

[2] St. Matt. xxiv. 31; xxv. St. Mark xvi. 16, &c.

[3] St. Matt. xxii. 23, &c.   [4] St. John xiv. 3, 18, 28.

[5] Acts i. 11.   [6] Ib. ii. 24.   [7] See note 4, p. 55.

have already seen how the doctrine of a power inherent in Jesus pervades the Acts of the Apostles; and if it be argued that this power is in no way specially connected with the resurrection of the dead, we may frankly admit that this is so. Our argument is not much affected by the fact. If repentance and remission of sins are given not only through, but by Jesus Christ;[1] if health and recovery be due to Him;[2] if the Holy Ghost be sent by Him; if He be the worker of all that is done in His name by His Apostles;[3] if He be appointed to judge the world;[4] if the faith which is offered to all men be said to be due to His Resurrection,[5] it is at least hardly incompatible with these strong expressions to suppose that the Resurrection itself was His work.

But when we turn to St. Paul, in whose company the Acts of the Apostles was unquestionably written, we shall see that St. Luke's silence on this point is not the result of ignorance or disagreement. That St. Paul believed in a future judgment there is no necessity to prove. The first two chapters of his Epistle to the Romans afford us abundant evidence that he did so; and it is the main subject of his Epistles to the Thessalonians.[6] But the whole argument of the first two chapters of the Epistle to the Romans proceeds on the assumption of the doctrine contained in the fourth Gospel. Judgment is declared to have been already passed by God upon the sins of men, both by the testimony of their own consciences and by His abandonment of them

---

[1] Acts ii. 38; v. 31; x. 43.   [2] Ib. iii. 6; ix. 17, 34.
[3] See Wordsworth. 'Introduction to Acts.'
[4] Acts x. 42; xvii. 31.   [5] πίστιν παρασχών, chap. xvii. 31.
[6] See also 2 Cor. v. 10, &c.

to the evil which they had embraced, and which was desolating their whole moral nature. The righteous judgment of God is but a revelation of the wrath He ever bears towards sin.[1] That judgment is well known to themselves, if they only chose to acknowledge the fact.[2] The law has already declared the guilt of those who lived under it.[3] The salvation by Jesus Christ is a means of deliverance for all those who desire to accept it, but it is not a dispensation of wrath upon mankind. By the obedience of Jesus the many were to find their righteousness established, and in the place of the reign of sin, resulting in death, was substituted the reign of favour and loving-kindness unto eternal Life, by means of Christ Jesus our Lord.[4] Henceforth there is no condemnation for the Christian.[5] He has been set free from the law of sin and death, which had been condemned by the mere appearance of the Holy Jesus in the likeness of humanity.[6] So, in the Second Epistle to the Thessalonians, men are described as perishing, because they did not receive the love of the truth, so that they might be saved.[7] The expression in the Epistle to the Hebrews, drawing back unto perdition;[8] in fact, the very term salvation[9] involves the idea of a rescue from a state of things already existing —a state most graphically described in the seventh chapter of the Epistle to the Romans; and the whole tone of the Sacred Scriptures is in favour of the doctrine enunciated in St. John, that he who will not accept

---

[1] Rom. ii. 5.   [2] Ib. i. 28, 32.   [3] Ib. iii. 19.
[4] Ib. v. 19, 21.   [5] Ib. viii. 1.   [6] Ib. ver. 3.
[7] 2 Thess. ii. 10.   [8] Heb. x. 39.
[9] And redemption also. See, for instance, Titus ii. 14.

Doctrine of the Resurrection, &c. 165

the salvation offered to him by Christ, incurs, not a new condemnation, but one pronounced by God on all transgressors from the very first. That the rejection of Christ may be an aggravation of such transgression is implied by St. John himself;[1] but the Gospel is in no sense a proclamation of the wrath of God, but only of His infinite mercy: a fact implied by the continual repetition in the New Testament of that much-abused word grace.[2]

St. Paul's doctrine of the Resurrection, again, differs in no respect from that of St. John. Christ does not only proclaim, He is the Resurrection. Nowhere is this more clearly set forth than in the great discourse on that subject in the Epistle to the Corinthians. It is an elaborate commentary on the words, "I am the Resurrection and the Life." All hinges upon Jesus our Lord. If He be not raised, there is no resurrection for us. We are not delivered from our sins; we shall sleep an everlasting sleep.[3] Christ is not merely the "first-fruits of them that slept:" we shall all be made alive in Him, that is, by participation in His nature.[4] He is the "corn of wheat," which by falling into the ground and dying shall "bear much fruit,"[5] for He is the quickening Spirit by whom our bodies, sown in corruption, are raised in incorruption[6]—sown in the possession of a mere natural and earthly life,[7] are raised with the Life of the Spirit fully developed within them.[8] It is His image, that of the Lord from heaven, that we shall bear.[9] It is through Him that we obtain this victory over our

---

[1] St. John v. 40.   [2] See Appendix I.   [3] 1 Cor. xv. 18.
[4] Ib. xv. 22.   [5] St. John xii. 24.   [6] 1 Cor. xv. 42.
[7] σῶμα ψυχικόν.   [8] σῶμα πνευματικόν.   [9] 1 Cor. xv. 47, 49.

mortal selves; the corruptible putting on incorruption, and the mortal putting on immortality. To the same effect are other declarations of the Apostle. It amounts to the same thing when he declares that we shall be raised up from the dead by means of, or as some copies of the New Testament read, in virtue of, the Spirit of Christ which dwells within us.[1] It is by the power of Christ, whose members we are, that we shall be raised up.[2] He it is who alone can "change our vile body, that it may be like unto His glorious body;"[3] for if we "appear with Him in glory," it is because He is "our life."[4] Nay, even in this life we enjoy the earnest of our future resurrection, for already we are quickened with Christ, and raised with Him, and made to sit with Him in the heavenly places in Christ Jesus.[5] This is why we are said already to possess in the heavens a house not made with hands.[6] What is all this but an expansion of the doctrine of St. John, who tells us that Jesus is the Life, and that among the many powers derived by Him from His Father, is that of quickening whom He will?[7]

St. James is almost entirely silent on this head. Almost the only intimation of a future judgment to be found in his Epistle is in the passage where he tells us that the coming of the Lord draweth nigh, and that the Judge standeth before the door.[8] Nay, so rigidly

---
[1] Rom. viii. 11.
[2] 1 Cor. vi. 14, αὐτοῦ surely refers to Christ. See 2 Cor. iv. 14.
[3] Phil. iii. 21.   [4] Col. iii. 4.   [5] Eph. ii. 5, 6.
[6] 2 Cor. v. 1.   [7] St. John v. 21.
[8] St. James v. 8, 9. Cf., however, ii. 12, 13. We may perhaps be allowed to argue from ch. v. 20 that sentence of death had been already pronounced upon the world, and that the only way of deliverance was

practical is his object, that he makes the very barest allusion to a future life. In this fact we may find the completest refutation of the theory that St. James was ignorant of, or opposed to, sundry doctrines of the Gospel which do not find a place in his Epistle. It is hardly to be supposed that he had little or no idea of a future state; yet his only reference to it is in two brief sentences, in which he speaks of the "crown of life," and "the kingdom which God hath promised to those that love Him."[1] The occurrence, however, of the expression, "the Lord hath promised," in the first of these passages, implies that Christ, to whom the title "the Lord" is usually given,[2] contains, by implication, the doctrine of our resurrection in Christ, if even it may not be pressed so far as to indicate an equality with God, who is, in the other passage, spoken of as making the same promise.

St. Peter is more explicit. Not only does he speak in the plainest terms in each of his Epistles of the coming of a day of judgment,[3] but he declares the Resurrection of Christ to be the efficient cause of our own,[4] for we are not only "begotten" by it "unto a lively hope," but also unto "an inheritance incorruptible, undefiled, and that fadeth not away, reserved

---

that revealed by Jesus Christ. There is moreover an allusion to Gehenna in chap. iii. 6, and to a lawgiver able to save and to destroy in iv. 12.

[1] St. James i. 12; ii. 5.   [2] See Acts, *passim*.
[3] 1 Pet. iv. 5. 2 Pet. ii. 9; iii. 7-12. It is worthy of remark that the conceptions of the second Epistle are less advanced than those of the first. We are therefore, I presume, entitled to conclude that it was written earlier.
[4] 1 Pet. i. 3, 4. So also Christ's Resurrection gives to Baptism its saving efficacy.—Ch. iii. 21.

in heaven for those who are kept by the power of God through faith unto salvation." Has not such a passage as this some connection with the declaration, " I am the Resurrection and the Life; he that believeth in Me, though he were dead, yet shall he live?" The other allusions to Christ as the living and energizing principle of the Gospel have already been discussed.[1] It is sufficient here to call attention to them, as affording additional proof that Christ, who is our Life, is also our resurrection. For as St. Paul reminds us, and as St. Peter more than implies, " He is before all things, and by Him all things consist; and He is the Head of the Body, the Church, who is the beginning,[2] *the firstborn from the dead,* in order that in all things He might have the pre-eminence,[3] for it pleased the Father that in Him should all the fulness dwell."[4]

We have now passed in review the main doctrines of the Gospel. We have found nothing to justify the assumption that the Synoptists and St. John are at variance with one another on the Gospel scheme, while, on the other hand, we have found much to support the hypothesis that where the former were silent with reference to those important doctrines which St. John proclaims, it was a silence of intention, and not one either of ignorance or hostility. This conclusion is strengthened by the fact that St. Peter, who was responsible, according to the best and earliest authorities, for the Gospel of St. Mark, and St. Paul, who was the " guide, philosopher, and friend" of the writer of the third Gospel,

[1] Above, chapter ii.
[2] ἀρχή. Compare ἀρχηγός. Acts iii. 15; v. 31. Heb. ii. 10.
[3] Or pre-existence, πρωτεύων. [4] Col. i. 17–19.

Doctrine of the Resurrection, &c. 169

reflect most definitely in their writings the system of St. John. The result, therefore, of our inquiries has been to divest the argument derived from the supposed contrariety of the Synoptists and St. John of a great deal of its force. It is at least clear, that if the teaching contained in his Gospel be less fully set forth than in the narratives of St. Matthew, St. Mark, and St. Luke, that such teaching was fully accepted in the Apostolic age, and even by the Apostles themselves. It is further clear, that two out of the three Evangelists just named were aware of the existence of such teaching. It is necessary, therefore, in order to establish the spuriousness of St. John's Gospel, on the ground of its containing matter not found in the rest, that the two Evangelists in question should not have been content with silence on such points, but that they should have energetically borne witness upon them to what they believed to be the truth. The exact contrary of this is the case. They not only do not disavow such principles, but they do a great deal to suggest them. Such conduct, if it can be proved against them, is, on their part, highly culpable. To be aware that Christ was not merely represented as a man of surpassing merit, an example to all His fellows, but as actually God, and as a source of new Life to all who believed in Him, and to say nothing but what would tend to encourage a doctrine they knew to have been put forth without authority from Christ, would have been in them an offence of a very grave kind. To associate themselves in work with men who, to their certain knowledge, were setting forth, in the name of Christ, doctrines which, had He

170 *The Doctrinal System of St. John.*

heard of them, He would indignantly have repudiated, would be absolutely inexcusable on their part. Whereas, on the contrary, the principle of unfolding the truths of Christianity by degrees, as the weak, and ignorant, and prejudiced human mind was able to bear it, was in exact accordance with the method of their Teacher. We have, then, to choose between two explanations of a phenomenon admitted on all hands: the one, an explanation which supposes the Evangelists to have acted according to the example[1] and express directions of their Divine Master; the other, an explanation which attributes to them conduct not only inexplicable, but in a high degree reprehensible. In fine, we arrive at two conclusions from this portion of our investigation; first, that the differences between the fourth Gospel and the other three have been greatly exaggerated, and next, that we cannot attack the Gospel attributed to St. John without assailing the judgment and the character of two at least, if not all, of the remaining biographers of Christ. But the argument against St. John's Gospel, from the silence of the other three on certain subjects, derives all its force from their supposed truthfulness in the main. We may therefore with confidence assert, that a careful review of all the phenomena presented by the literature of the Apostolic period is sufficient to dispose of the apparently formidable objections raised against the authenticity of the Gospel according to St. John.

[1] 'Without a parable spake he not unto them.' See above, p. 74.

PART II.
THE PRIORITY OF THE DOCTRINAL SYSTEM OF THE FOURTH GOSPEL.

CHAPTER I.
ST. JOHN AND THE THEOLOGY OF THE SECOND CENTURY.

THE result of our previous investigations has been to establish the fact that there is a general agreement, tacit or expressed, between the various writers of the New Testament. Such a discovery is sufficient to neutralize the force of objections derived from the alleged want of harmony between the first three Evangelists and the fourth as regards their conceptions of Christ. But while this argument is negatively of considerable force, it does little to determine positively the date of the Gospel. The agreement between the supposed St. John and his brother Evangelists and Apostles may have been due to the readiness and docility with which he imbibed their principles. But in such a case we shall expect to find in his pages traces of their influence. If it be really true that, though writing with such exact and scrupulous orthodoxy, he wrote in the middle of the second century, and compiled memoirs of Christ which were to a great extent imaginary, we cannot fail to detect in them the influence of the theological schools which had arisen previously. Or if we suppose him to be able to shake himself free from such an influence—a supposition which makes considerable demands upon the faith of those who entertain it—we can hardly suppose that even the master mind of St. Paul had left no mark upon him. If so, he alone, of all the early Christian writers, had been able to achieve so remarkable a feat. Those who assign the Epistle to the Hebrews to Apollos or Clement are obliged to explain the points of similarity between that powerful and strikingly original treatise and the Epistles of St. Paul, by the ascendency of the mind of the great Apostle over all those who had come into contact with him. The Second Epistle of St. Peter, if genuine, shows that not even St. Peter could quite free himself from the spell cast over him by his great fellow-worker. Over the pages of Clement, Ignatius, Polycarp, Justin Martyr, the signs of Pauline influence are innumerable. If then the fourth Gospel be a production of post-Apostolic times, we may fairly contend that its author would have found it impossible to emancipate himself altogether from the ideas and phraseology of St. Paul.

We propose, therefore, to inquire, first, whether we can detect any Montanistic or Gnostic conceptions in the fourth Gospel. Next, we shall compare the Gospel which goes by St. John's name with others admitted to be Apocryphal. Lastly, we shall inquire what evidence there is in it of the influence of the writings of St. Paul. And here we may advert at the outset to a very remarkable fact. In the Apocalypse, and in the writings of Justin Martyr and others, we find distinct traces of the

St. John and Theology of the Second Century. 173

terminology of St. John's Gospel.[1] These, however, are disposed of by the argument that they were mere indications of the existence of a stream of thought which eventually matured itself in the production of that Gospel. That this line of defence is regarded as scarcely satisfactory by those who take it is made clear by the admission on the part of later assailants of the Gospel, that there was a mass of unwritten but authentic tradition to which the writer of the fourth Gospel had access.[2] Such a solution of the difficulties attendant on the supposition of its spuriousness bears a strong resemblance to the contrivances with which Tycho Brahe and others defended the Ptolemæan hypothesis of the motions of the heavenly bodies against the innovating theories of Copernicus.[3] Yet, of course, it is possible that

---

[1] See Appendix III. The application of the term Logos to Christ is an instance which has been already mentioned. We have also instanced the use of the expression ἀρνίον, and such words as ὁ νικῶν, μαρτυρία and the like. And though it is somewhat outside the range of my subject, I cannot help noticing the remarkable reference to the piercing of Jesus in Rev. i. 7, in which precisely the same word is used as in the Gospel. See Alford *in loc.* Hengstenberg, in his Commentary, remarks continually on the verbal and other coincidences between the fourth Gospel and the Apocalypse.

[2] "Nevertheless, I hesitate to regard him as having absolutely forged all the incidents which are to be found in his Gospel alone. How much more plausible the supposition would be, if we were to discover a collection of traditions concerning the history of Jesus which the editor had determined, towards the commencement of the second century, to snatch from the oblivion of the episodes, or the words which the former documents had ignored or omitted!"—M. Reville, 'Revue des Deux Mondes,' Mai 1866, p. 118.

[3]   "Perhaps to move
  His laughter at their quaint opinions wide
  Hereafter, when they come to model Heaven
  And calculate the stars, how they will wield
  The mighty frame, how build, unbuild, contrive   [To

it may be the true solution. We proceed, therefore, to inquire what traces can be found of the influence of second century thought upon the Gospel of St. John. We are told with the utmost confidence that it was written to effect a reconciliation between Gnosticism and the Church. For this purpose it not only adopted the Gnostic terminology to a great extent, but gave its sanction to some of the principal doctrines of the Valentinian and Basilidian sects. What those doctrines are we are not very plainly informed. It is somewhat singular that the principal opponents of the Gospel should be so obscure and oracular on the subject. It is usual with them to dispose of it in a few lines, and to adduce no arguments, save one which will be considered shortly, in proof of their dogmas.[1] But the question most certainly does not thus lie in a nutshell. There are difficulties of the gravest kind in the way of their theory. If it be true that the Gospel was written to mediate between Gnosticism and the Church, it is surely most extraordinary that the prologue to St. John's Gospel should contain a most emphatic negation of all

To save appearances, how gird the sphere
With centric and eccentric scribbled o'er
Cycle and epicycle, orb in orb."
Milton, 'Paradise Lost,' book viii. l. 78-84.

[1] See Reville, Strauss, Schenkel, in reference to this. The Gospel finds a more indulgent critic in M. Renan, and has recently secured a new ally in the person of Mr. Matthew Arnold. But even these last two patrons of the Gospel are at issue on a point of some little importance. One thinks that St. John invented the discourses, the other the history. See Renan, 'Vie de Jésus,' Introd. p. 68, 3rd edit. 'Literature and Dogma,' ch. vi. sect. 4. Dr. Keim holds that it is quite impossible that the Gospel appeared in the days of Valentinus or Marcion: 'Jesus of Nazareth,' vol. i. p. 203. The author of 'Supernatural Religion' wisely avoids committing himself to any theory on this point.

the principal doctrines of the Gnostic sects. Amid their almost infinite variations of opinion they were all true to the following fundamental propositions: first, the gradual evolution of the various forms of the higher existences from the Supreme Power by a series of Æons; secondly, the absolute incompatibility of matter and spirit; thirdly, the creation of the world by a being either actually antagonistic or at least markedly inferior to the true God, so that He needed to interfere to counteract the malice or the blunders of a being who had allied himself with matter, the natural enemy of all that is Divine.[1] The prologue of St. John's Gospel, short as it is, absolutely repudiates each of these doctrines. In the place of the succession of Æons, we meet with the assertion of the existence of one being only—the Word, who was in the beginning with God, and who was himself God. In the place of the impossibility of the union of spiritual beings with matter, we have the curt and unqualified declaration that "the Word was made (or rather became, ἐγένετο) Flesh." In the place of the Demiurgus, whose ignorance, or folly, or innate malevolence brought him into contact with matter, and so produced the world in which we live, we have the naked and explicit assertion that the only Begotten Son, existing in the bosom of the Father while yet He declared Him to mankind, was the Creator of the world and all that was therein. So far from there being here any evidence of an intention

---

[1] See a full account of the various Gnostic systems in Irenæus' first book. Also the summary in Hippolytus, 'Philosophumena,' book x. I regard the position of Marcion as intermediate between Gnosticism and the Church. See below, p. 189, note.

to conciliate the Gnostics, the object would appear to have been the very opposite. Nothing could have tended more to sharpen the antagonism already existing between Gnosticism and the Church than the publication of a Gospel with such an introduction, and it is not easy to see how its writer could have conveyed with greater clearness his unconquerable aversion to the tenets of the Gnostic schools. Nor does a more minute scrutiny of the relations between the fourth Gospel and this class of heresies bring out any hidden bond of union between them. On the contrary, it rather leads to the conclusion that while the writer of the fourth Gospel and the Epistles knew nothing of the Gnosis of the second century, he knew a good deal of its adumbrations in the first, and disapproved very much of what he knew. There can be no mistake whatever about the language of the Epistle as regards these heresies;[1] and if the Gospel be less directly polemical, it is because the writer believed the words of Jesus Christ to be the best antidote to the errors which he dreaded.

Let us examine the matter more in detail, in the order in which we have compared the systems of the writers of the New Testament. To begin with the doctrine of the being of God. What more simple, more elementary, more redolent, moreover, of the Jewish idea of an universal Father, than the conceptions of St. John?[2]

[1] 1 John ii. 18, 19, 22; iv. 1-3. "Every spirit that confesseth not Jesus Christ, *come in flesh*," is not of God.

[2] The idea that St. John was a disciple of Philo does not gain much countenance from an examination of his doctrine concerning God. The Platonic idea of the Absolute, the τὸ ὄν, as we have seen, is not to be found in his writings. There is nothing beyond the simple Jewish con-

What more thoroughly in accordance with Jewish conceptions than the manner in which the doctrine of the Trinity in Unity is indicated rather than unfolded in his pages? On the other hand, what more complex, more extravagant, more ideal, than the Ogdoad and Abracax of Basilides, and the elaborate system of evolution by pairs that was invented by Valentinus? God, whose unsearchable and mysterious nature is but hinted at by St. John, becomes in the one great Gnostic leader the Unnameable One, the πρώτη δύναμις, who evolves from himself the living and energizing powers by which the world, intellectual and spiritual, is directed, and in the other, Bythus, the abysmal depth which no created being can sound, from whom proceed, by the mutual action of the active and the receptive elements of being, a chain of Æons, thirty in number, who constitute the Pleroma, which is itself the complement of Bythus. Valentinus introduces us, moreover, to a being or principle called Horos, whose sole business it is to keep all the Æons in their place, and it is only by eluding his action that the Æon Sophia, coming in contact with matter, produces this lower world. The Valentinian and Basilidian systems, in fact, endeavoured to offer some explanation of the

---

ception of the Divine Being. In the use of the expression Logos alone do we find any trace of that blending of Judaism with Platonism which was the characteristic of Alexandrian thought. Besides, Philo, in his treatise 'De Vitâ Contemplativâ,' says that "the Absolute is better than the good, and purer than the One," *i.e.* above unity and goodness. How does this agree with St. John's doctrine? And how is it that St. John and St. Paul, while they borrow such expressions as Logos and εἰκών θεοῦ, carefully avoid such terms as ὀπαδός or ὑπηρέτης θεοῦ, or such assertions as that the Son was "a second God," or intermediate (μεθόριος) in nature between the Absolute and created intelligences?

origin of evil, of the cause of the estrangement between God and man, other than the simple narrative which satisfied the Jew, and they found it in the theory of an intermixture between antagonistic worlds of good and evil. There is not a word of all this in St. John. It would seem hardly possible for him, with a mind so actively employed upon the false impressions abroad in his time,[1] to have avoided any allusion to theories so plausible and so attractive for the minds of that age, had he been engaged in manipulating a mass of traditions to suit the theological needs of the second century. He must have been prepared to meet the Gnostics half way with a new theory of the origin of the world, and of evil, or have adapted theirs to his purpose. He must have invented a system of Æons of his own, or have put into the mouth of Christ solemn warnings against the "endless genealogies" which, even in St. Paul's time, threatened to entice the disciples from the faith. He must have endeavoured to rival the Gnostic leaders in the depth of his intellectual conceptions, as Clement and Origen did afterwards; and he must, therefore, not only have laid the foundations of a Christian philosophy, which he undoubtedly did, but have proceeded a long way with the superstructure, or else he must have filled his pages with denunciations attributed to Christ of "philosophy falsely so called." He does neither. He simply takes the old Jewish traditions for granted. He has no theory about the creation of the world save that, like Moses, he supposes it to have been the work of God's Word. He

---

[1] See not only the prologue to the Gospel, but the strong remarks on the prevalence of antichristian doctrine in the Epistles.

St. John and Theology of the Second Century. 179

says nothing about Adam's fall, but his very silence, under the circumstances, is a proof that he accepts it as truth.[1] His Pleroma is that which dwells within the Word, which He imparts to all who believe in Him.[2] He does not even go as far as St. Paul, who assigns a Pleroma, or complement to Christ in the person of His Church.[3] The only innovation on the Jewish idea of God in his system is a more direct assertion of God's love for mankind, and the doctrine of His Personal inhabitation of the human soul. But these are only expansions of the Jewish idea. They only intensify and extend to all mankind the tender and parental relations in which the Jew conceived himself to stand to a Being essentially personal.[4] The Gnostic conception of God was as different as possible from this. Like the Platonists and the Oriental Mystics, from whom the Gnostic doctrines were derived, their God. instead of being a Person, was an inscrutable and impenetrable principle, dwelling apart in a world of his own. The simplicity and tenderness of the Jewish idea of God was a thing unknown to Gnosticism. They could only conceive of their Deity as coming even into the most distant relations with humanity through the

---

[1] See, however, St. John viii. 44.   [2] Ib. i. 16.   [3] Eph. i. 23.
[4] I fear I am incurring the wrath of Mr. Matthew Arnold by re-inculcating after the "Bishops of Winchester and Gloucester" this altogether exploded doctrine. My only excuse must be that God is spoken of throughout the Bible as a Father, a fact which Mr. Arnold seems to have overlooked. Whether a father can possibly be only "a deeply moved way of saying conduct or righteousness," or "the not ourselves which makes ◉r righteousness," I will not undertake to say. But if a father can be this, and need not be a "person," I would humbly suggest that we require a new dictionary of the English, and possibly of some other languages.

intervention of a chain of Æons. Thus in the first and fundamental doctrine of all religion there is a chasm between the fourth Gospel and the Gnostic systems, which makes it impossible to conceive that the former was written with the intention of effecting an accommodation between the latter and the Christian Church.

We have already remarked on the doctrine of the Trinity, as it is conveyed to us in the fourth Gospel. Though not perhaps enunciated in such distinct terms as in some other portions of the Christian Scriptures, we have at least no more than three Divine Persons introduced to us. We hear nothing of the strings of Æons in which all the Gnostics delight. There is nothing, moreover, in common between the Paraclete of Valentinus and the Paraclete of St. John. The Paraclete of the latter is the Holy Spirit. The Paraclete of the former is one of a number of intelligences who go by the names of Righteousness, of Peace, of Grace, of Wisdom, and of other abstract qualities of which Pneuma, or Spirit, is the underlying principle of existence. Here again St. John, in spite of the marked individuality of his language, is in substance precisely at one with his brethren, and utterly at variance with every one of the Gnostic sects.

There is just as wide a divergence between the Gnostics and the fourth Gospel with regard to the Incarnation and the Atonement. St. John, as we have seen, starts with the axiom that the "Word was made flesh."[1] He does not even hint at any future solution of

[1] The author of 'Supernatural Religion' would no doubt contend that St. John's Epistle was by a different hand to the Gospel, because

continuity between these two elements of His Personality. Christ speaks of His Ascension as one would speak who possessed a human body. His Divine Nature, He tells us, was still in heaven while He was on earth. But there are more conclusive statements still. It was He, and not a part of His composite being, that was to be "lifted up" on the Cross. His Life was to be laid down for the sheep, and above all, His Flesh, which was henceforth to be the Life of the world for evermore. Not only was the union of His Flesh with His Godhead perpetual, but that perpetuity was the only assurance He gave for the salvation of the human race.[1] There is no trace of faltering, of embarrassment, of the shifts to which men are reduced who wish to blend in one system the conceptions of opposite schools of thought. All the confusion and embarrassment is on the other side. While St. John is clear, coherent, and intelligible, only desirous that his converts should hold fast "that which was from the beginning," the Gnostic systems are chaotic and inconsistent with themselves. Starting with the endeavour to combine detached portions of Judaism, Christianity, Platonism, and Oriental mysticism, they found themselves immediately hampered by insuperable difficulties. They believed in the irreconcilable antagonism between spiritual intelligences and matter, and yet they had to find some sort of place in their system for the distinctively Christian doctrine that the "Word became

---

the former, instead of saying that Jesus Christ "was made," or became, flesh, uses the expression, "come in flesh." See Appendix III.

[1] See chapter vi. throughout.

Flesh." They were driven by an imperative necessity to a sort of compromise. Salvation was not conveyed to man by the Supreme Being Himself, but by a kind of representative called an Æon. The Æon Christ descended upon the man Jesus at His Baptism, and left Him before His Crucifixion. The appearances after the Resurrection were those of a phantom. The revelation of the truth was somehow connected with Jesus, but it was difficult to give a sound logical reason why it should have been so. For man's whole being was not, and could not be, regenerated; all that could be done was to purify his spirit from the intrusion of the lower influences of matter. We can easily explain this if the doctrine of salvation by the God-man be anterior to Gnosticism. The Gnostics had, as we have said, to do their best to fuse hostile conceptions into a system. The result was in the highest degree capricious, fantastic, and absurd; but it suited the age, which, while it was incapable of accepting what seemed to it the astounding audacities of the Christian scheme, yet could not bring itself entirely to reject them. It could not endure to hear that God Himself became man: it could tolerate the idea of such a degradation of the Divinity when ascribed to an Æon. It could not regard spirit and matter as entering into an eternal union: to a temporary one, for a special purpose, it flattered itself there could be less objection. On the whole, we are led to the conclusion that the doctrine usually ascribed to the fourth Gospel, so far from being of later, must have been of earlier origin, not only than the systems of Valentinus and Basilides, but of Cerinthus also—for most of the characteristics of Gnosticism are to be found in Cerinthus.¹ It is clear, therefore, that we have no reason to conclude that the very opposite was the case with the Gospel which first ascribes that doctrine to Christ.

The Gnostic doctrine concerning man, again, does not appear to have suggested anything to the writer of the fourth Gospel. The threefold division of mankind into σαρκικοί,² ψυχικοί, and πνευματικοί seems to be unknown to him. The opposition between σάρξ and πνεῦμα, which he admits, is nullified by a communication through πνεῦμα of σάρξ³—a doctrine in every way most abhorrent to the Gnostic mind. Faith, the one foundation of the renewed life of man, according to St. John, and, in fact, to all the writers of the New Testament, becomes Gnosis in Valentinus, while Basilides here accepts the definition of St. Paul.⁴

The doctrine of the intimate inward union of the believer with Christ is, as we have seen, not peculiar to St. John among the Apostles. The writings of later Gnostics have every appearance of being an attempt to engraft this simple doctrine upon their more complex schemes. Not only those who lay hold upon the communication of life from above are admitted into an intimate fellowship with the Divine, but, according to Basilides, the Creator of the world Himself partakes of this purification; while Valentinus teaches that the

¹ Cerinthus felt the impossibility of an eternal union between spirit and matter, and avoided it by Docetism.
² Or rather ὑλικοί, a word unknown to St John.   ³ St. John vi.
⁴ Heb. xi. 1. Neander denies that St. Paul regards faith as an intuition. See his account of Basilides, 'Ch. Hist.' vol. ii. Yet, as is generally admitted, the Epistle to the Hebrews is a production of the Pauline school, and would hardly take up an independent position on so fundamental a question as that of faith.

possessor of redemption, so far from being united to the world's Creator, is, on the contrary, released from his power. In St. John, again, the Holy Spirit has a vast share in the salvation of man. In Valentinus we have the word Paraclete used as the name of an Æon, but without the office assigned to the Paraclete of St. John; while in Basilides He disappears altogether. We have already observed how little foundation there would seem to be for the statement that St. John borrowed his Paraclete from Valentinus. It may not be amiss to add here, that not only does St. John make a very sparing use of the term, but he applies it to Christ as well as to the Holy Spirit: in fact, it is intended to signify an office rather than a person. This is rendered clearer still by the fact that Christ declares His intention of sending *another* Paraclete in the place of Himself. We can scarcely hesitate therefore, if we are called upon to decide whether St. John borrowed his Paraclete from Valentinus, or Valentinus from St. John, to pronounce in favour of the latter hypothesis. It is surely more probable that Valentinus had found some difficulty in providing names for his thirty Æons, and had therefore, without any special reason, adopted the word Paraclete from St. John, than that the Gospel should have been indebted to a list of Valentinian Æons for a word which so precisely expressed the threefold function it was desired to describe.

The doctrine of the Atonement brings out into strong relief the irreconcilable difference between the Gnostics and the fourth Gospel. It is unnecessary to repeat here what has been before shown to be the doctrine of the Epistle and Gospel ascribed to St. John on this point. There can be no doubt that in both the death of Christ is regarded as a sacrifice of propitiation for sin. But the Gnostics had no such idea. Basilides regards the man Jesus as a sinner, Himself needing redemption, and His death as the penalty of His sins; while Valentinus not only denied a real human body to his Messiah, but regarded the Crucifixion as a symbolical representation of the action of the Æon Soter upon the Æon Sophia, in bringing her again into union with the Pleroma. The act of the Crucifixion, however, was held to have some actual virtue by reason, of its union with the work of the Soter in the unseen world, so that in some mysterious way it could be said that the Cross of Christ destroyed evil, and was necessary to the purification of the Church. But here again we see the embarrassment which results from the attempt to blend discordant elements into a system. Here again we discover traces of the influence of Christian thought upon the founders of a later school, while we look in vain for any influence of that later school upon the Gospel which is the subject of our inquiries.

St. John's doctrine of the Resurrection implies, though it does not assert, the Resurrection of the Body. The famous utterance, "I am the Resurrection and the Life," is put into the mouth of Christ at the raising of Lazarus, who was certainly raised in body as well as soul. The statement that "they that are in the graves shall *come forth*," is one which points in the same direction. The Ascension of Christ in His Human Body is more than intimated in this Gospel, and it is connected with the taking others to dwell with Him hereafter. The Epistle affirms the future likeness of the disciples to their Lord. None of these sayings are compatible with any other belief than that of the Resurrection of the Body. And this was precisely the doctrine which it was impossible for the Gnostics to accept. A Resurrection there might be, but it must be entirely free from all connection with matter. The psychic and spiritual elements of man's nature would subsist, but purified from all grosser hylic properties. Once more, therefore, we miss all those indications of the supposed mediation between Gnosticism and the Church which are so confidently, and at the same time so vaguely, announced.

It is not only among the main doctrines of Christianity that we may seek for evidence of the radical differences between the writer of the fourth Gospel and the Gnostics. These differences are quite as marked in what may be regarded as his secondary and subordinate utterances. We may refer, as a confirmation of our view, that he could have had no intention of effecting a reconciliation between Christian and Gnostic thought, to the peculiar twofold conception attached in the fourth Gospel to the word κόσμος. The very word bears in it undoubted evidence of the Jewish conception that the world was created by God, that it was originally very good, and that it had been corrupted by some evil agency. And if we admit that the word, being Greek, has no connection with Jewish ideas, yet we shall still be able to contend that there is some significance in the fact that it is selected to express the doctrine which the fourth Gospel adopts, and which is entirely Jewish in its character.[1] Now this conception of the world as the work of God, but so fallen from its original perfection as to display few traces of the Creator's Hand, is the very antipodes of the Gnostic theory on the point. With one consent they adopt the explanation that the anomalies and confusions of this lower world are due to its creation by some other than the Supreme Being. Here, therefore, in the important question of the relations of the Supreme Being to the world in which we live—a question upon which hinges our whole view of sin, of redemption, of our present condition and future prospects—we find St. John and the Gnostics in the most thorough and absolute antagonism. It is impossible to conceive of his Gospel being forged in the second century without reference to a doctrine so fundamental as this. Either he must have put into the mouth of his Christ some references to the true doctrine to be held on this point, or his work would be discredited alike by both parties as a lifeless, colourless biography, which threw no light upon the great questions of the day, and which, by the peculiar form in which it was cast, did but "keep the word of promise to the ear, and break it to the hope."[2]

[1] According to the discourses of Christ in the fourth Gospel, the world is at once loved and condemned by God. It had a prince of its own, from whose subjects the disciples of Christ were to separate themselves, and yet Christ loved it, and came to save it.

[2] It is worthy of remark that in ' Supernatural Religion' this aspect of the question is altogether ignored. The author does not attempt to explain the relation of the fourth Gospel to schools whose teaching agitated the Christian Church to its depths at the time when he supposes it to have appeared. He discusses, it is true, sundry alleged quotations from the Gospel in the writings of Valentinus or Basilides, but not the certainty that some allusion to their teaching would be

There is another point, which may be regarded as a crucial test of the date of the fourth Gospel, and that is its conceptions regarding the Devil. For among the Gnostics there were two conceptions of the principle of evil. With the one party it was the ὕλη, the world of matter, which was at war with the spiritual world, with which, therefore, any communication was fatal to spiritual life. With the other it was the principle of evil, the second god, the Ahriman of the Zoroastrian creed, between whom and Ormuzd there was an eternal conflict. St. John does not even hint at such ideas, still less does he attempt to harmonize them with the theology of Christendom in his own time. He refers to the Devil as a being well known among Christians, and his conception of him is in no way different from that contained in the Scriptures of the Old Testament, or of his fellow-labourers in the New. It is quite inconceivable that writing in the second century a narrative to a large extent entirely fictitious, and to subserve a definite theological purpose, he should have thus almost contemptuously ignored one of the

---

found in it if it had been composed subsequently to their era. He believes that its terminology was "in current use long before that Gospel was composed;" but with a singular forgetfulness of the castigation he bestows on Tischendorf and Canon Westcott for making unsupported assertions, he informs his readers that "there is no evidence whatever that Valentinus was acquainted with such a work" (p. 372). [I quote from the first edition.] It is instructive to find that the only evidence necessary, in his opinion, for the assertions he makes that Basilides flourished about A.D. 125 and Valentinus about A.D. 150 are, for the former, "Eusebius, II. E. iv. 7, 8, 9," and for the latter, "Irenæus, Adv. Hær. iii. 43; Eusebius, H. E. iv. 11." On his own principles of criticism such evidence is wholly and hopelessly insufficient.

leading features of the school to which he was anxious, on the part of the Church, to make overtures of peace. If his Gospel be indeed the Eirenicon of the second century, it was certainly as ill adapted for its purpose as any that could have been conceived. That attempts at such a reconciliation should be made is by no means surprising. Not only were they to be expected, but they were actually made by Marcion and Tatian.[1] The results of such attempts, however, were not such as to confirm the hypothesis that St. John's Gospel was one of them. They invariably ended by the fierce rejection of their authors by the Church.[2] But the hypothesis of the spurious origin of this Gospel assumes its success. It was accepted by both sides, we presume, at least by the Christian Church, as an authentic document, on account of the skill with which it accommodated Gnostic opinions to Christian prejudices. Such a theory can hardly fail to excite a smile in any one acquainted with the Christian theology of the second century—its suspicion of novelties, its intolerance towards all who did not accept the genuine traditions of the Church.[3] But when we add

[1] Tatian unquestionably intended to graft Gnostic ideas upon his previous Christian belief. The acceptance by Marcion of portions of the Christian Scriptures, and his apparent abandonment of the emanation systems, seems to point in the same direction. All the early authorities are extremely vague on the subject of Marcion's doctrine of Æons.
[2] The well-known anecdote of Marcion and Polycarp related by Irenæus and Eusebius is a proof of this.
[3] 'Supernatural Religion,' though it unhesitatingly affirms the fourth Gospel to be subsequent to Valentinus, does not contain even an effort to deal with the somewhat difficult problem of its immediate reception into the sacred Canon. Irenæus and Tertullian were not exactly ignorant men. Yet they express themselves in terms which show that not the shadow of a doubt of its authenticity had ever crossed their

to this that such a reconciliation was effected by a work singularly ill-adapted to its purpose, a work which studiously avoided all reference to the leading doctrines of the Gnostic sects, which assumed, without examination or explanation, the truth of a large number of Christian traditions utterly at variance with those doctrines, this theory of the origin of the fourth Gospel, however plausible at first sight, would seem, upon examination, to be utterly untenable.

We might pursue this inquiry further. We might show how entirely Jewish was St. John's conception of angels and their work; how entirely it reflects the doctrine of the Psalmist on this point;[1] how exactly it corresponds with their employment as described by the Synoptists; how completely their nature and office was superseded in the Gnostic systems by the Æons, or by the strange beings to which some of the more extravagant of these heretics ascribed their magical powers. We might discuss the discrepancies between the Christian and the Gnostic view of sin, and show how those Gnostic leaders who were orthodox on this point were not a

---

mind. One observation, however, is to be found which is apparently intended to dispose of the whole question of admission into the Canon. It is to be found in the remark (vol. ii. p. 394) that "it is an undeniable fact that not a single trace exists of the application of historical criticism to any book of the New Testament in the early ages of Christianity." This is rather a bold assertion to come from one who professes to be acquainted with the writings of Tertullian, Clement of Alexandria, and Origen. Jerome, too, I presume, is not to be included in the category of early writers.

[1] "Who maketh His angels spirits, and His ministers a flame of fire," Ps. civ. 4. It must be remembered, however, that the genuineness of the most important of these passages, that in St. John v. 4, is denied by many.

St. John and Theology of the Second Century. 191

little indebted for their opinions to St. John. But such an inquiry would be tedious, and seems to be hardly necessary. Upon none of the fundamental doctrines of the faith is St. John at one with the Gnostics and opposed to the Christian Church. Upon none of them does he present, to a close examination, even the semblance of an attempt either at compromise or conciliation. That there was any such attempt no assailant of the authenticity has even tried to prove. They have been content with the bare assertion. And it may be safely affirmed that on the slightest examination their case breaks down.

Upon what grounds, then, has this theory been advanced? Upon what points has any evidence been offered? The only allegation which approaches to an argument is grounded on the use made by St. John of the supposed Gnostic terms, Life, Light, Truth, Grace, Peace, Pleroma, Paraclete, and the like.[1] It is obvious that it is abstractedly quite as possible that the Gnostics may

[1] M. Reville regards them as borrowed from Philo. "In the place of the Greek of the Synoptists," he says, "popular, very simple, very realistic, concise, rapid, full of Hebraisms, the fourth Gospel speaks a philosophic language. It is mystical, not a little prolix, often elevated in style, and interwoven with abstract and scholastic expressions. These terms, the Word, Life, Light, Paraclete, Truth, employed in the sense of the Alexandrian philosophy, denote a phraseology strongly marked with the stamp of a particular school, of which, in the first century of our era, Philo of Alexandria may be considered the most eminent organ."—'Revue des Deux Mondes,' Mai 1866, p. 91. But if this be all, there is nothing to hinder the Gospel from having been written by St. John. Dr. Keim, as we have seen, admits that St. Paul owed much to Philo. M. Reville, however, soon forgets what he has said, and tells us (p. 115) that the "most ancient traces of the usage" of St. John, Logos, Arche, Zoe, Truth, *Grace*(!!), Paraclete, Pleroma Monogenes, are to be found in the school of Valentinus.

192   *The Doctrinal System of St. John.*

have borrowed these words from St. John as that he borrowed them from the Gnostics. But the former hypothesis seems infinitely the more probable when we find that all these words, with the single exception of Paraclete, are to be found almost with equal frequency in St. Paul,[1] and that the term Paraclete is made use of by St. John rather to denote an office than a person.[2] And when we trace these words to their real source, the assumption that St. John was adopting Gnostic philosophy in his Gospel is shown to be utterly baseless; for with the single exception of Paraclete, all these words are derived from the Hebrew Scriptures, and their use there is precisely in accordance with their use in St. John. The probability that the Gospel was written by a Jew well versed in the sacred writings of his nation derives immense additional confirmation from this fact.[3] And that it is a fact will need little demonstration. Life, one of St. John's fundamental attributes of God, meets us in the second chapter of the book of Genesis, where God breathes into man's nostrils the Breath of Life, and man becomes a living soul.[4] Life and Light are combined together not only by St. John, but by the Psalmist, in the passage, "For with Thee is the well of Life, and in Thy Light shall

---

[1] Grace is only to be found in the Prologue to St. John's Gospel. Pleroma is used by St. Paul, we have seen, in a sense more nearly corresponding with that of the Gnostics than that in which it occurs in the fourth Gospel.

[2] See above, p. 184.

[3] It would be more correct to say, is a faithful report of the sayings of One who could not fail to be well versed in the Hebrew Scriptures, and was careful to build upon the foundation of a knowledge already possessed by His hearers.

[4] Gen. ii. 7.

we see Light."[1] Light and truth are found together in the prayer, "O send out Thy light and Thy truth, that they may lead me, and bring me unto Thy holy hill, and to Thy dwelling."[2] Spirit ($\pi\nu\epsilon\hat{\upsilon}\mu\alpha$) is the רוח of the Old Testament, in the double sense of the immaterial part of man's nature, and of the Third Person in the Trinity, "Who spake by the prophets." We have already called attention to the fact that heathen philosophy knew nothing of this doctrine. The Gnostics, therefore, must have acquired their notions of Spirit from Judaism, either directly, or indirectly through the Evangelists and Apostles. Righteousness, again, introduced into Gnostic systems as the Æon Dikaiosune, is one of the first principles of Hebrew theology. "The Lord is righteous[3] in all His ways, and holy in all His works;" "Righteous art Thou, O Lord, and upright are Thy judgments,"[4] are the pious ejaculations of the Psalmist, and Moses stamps them with the sanction of his authority when he declares, "A God of truth, and without iniquity, just and right is He." Nor was even the doctrine of a righteousness imparted from God to man entirely foreign to Jewish ideas, as may be seen from a comparison between Jeremiah xxiii. 6, and xxxiii. 16.[5] Grace is by no means an idea foreign to the Old Testament,[6] nor is Peace alien from the conceptions of a

[1] Ps. xxxvi. 9; cf. Ps. xxvii. 1.   [2] Ib. xliii. 3.
[3] Or "righteousness," Ps. cxlv. 17.   [4] Ib. cxix. 137.
[5] Cf. Ps. lxxxv. 9-11, where we have Dikaiosune, Eirene, Aletheia, as well as mercy and salvation. Truth is to spring up from the earth, and Righteousness to descend from heaven. Were the Psalms an attempt at mediation between Gnosticism and Christianity? They are teeming with Valentinian ideas and expressions.
[6] As, for instance, Ps. lxxxiv. 11, and Zech. iv. 7.

194 *The Doctrinal System of St. John.*

race whose chief city bore its name, and whose most powerful monarch bore the name of The Peaceful.[1] Truth, closely connected with Light in the Old Testament, and constantly spoken of as an attribute of God, is, moreover, the Septuagint translation of the Hebrew Thummim, which, even if incorrect, was at least widely received in St. John's day. Even Pleroma, the term which is presumed to be so essentially Gnostic, must be admitted to be a phrase of Hebrew origin. It is the Hebrew מְלֹא. We find it over and over again in the Psalms: "The earth is the Lord's, and the fulness thereof;"[2] "In Thy presence is fulness of joy."[3] Isaiah uses it: "The fulness of the whole earth is His glory;"[4] and his language is repeated by his successors.[5]

We are now in a position to estimate the slender foundation on which this theory of the origin of the fourth Gospel has been raised. The whole argument in favour of the theory that this Gospel was an attempt to reconcile Gnosticism and the Church is grounded upon the occurrence of certain words in the writings of the Gnostics of the second century and in St. John. These words have now been shown to have been quite as freely in use in the Hebrew Scriptures, and in the other books of the New Testament, as in St. John. We have only to add that their use by St. John is in perfect harmony with their use elsewhere in the Scriptures, to denote, that is, abstract qualities, and not the personifications

---

[1] שְׁלֹמֹה   [2] Ps. xxiv. 1.   [3] Ib. xvi. 11.
[4] Or, "His glory is the fulness of the whole earth" (Is. vi. 3). Cf. viii. 8; xlii. 10.
[5] Jer. viii. 16. Micah i. 2. For a fuller statement of this argument see Appendix IV.

of abstract ideas, and that this tendency to personification appears first in the systems of Basilides and Valentinus, to make it clear that the arguments against the genuineness of the Gospel derived from this source are of the slightest and most superficial nature. They are by no means of the kind which we declared at the outset to be necessary in the absence of historical evidence. On the contrary, they are surmises of the barest kind, derived from a similarity in phraseology, which, if it existed between St. John and the Gnostics alone, would not be sufficient to determine the priority of the latter; which does not exist only between St. John and the Gnostics, but also between St. John and the Scriptures as a whole; and which, inasmuch as the first trace of the employment of these similar phrases in a new sense is to be found in the Gnostics and not in St. John, is in itself decisive evidence of the priority of the former. We may add another fact, not less significant than those to which we have already referred. Clement of Rome was contemporary with St. John. It is possible that the former wrote his Epistle before the latter published his Gospel. But Clement makes use of a term—Demiurgus—to denote the Creator[1] which is not in use in the Old Testament Scriptures, and is an essential feature of the Gnostic system. Did Clement write to " reconcile Gnosticism with the Church," or is his Epistle necessarily spurious, or have we here again a proof of the readiness of the Gnostics to borrow their terminology from the accredited teachers of the Church?[2]

[1] 'Clem. Rom.' Ep. i. 26. Cf. c. 20.
[2] The Epistle of Clement, Eusebius tells us, was held in the highest

196 *The Doctrinal System of St. John.*

An examination, therefore, of the mutual relations between St. John's Gospel and the Gnosis of the second century leads us to the belief, independently of historical evidence, that the former preceded the latter. We now proceed to inquire what reason there is for the supposition that the fourth Gospel was published subsequent to the origin of Montanism. A few words will be sufficient to deal with this question. The doctrinal differences between Montanism and the Church were not numerous, nor is it necessary to enter into a very close analysis of the relations of the two. For unless we discover in the Gospel of St. John indisputable traces of Montanistic modes of thought, we are bound to dismiss the hypothesis of its post-Montanistic origin as "not proven." The main doctrines of Montanism were the existence of the Paraclete in a human form in the person of Montanus, and the necessity of a certain condition of physical exaltation and excitement as a condition of salvation.[1] There is nothing uncommon in such views. They have appeared and reappeared continually during the history of the Christian Church. But it is not to the fourth Gospel that they appeal for confirmation.[2] We have already seen that

---

repute, and was read publicly in the churches like the books of the New Testament. The 'Codex Sinaiticus' contains it, in addition to the canonical books.

[1] See Eusebius, H. E. v. 16.

[2] Take, for instance, the history of the origin of what is called Irvingism. The Acts of the Apostles and the First Epistle to the Corinthians were the sources from which the followers of Irving derived their ideas about spiritual manifestations. They have never, so far as I am aware, been accustomed to defend them out of the Gospel of St. John. And what is true of the Irvingites is equally true of their precursors, the Montanists.

in the mind of the writer the term Paraclete referred not to a Person but to an office ; and that therefore it was used to denote, not the appearance of the Person so described in a visible form, but the nature of His operations. And, moreover, the Paraclete thus promised is described as a spirit, and flesh and spirit are sharply contrasted in more than one passage in St. John. The influences of the Paraclete, so far from being visible, are to be discerned solely by their effects.[1] And there is absolutely not a single passage in St. John—and it may be observed in passing that the number of passages in which the Holy Ghost is mentioned are far fewer in his Gospel than elsewhere in the Scriptures—which either countenances or discountenances that idea of strong physical enthusiasm which was the chief characteristic of Montanism. Neither is there a single allusion to the assumption of superiority with which the Montanist regarded his calmer brethren in the bosom of the Church. Tertullian, as we know, dilates with complacency on the higher gifts of the Montanists,[2] their more frequent fasts,[3] their loftier ideal of Christian holiness.[4] It is scarcely conceivable that a Gospel compiled for a purpose in the second century could have come into being without some reference to this class of ideas. They were in some degree countenanced by passages in the Acts of the Apostles and in the Epistles of St. Paul. If it had been the intention of the writer of our Gospel to lend his support to a scheme for including these sectaries within the pale of

[1] See above, part i.
[2] Tert., ' De Pudicit.' xxi ; ' De Virg. Vel.' i.
[3] Id. ' De Jejuniis,' throughout.
[4] Id. ' De Ex. Cast. ;' ' De Monogamiâ ;' ' De Pudicitiâ,' throughout.

the Christian Church, could he have so studiously avoided all reference to their views? Or even, if he wished to silence them—a theory of the origin of the Gospel which has not yet been advanced—is it conceivable that he would have refrained from any mention, in the form of prophecy or otherwise, of their excesses? The only conclusion to which we can come, after remarking the reticence of the Gospel on these subjects, is that the author of the Gospel knew nothing of Montanus or his doctrines. We may go further; we may assert that the references of St. Luke and St. Paul to spiritual manifestations,[1] as compared with the silence of St. John, is a decisive proof that he is relating genuine discourses of Christ, uttered before such manifestations had ever occurred. And we may add that the obvious and grotesque perversion of the promise ascribed to Christ by Montanus is in itself an argument for the prior origin of the Gospel. Would Montanus have announced himself as the Paraclete if it were not well known to Christians that a Paraclete was to appear? And is not the discrepancy between the statement of the Gospel that the Paraclete was the Spirit of God, a Being thoroughly known to and acknowledged by Jews as well as Christians, and the statement of Montanus, that He was a human being, a clear proof that the assumption of the title by the heretic was a bold, but hopeless attempt to obtain a Scriptural sanction for his claims?[2]

---

[1] Acts ii. 4; x. 46; xix. 6. 1 Cor. xii. xiv. A prophecy of our Lord to this effect is recorded in the last chapter of St. Mark.

[2] Yet M. Reville can write, "now it is in the doctrine of the Paraclete that Montanism and the fourth Gospel approach most nearly to each other. They both wish to teach that the Holy Spirit will continue His work in the Church, and be partaken of by all the truly

St. John and Theology of the Second Century.

One question of paramount importance remains still to be asked. We are told that the fourth Gospel was composed in the second century. If so, to whom is it to be ascribed? The hypothesis demands that he should be a man of singular courage, consummate art, commanding intellect. He must have possessed the finest tact, the most unerring judgment, the most extraordinary powers of persuasion, and, as we shall see hereafter, an unusual capacity of epitomizing in a single sentence the substance of other men's teaching. His faculty for deep abstract meditation has been admitted on all hands. To this must be added opportunities of an unprecedented kind for the successful perpetration of an ingenious literary fraud, in a period when men were sensitively jealous of the purity of Christian tradition, and severe to a degree upon those who transgressed against that purity. This is no ordinary combination of qualities, and nothing less could be required in a man who, as we have seen, steers his way so dexterously among the rocks and quicksands of theological controversy in his time. It is difficult to imagine that a writer who took up his pen when the Church was agitated to her depths by disputes relating to her fundamental doctrines, and confused by the strangest distortions of her elementary principles, could have retained the coolness of head to avoid all these disputes and keep clear of all these confusions; that he could have evolved from his own inner consciousness a

---

faithful." As if St. Paul or the Synoptists had taught any other doctrine, and as if M. Reville had not said, two lines previously, that one of the chief features of Montanism was the Holy Spirit speaking by the instrumentality of prophets and prophetesses in ecstasy!

conception of Christ and His doctrine rigidly and successfully confined within the limits assigned to it by the original preachers of the Gospel. The question irresistibly forces itself upon us—who was this writer, endowed with powers so uncommon ? Call in review the best-known names of the period : Papias, Justin Martyr, Irenæus, Hegesippus—all fail to satisfy the conditions of the problem. There is nothing of the poverty of intellect attributed by Eusebius to Papias. We find in the Gospel no traces of the interminable discussions and philosophical refinements which are apt to weary us in Justin Martyr. The shrewd good sense, the caustic humour, the homely and practical turn of Irenæus are nowhere reflected in its pages. A careful investigator of original traditions like Irenæus, unlikely as he was to have composed the Gospel himself, was still more unlikely to have been imposed upon by his contemporaries, such as Claudius Apollinaris, Apollonius, Miltiades, Athenagoras, Theophilus of Antioch, Pantænus and the rest. What we read of the somewhat gossiping historical chronicle of Hegesippus, painstaking and careful as it is, will hardly lead us to ascribe to its compiler a hand in the composition of the fourth Gospel. If it were written by any of those early apologists, such as Quadratus or Aristides, it is a marvel that their works have not been preserved, for they would naturally have presented the same features as the Gospel.[1] The serene calm, the air of lofty contempla-

[1] As so little is known of Quadratus, we may perhaps expect some day to find the fourth Gospel assigned to him. The two sentences which Eusebius preserves have all the simplicity of the Gospel narratives, and, moreover, (1) imply the fact of the raising of Lazarus, and (2)

tion, the habit of repeated meditation upon Divine truth in all its aspects, the entire abstraction from all controversy, the spirit saturated with the two ideas of love and the Divine indwelling, are characteristics perfectly unique. The existence of such a writer, if he be not the person he professes himself to be, is a standing miracle.[1] He has achieved a feat which must be confessed to be unparalleled. He has successfully palmed off a literary forgery on the world for seventeen hundred years, and has shrouded himself in a mystery which the acutest critic has failed to penetrate. Among the many who have confidently assumed to have demonstrated the spuriousness of his Gospel, there is not one who has ventured to tell us his name.

---

supply us with the reason why no allusion is made to it by the Synoptists. See Eus. H. E. iv. 3.

[1] Dr. Davidson, in his 'Introduction to the Study of the New Testament,' speaks of the "miraculous concealment" in which the author has remained. Vol. ii. pp. 4 and 6.

CHAPTER II.

ST. JOHN AND THE APOCRYPHAL GOSPELS AND ACTS.

OUR investigation would hardly be complete without some notice of the Apocryphal Gospels, among which the Gospel of St. John, as we have seen, is ranked by many critics. And yet in truth there is little to be said from the point of view in which we have been regarding the question. Points of contact in a doctrinal direction there are literally none. The Apocryphal Gospels never touch on doctrine. They differ *toto cœlo* from St. John's Gospel in subject, in plan, in composition—in fact, in everything. They are either expansions of the history of the Incarnation, with many marvellous details regarding the infancy of the Saviour and the Nativity of His Mother, or they are expansions of the history of the Passion. Of the former the Protevangelium of St. James[1] is probably the earliest, as may be inferred from the diction and the nature of its contents. It seems to wear the impress of a strong Judæo-Christian tendency, both in the form of the narrative and in the cast of the songs of triumph with which it abounds—these having manifestly been derived from a careful and continual study of the Old

[1] So called because its discoverer in modern times, Postel, regarded it as the missing basis and foundation of the Evangelic history.

Testament. While other Apocryphal narratives bear so strong a resemblance to the Protevangelium of St. James as to make it certain that all these Gospels had a common origin, we find the circumstances recorded in the Protevangelium modified in its successors to suit the class of readers for whom they were intended. The Jewish respect for marriage displayed in the Protevangelium seems to assume a half apologetic tone in the other Gospels, and is explained to be due to the customs of the Jewish people. The praises of chastity and virginity, absent from the Protevangelium, are introduced both implicitly and explicitly in its companion myths. In the Protevangelium we are informed with much emphasis that the state of virginity is a new order of life discovered by Mary alone,[1] and apparently not intended to be widely practised by others even after she had set the example. But in the others we hear of the "crown of virginity," and the like. Mary's weeping and smiling at the sight of the two peoples, recorded without comment in the Protevangelium, receives another turn in the spurious Gospel of St. Matthew. The people themselves are weeping and rejoicing; the former being the Jews in their rejection, the latter the Gentiles in their acceptance. Again, in the later narratives the prodigies related of the Virgin and her Son are continually growing in number, and, it may be added, in absurdity. Stories of clay turned into sparrows, of palm-trees bending to offer their fruit to the Divine infant, of lions fawning on Him, of schoolmasters falling down dead for daring to strike Him, abound in these Pseudo-

[1] Protevangelium of St. James, c. 8.

Gospels.[1] And what is more to the purpose still, fragments of the genuine Gospels are imbedded in them, forming, as is clear enough, the nucleus of truth round which the accumulation of legend has gathered. It scarcely falls within our present province, but I cannot forbear remarking that St. John's Gospel presents phenomena the very opposite of these. While manifestly supplementing, and intending to supplement the former narratives, he never quotes them, nor, when relating events which they have described, does he fail to produce an entirely independent account, which while fully coinciding in all material respects with theirs, amplifies their statements in the direction he requires with the combined precision and freedom to which only an eyewitness could pretend. His miracles, again, are no mere childish prodigies, but though usually different to those recorded by the Synoptists, they are of precisely similar character. Another remark may perhaps be added. These Gospels of the infancy betray a very slight acquaintance with the Gospel, and none with the theology of St. John.[2] If we are not entitled to conclude, as has been done in these pages, that this was simply because it did not enter into the plan and purpose of the writers, we are driven to the conclusion that St. John's Gospel had

---

[1] It is beside the purpose of this Essay, but the subject of the difference between the character of Jesus as depicted in the Apocryphal Gospels and those usually regarded as genuine has been discussed by the Rev. C. A. Row, in his 'The Jesus of the Evangelists.'

[2] There are allusions in these Gospels to St. John's narrative in ch. viii. 56; xii. 5; xviii. 36, and xix. 34. But these may surely be the "traditions" of which we have heard, to which the compiler of the fourth Gospel had access.

not been published when they were composed—that is, that either they originated in the first, or the early part of the second, or that St. John's Gospel was written in the fourth or fifth century of the Christian era.

When we turn to the Acts of Pilate and the other Gospels of the Passion, the phenomena presented are but slightly modified. The four Gospels are very impartially employed in the construction of the narrative, and a kind of harmony of the Passion constructed from them is the substratum of the narrative, to which a large quantity of legendary matter is added. But we look in vain for the peculiar characteristics of St. John, while those of the Synoptists are caricatured and exaggerated. There is less of teaching and more of narrative than in any one, even of the first three Gospels. So that a comparison of St. John's Gospel with the other compositions which are placed in the same category with his only increases our admiration for the daring originality of the author. He alone ventures to intrude boldly into the dangerous region of doctrine, into which so many thinkers, ambitious of the credit of originality and invention, had already ventured to their own confusion. He alone dares to put in the mouth of the founder of Christianity sayings of unparalleled depth, sublimity, and we may add audacity, concerning the root-principles of the Christian faith. And he does so with the most complete success. While the harmless purveyors of innocent legend are rejected with disdain, this unblushing fabricator of a doctrine for Christ, which He would have spurned with all the energy of His exalted character, is received with open arms, and acknowledged as the mouthpiece of the Spirit of God.

One word as to the Apocryphal Acts may conclude this section. A comparison of their contents with those of the fourth Gospel does but add strength to what has just been said. The compilers of these narratives seem rather to have had the amusement than the instruction of the Christian Church in view. Like the rhapsodists of old, and the romance-writers of later times, they seemed to desire to interweave their own fancies with the substantial facts of authentic history that they might impart the pleasure usually derived from works of fiction. There is scarcely any didactic element in the whole of the Apocryphal Acts. An unmistakeable *cento* from St. Paul's Epistles, and a feeble reproduction of his theory on the relation of the Jew and Gentile Churches, are all that can be extracted out of the whole mass of these legendary productions. Therefore we rise from their perusal with an increased sense of the uniqueness of the spectacle which the fourth Gospel presents, if it be indeed Apocryphal. In fact, we are asked, without any evidence but such as is derived from a very superficial comparison of the contents of that Gospel with the others and with the rest of the New Testament Scriptures, to accept a theory which is not only destitute of all historical foundation, but which is in direct opposition to all the evidence we have before us, whether it be drawn from the genuine or the spurious writings which have come down to us. Whatever difficulties a comparison of St. John with the Synoptists may suggest to the mind, they are as nothing by the side of those which present themselves when it is desired to include his among the Apocryphal Gospels. A more glaring discrepancy in tone, substance, character, style, power, spiritual and mental, can hardly be conceived. And those who would impose on us such a classification have not only to explain how so extraordinary an event took place as the reception of this Gospel into the canon; they have also to explain how it is that the Gospel stands absolutely alone. They have to account for the fact that no phenomenon of the kind has ever been witnessed before or since. They have, moreover, to make it clear to us why they adopt such principles of classification — why, to borrow a metaphor from physical science, they thus rank the lion in the same class with the mouse, the oak among the grasses of the field. In fact, the moment their theory presents itself in a constructive rather than in a destructive aspect, its enormous difficulties flash upon us at once. Banish St. John's Gospel from among the sacred Scriptures; publish it in the next collection of Apocryphal Scriptures that appears; and unless you are careful to surround it with his own Apocalypse, with half the Epistles of St. Paul, and one or two Epistles of St. Peter, you will have presented the world with a greater literary monstrosity than has ever yet been known.[1]

[1] The author of the last new assault on Christianity boldly assails all the Gospels. He omits to deal with the difficulty his theory suggests—the inconceivable perversity of the Christians in preferring apocryphal to genuine biographies. In the case of other great moral and religious teachers personal and contemporary details have been preserved with an extraordinary eagerness. We have only to refer to Socrates, Mohammed, Dominic, Francis, Luther, Loyola, Wesley, Irving, as examples. But the disciples of Jesus Christ waited for nearly one hundred and fifty years before they cared to preserve any details of His life. Such is the theory of the author of 'Supernatural Religion!'

CHAPTER III.

THE FOURTH GOSPEL AND THE EPISTLES.

THE last point which will engage our attention will be the attempt to discover whether a comparison between the Epistles and the fourth Gospel will lead us to a discovery of their relations to each other in the order of time. It is admitted on all hands that the Gospel was written last. But, with the exception of the prologue and a few comparatively unimportant passages in the course of the narrative, the Gospel professes to be a record of the *ipsissima verba* of Christ. We should naturally expect to discover in these, if genuine, the groundwork of the theological system of the Epistles. If, on the contrary, we find clear traces of the priority of the Epistles; if we find the discourses attributed to Christ based upon the writings of St. Peter or St. Paul, we can come to no other conclusion than that, so far from their being genuine, they have been put into His mouth by a later writer, for the purpose of obtaining the sanction of His authority for a teaching which was invented after His departure from among mankind.

That there are clear indications of a development in the prologue is admitted on all hands. We have traced the growth of the tendency to apply the Philonian appellation Logos to the Son of God, as St. Paul had previously availed himself of the Philonian expression εἰκὼν θεοῦ. The question, however, with which we have now to deal is, whether such signs of development are to be found in the discourses attributed to Christ. And, in the first place, we must ask whether the phraseology of the fourth Gospel shows any evidence of being cast in a Pauline or a Petrine mould. We are not aware that any assertion to that effect has ever been made. On the contrary, much has been said in many quarters of the essential differences between Pauline, Petrine, and Johannean theology. It has been universally admitted that the fourth Gospel bears the stamp of a profound originality, and that, even where it treads on ground common to all the Apostles, its step is one peculiar to itself. The phrases which naturally belong to a more advanced stage of the history of the Christian Church, when the principles which lay at the root of its Life were translated into the language of experience, are unknown here. We read nothing about Justification, Sanctification, Adoption, Election, Grace,[1] and the like. And not only are the phrases absent, but also the systematic teaching which those theories imply. St. Paul's Epistles are full of such systematic teaching. In the Epistle to the Romans he treats at length of Justification, of the relation of the law to the Gospel, of the position of the people of Israel in reference to the later and more expansive covenant. In the Epistle to the Corinthians he applies the principles of the Gospel to questions of Church life and order,[2] and

---

[1] Grace, we have already remarked, is only mentioned in the Prologue.
[2] The Sermon on the Mount, and the exhortation to hear the Church —which, as has been before remarked, would hardly have been recorded if it related to a state of things which was fast passing away—indicate a more advanced stage of thought than the fourth Gospel on these points.

concludes with a long argument setting forth the certainty of a resurrection. The Second Epistle relates chiefly to the duties of the ministers of Christ. The Epistle to the Galatians deals with the relation of Christians to the Jewish law, and of that law to the earlier dispensation of promise. The Epistle to the Ephesians, taking for granted the doctrines of election, sanctification, redemption by Christ's blood, and His indwelling in the soul, proceeds to unfold their practical results, the perfection, first of the individual, and through him of the body which such individuals compose. In the Epistle to the Colossians the same doctrines are used to confute the false teaching of those who were seeking to pervert the Colossian Church. A simpler note is struck by St. Paul's earlier Epistles—the Epistle to the Philippians alone of the later ones displaying any approach to that simplicity of tone. But though the Epistles to the Thessalonians are redolent of an earlier period of the Apostle's ministry, when even his luminous apprehension of the doctrines of the faith as yet lacked the fulness and depth to which it afterwards attained, yet even in them we detect the evidences of a period when the principles of the Gospel had begun to be formulated in words and phrases. It is needless to do more than simply mention the Pastoral Epistles, where the practical problems of Church administration are solved by a similar reference to first principles, and the Epistle to the Hebrews, where the doctrine of the Sacrifice of Propitiation on the Cross is proved to have been foreshadowed by the law. In the Epistles of St. Peter, moreover, the same advanced condition of the Christian Church is presupposed. The practical exhortations to a settled community are in each case enforced by the appeal to a set of doctrines admitted on all hands. Redemption, regeneration, the effects of baptism, the union between Christ and His people, are all assumed as truths too well known to need more than an allusion, while the Epistle is not allowed to conclude without a word of advice to the rulers of the Christian community. There is nothing of this in St. John. There are unquestionably, as we shall see, the germs of the doctrines which are capable of being expanded into the fuller teaching of the Apostles after the Ascension. But in the discourses attributed to Christ there is not one word, either relating to theory or practice, which justifies any supposition but that which regards them as spoken in the infancy of the Church, and as containing only the first principles of the dogmatic and practical theology of later ages. We have seen that not only is there no theory of Justification, Sanctification, nor Election, but the words themselves are nowhere to be found. There is no reference to the Church, except as a body hereafter to be organised. If the Sacraments are spoken of, it is with reference to their primary principles only. We are not asked to look back on them as the symbols and pledges of an initiation and incorporation into a body already existing. We are simply told that we must be born again of water and the Spirit, and nourished after that new birth by the Flesh and Blood of Christ. And if there be any exhortations which treat of the inner life of the believer, and his corporate union with his brethren and with his Lord, they rather bear an inchoate and anticipatory character than present these truths to us as realised facts. In fact, all the discourses of our Lord recorded by St. John seem to reflect the spirit of the words recorded by St. Luke: "Fear not, little flock; it is your Father's good pleasure to give you the kingdom."

We will enter upon the proof of these assertions. We shall find, if we compare the subject-matter of this Gospel with the writings of the Apostles, that while it is identical in spirit, it is invariably more elementary in form. Let us compare the doctrine of the nature of God, as taught in the other books of the New Testament, with the same doctrine as set forth by St. John. We find St. Stephen entering into an argument, wherein he shows the temporary nature of the Jewish covenant, the entire impossibility of its finding a root in the essential nature of God, the certainty of the fact that it was only a step in the education of the world, and concludes with the bold declaration that "God dwelleth not in temples made with hands." St. Stephen's yet more renowned disciple repeats this declaration in almost the same words; and again, when enlarging on the truth that the Mosaic dispensation must needs come to an end, tells the Corinthians that the Lord is the Spirit, and that it is the Lord, the Spirit, who will secure our salvation rather by the inward change of our hearts than by our actual obedience to an external enactment. What right had they to make such statements? None whatever, if St. John's Gospel be not authentic. But the whole substratum of their teaching is given in the brief but pregnant utterance, worthy, in its exceeding breadth and depth, of the Divine lips that uttered it, "Believe Me, the hour cometh when ye shall neither in this mountain, *nor yet at Jerusalem*, worship the Father. . . . The hour cometh, and now is, when the true worshippers must worship the Father in spirit and in truth. . . . *God is Spirit*, and they that worship Him must worship Him in spirit and in truth."

Another instance may be taken, among many, of the weighty utterances recorded by St. John, which were either genuine words of Christ Himself, or else display a power of epitomising in a single sentence the teaching of whole pages of the New Testament, which is absolutely unparalleled. St. John remarks in his prologue that, "No man hath seen God at any time; the Only Begotten Son, who existeth in the bosom of the Father, He hath declared Him." In this he is but expanding those mysterious sayings of Christ recorded elsewhere in his Gospel, which, when their inner meaning was unfolded, became so full of instruction. "Not that any man hath seen the Father, save He Who is with God, He hath seen the Father." "Ye have neither heard His voice, nor seen His shape," Christ says to the Jews; and again to Philip, "He that hath seen Me hath seen the Father, and how sayest thou then, show us the Father?" Here we discover the germ of the doctrine of the Christian Church, taught explicitly by her Apostles and enforced by her divines, that God dwells apart, in light that no one can approach, and that it is through the intervention of the Eternal Son alone that He has been pleased to reveal Himself to mankind. This teaching, whether promulgated by St. John or his brother Apostles, is based upon words of Christ, recorded by him alone. No Synoptist contradicts, or appears to contradict him; no Synoptist has unfolded a doctrine[1]

---

[1] There is one exception to this statement, and it is remarkable that the exception is the solitary instance to which we have above referred,

which is universally accepted by the Church of Christ. We need not repeat again the contents of Chapters I. and II. of this Essay to show that God the Father is regarded in the Epistles at least of St. Paul, as invisible and inscrutable, save through the revealing power of the Son.[1] But we would here call attention to the fact that the discourses of Christ, in which we find the proclamation of this truth, are recorded by St. John, and by him alone.

In regard to the person of Christ, it is equally impossible, if we except the Prologue, to find any traces of a development in the Gospel of any statements in the Epistles. Even in the Prologue itself the only evidence of a later date is the adoption of a single term to express a doctrine universally accepted before. On all other points the contents of the Gospel point to an earlier origin than the Epistles, inasmuch as what Christ says concerning Himself, though identical in substance, is on this point also more elementary in form than that of the Epistles. The humanity of Christ is but glanced at in the latter. It is His Divinity, His Lordship, His indwelling in men through His Divine power, which are most insisted on. Such points we should expect to find especially dwelt on in a Gospel devoted to an establishment of His Divinity. We should expect to find a jealousy displayed of the encroachment of the human element, to which already more than sufficient prominence had been given in former biographies. But the contrary, as we have already seen, is the fact.

---

where the Synoptists, for the moment, adopt the very phraseology of St. John.

[1] It may be inferred from the original Greek of such passages as 1 Pet. i. 13, 21, and ii. 9, that St. Peter held the same doctrine.

Christ's own claims to Divine authority are not, after all, so very much more marked in the fourth Gospel than in the rest. But the traits of His humanity are numerous and striking. We need only refer to what has been said above [1] to make it clear that St. John was as fully penetrated with the conviction of the humanity of the Saviour as any other Evangelist, and as eager to convey this his conviction to others. Nay, in some points his teaching is less advanced than that of the Synoptist. The doctrine of Christ's sinlessness was a vital one in the Apostolic Church. St. Peter and St. Paul lay especial stress upon it.[2] Yet in the Evangelists we find the first and third more emphatic than the fourth. "Take My yoke upon you and learn of Me," says St. Matthew.[3] "This man hath done nothing amiss," says the penitent thief in St. Luke. St. John does but once intimate a conviction of the sinlessness of Jesus,[4] and never sets him up as an example, save on one particular point.[5] These are hardly the phenomena which would be presented us in the pages of a biographer who was writing for a purpose, and that purpose the apotheosis of Jesus Christ.

We proceed to apply the same test to the relations of the Epistle writers to the Gospel on the doctrine of the Incarnation. The scanty hints which the Gospel supplies of man lying in darkness and under condemnation, and of the Life, Light, and forgiveness revealed in Jesus Christ, are expanded into a complete system in the Epistles. And it is to be observed that these hints are found in the fourth Gospel, and nowhere else.

---

[1] Pp. 43, 44. [2] 2 Cor. v. 21; Heb. iv. 15; 1 Peter ii. 22.
[3] St. Matt. xi. 29. [4] St. John viii. 46. [5] Ib. xiii. 15.

If Christ did not utter the words attributed to Him there, then the whole system of the restoration of man to purity, through the communication of life through Christ, was invented by the Apostles, and attested afterwards by a fictitious narrative of the second century. Let us see how the facts bear out such a supposition. If it were true, we should expect to find the Saviour in the fourth Gospel making an awkward use of the writings of St. Paul and St. Peter. Their favourite turns of expression would be found in His mouth, repeated with a laboured anxiety to demonstrate the authenticity of their doctrine. Such are the usual features of forgeries and interpolations written for polemical purposes.[1] Is anything of this kind to be detected in the phenomena before us? On the contrary, the language put in the Saviour's mouth in the fourth Gospel is of the simplest kind. There can be no doubt that it may have served as the storehouse whence the arguments and illustrations in the Epistles were drawn, but evidence for the contrary supposition there is absolutely none. To begin with the anthropology of the Gospel of St. John. The alienation of man from God; his condition at Christ's coming; the sentence of condemnation under which he lay, are

[1] We have already drawn attention to the fact that Pauline expressions occur in every page of Clement, Ignatius, Polycarp, and Justin Martyr, in the Epistle to the Hebrews, and in the second Epistle of St. Peter. It is obvious that the argument derives additional strength if the latter be genuine (see p. 127, note) and the former be not written by St. Paul. Even St. Luke, in the Acts, introduces Pauline expressions in chapters xvii. xviii. (see Alford, Prolegomena to Acts), while in chapter xiii. we are introduced to his doctrine of justification by faith. If St. John alone displays no sign of the influence of the peculiar phraseology of St. Paul, it can only be because he is recording the genuine discourses of Jesus Christ Himself.

drawn in sharp, bold outline by Christ in the Gospel: the details are only to be found in the Epistles. Christ lays down the principles in authoritative apophthegms. "That which is born of the flesh is flesh : that which is born of the Spirit is spirit." "He that believeth on Him is not condemned : he that believeth not on Him is condemned already." "Because ye are not of the world, but I have chosen you out of the world, therefore the world hateth you." We have only to refer to what has been said above[1] to see how the teaching in St. John is expanded by St. Peter and St. Paul. The references of the former to a "vain conversation received by tradition," the allusion to a calling out of darkness into the "marvellous light" of Christ,[2] are sufficient indications of the fact that some such doctrine had been taught by Christ: we are told that He taught it, not by the Synoptists, but by St. John. In St. Paul we have the whole of three famous chapters in the Epistle to the Romans devoted to an exposition of the truth contained in the second of the verses we have cited from the fourth Gospel. The antagonism between the flesh and the Spirit, again, is enlarged upon in the eighth chapter of the same Epistle, after having supplied the Apostle with some striking ideas in the Epistle to the Galatians.[3] The opposition between Christ's disciples and the world out of which they have been called is a subject on which he is frequently

[1] Part I., chapter iii.   [2] 1 Pet. i. 18; ii. 9.
[3] The idea pervades St. Paul's Epistles. In 2 Cor. x. 3, he says, "though we walk in the flesh, we do not war after the flesh." In Eph. ii. he expatiates on the fact that he and his converts once had their conversation in the lusts of the flesh, but had now been made alive together with Christ; and, again, how those who were Gentiles in flesh (ver. 11), had now access in One Spirit to the Father.

accustomed to dwell,[1] nor is it absent from the Epistles of St. Peter.[2] In each case we seem to have the text in the Gospel, and its exposition in the Epistle. As yet unrecorded by any Evangelist, these root-principles of the Gospel sank deep into the minds of the Apostles, and formed the groundwork of their most striking exhortations. It is the same with the doctrine of the Life flowing from Christ to His disciples. We have seen how this doctrine, hinted at by the Synoptists, becomes the main subject of the Gospel of St. John. We have seen how fully, clearly, plainly, the truth is proclaimed that Jesus came to give Life to the world, and that this life was available by means of faith, and conveyed through the Sacraments. But when we scrutinize the way in which the truth is proclaimed, we shall be forced to admit that here we have not even the ablest of disciples endeavouring to manufacture a system for his master after he has long been laid in the grave, but the Master Himself laying solidly and strongly the foundations of His Eternal Work. For all the theology of the fourth Gospel is deep, shadowy, mysterious, as becomes the Infinite Wisdom Itself. In the Epistles we see the work of the Spirit, endeavouring in a measure to accommodate to the human intellect truths too vast for the human understanding. He supplies the glass by means of which, though as yet darkly, the outlines of

---

[1] In Gal. i. 4, St. Paul states that Christ delivered men from the present evil world, and in ver. 10, he remarks that if he pleased men he should not be Christ's slave. Cf. 1 Thess. ii. 4, and 1 Cor. i. 18, 23.

[2] 1 Pet. ii. 8, 12; iv. 14, 16; v. 9, 10. St. James is yet more emphatic. Whosoever will be a friend of the world is established as an enemy of God, iv. 4. Cf. St. John xv. 19.

The Fourth Gospel and the Epistles. 219

the mighty temple of truth may be discerned. Christ does not condescend to explain, He affirms.[1] Nor does He adapt His affirmations to human capacity. On the contrary, He invests them with an enigmatic character which frequently provokes the indignation or the ridicule of those who hear them.[2] He declares the broad principles of the Gospel: it is the office of the Spirit when He comes to unfold their meaning to the disciples. "I am the Life." "I am the Light," "the Way," "the Truth." "God so loved the world that He gave His only begotten Son, to the end that all whosoever believeth on Him should not perish, but have everlasting Life." "I am the Bread of Life." "Whosoever drinketh of the water that I shall give him shall never thirst." "Except a man be born again he cannot see the kingdom of God." "Whoso eateth My Flesh, and drinketh My Blood, hath eternal life." "I am the Vine, ye are the branches." "Without Me ye can do nothing." "I am the Resurrection and the Life." "The hour is coming, and now is, when the dead shall hear the voice of the Son of God, and they that hear shall live." "I am the Good Shepherd; the Good Shepherd layeth down His Life for the sheep." These, and such as these, are the utterances ascribed to Christ in the fourth Gospel. Are they, or are they not, such as the Founder of a religion was likely to make? There is no trace of an attempt to borrow the language or the ideas of other men: the words are originality itself. The

---

[1] Liddon's 'Bampton Lectures,' Lect. iv. p. 253.
[2] Both in the Synoptists and in St. John. St. Matt. xiii. 57; xv. 12; St. Mark vi. 3; St. John vi. 41, 52, 66.

doctrines are not elaborated into a system as in the Epistle to the Romans, or that to the Hebrews: they stand detached from one another, and are the more sublime for standing thus apart. They are not assumed as the basis of exhortations, nor adapted to the needs of this or that particular class of believers: all is simple elementary truth, addressed to all believers alike. They bear no marks of human feeling, like the fervid exhortations, the powerful arguments, which meet us in every page of the great Apostle of the Gentiles: they are delivered in a manner grave, calm, unimpassioned, as would beseem the lips of the Word Who became flesh. These voices of God are selected, it is true, by the Apostle—he tells us so himself[1]—and arranged in a certain order. The Master imparts the information in mystic phrase to His disciples that they must receive from Him a new life;[2] that they must stand in continual dependence on Him for the continuation of that life.[3] He tells them in what personal relation they henceforth stand to Him,[4] and how the life they receive from Him is able to triumph over death itself.[5] And then among his Apostles alone he unfolds the still greater mystery of the corporate life of His Church,[6] of the place held by the Spirit in the diffusion of that corporate life,[7] and the final effect of the Spirit's work in bringing them all, through inward sanctification, into complete oneness with God.[8] But throughout the whole narrative there is maintained, with the most perfect consistency, the

---

[1] St. John xx. 30, 31; xxi. 25.   [2] Ib. ch. iii.   [3] Ib. ch. vi.
[4] Ib. ch. viii., x.   [5] Ib. ch. xi.   [6] Ib. ch. xv.
[7] Ib. ch. xiv.—xvi.   [8] Ib. ch. xvii.

same indisposition to reason upon these truths, or to connect them by any other than the slightest and least obvious links with each other. Let us turn to the writings of the Apostles, and observe how they deal with truths common, as we have seen, to them and to the fourth Gospel. In all cases they are introduced as truths derived from some authority admitted by writer and readers alike. " When Christ our life shall appear, then shall ye also appear with Him in glory."[1] " Christ liveth in me, and the life that I now live I live by the faith of the Son of God, who loved me, and gave Himself for me."[2] God " hath shined in your hearts, in order to produce the enlightenment of the knowledge of the glory of God in the Person of Jesus Christ."[3] " Ye are light in the Lord."[4] " By whom we have boldness and access in confidence by the faith of Him."[5] These passages do not appear, even at first sight, to have that authoritative ring about them which we find in those contained in St. John's Gospel. And a reference to the context will show that in every case they are part of an argument in which the principles of the Gospel are referred to as the authority for the various dogmatic statements that are made, or as the basis of exhortations as to conduct. But this is not all. Whole passages of the Epistles seem to have flowed from these isolated utterances in St. John. Witness the Epistle to the Romans, in which the doctrines of man's condemnation, of deliverance through God's righteousness manifested in Christ, of Life in Christ,[6] of the

---

[1] Col. iii. 4.   [2] Gal. ii. 20.   [3] 2 Cor. iv. 6.
[4] Eph. v. 8.   [5] Ib. iii. 12.
[6] " The gift of God is eternal life in Jesus Christ our Lord," Rom. vi. 23.

agency of His Spirit in imparting "life on account of righteousness," of the function of the law in God's scheme, of the essential antagonism of the flesh and the Spirit, appear to be the expansion of a few phrases in St. John implying that man is delivered by Christ from a condemnation already pronounced, that Christ came to deliver them by the infusion of Life, that the Spirit was essentially antagonistic to and triumphant over the flesh, and that He should convince the world of righteousness because Christ had gone to the Father.[1] That noble piece of sustained argument on the Resurrection in 1 Cor. xv., as well as the references to the subject which are to be found elsewhere, are but a commentary on the saying, " I am the Resurrection and the Life," combined with the declaration regarding the corn of wheat in ch. xii. 24; for it is in Christ that all shall be made alive—by Him that the Resurrection cometh. He is the quickening spirit, whose image all the redeemed shall bear. The existence of a body in whose members one common Life dwells, and that Life the Life of Christ, is intimated under various figures, but never with the simplicity in which it is laid down in St. John xv. It is introduced not as a primary principle, but as an admitted fact, to clench an argument or encourage unity. The Gentiles are bidden to beware of pride, lest they should be cut off from the stock into which they have just been grafted.[2] Christ is one Body, and each disciple is one of His members; and therefore they are to cultivate mutual love,[3] to refrain from envying each other's spiritual

[1] This is equally true of the Epistle to the Galatians.
[2] Rom. xi. 17—24.   [3] Ib. xii. 4, 5.

gifts,[1] to speak the truth to each other.[2] He is the Head, and they all derive nourishment from Him; and while they can grow by means of the nourishment thus provided,[3] the neglecting to maintain this connection with the Head is the source of many errors.[4] Husband and wife are exhorted to live in mutual love, because their union typifies the mystic union between Christ and His Church.[5] And we cannot help observing on the remarkable manner in which the teachings of the 6th and 15th chapters of St. John's Gospel are combined in the words, " We are members of His Body, of His Flesh, and of His Bones."[6] So in like manner the memorable passage in which the Apostle celebrates the praises of love is, like the language of the other Apostles and St. John himself in his Epistle, prompted by the repeated injunctions to mutual love put in the mouth of Christ in the fourth Gospel. The theory of the Atonement put forth by the Apostles is a combination of the saying, " The Good Shepherd layeth down His Life for the sheep," with the announcement recorded in St. Matthew that " The Son of Man came to give His Life a ransom for the many."[7] If, again, in the discourse to Nicodemus, our Lord mysteriously connects the new birth of which He speaks with His Death and with His Ascension, He is followed by the Apostles. In a passage in which the language is singularly suggestive of the 3rd chapter of St. John,

[1] 1 Cor. xii. 12. [2] Eph. iv. 25. [3] Ib. iv. 16.
[4] Col. ii. 19. [5] Eph. v. 23—32. [6] Ib. v. 30.
[7] We may also compare the words, " Greater love hath no man than this, that a man lay down his life for his friends." But on this doctrine of propitiation the Synoptists are more explicit, and their doctrine more advanced than that of St. John.

the Apostle attributes the regeneration and renewing of the Holy Ghost to the Saviour, whose Ascension, as we have seen, procured for us this gift.[1] The first mention of baptism in the history of the Church after Christ's Ascension is connected with the descent of the Holy Ghost as the result of that Ascension; while both St. Paul and St. Peter connect baptism with the Resurrection,[2] and the former repeatedly with the Death of Christ. The doctrine of the Lord's Supper, if as expanded in the fourth Gospel as in the Epistles, is at least more recondite and mysterious, and it also serves to clear up a difficulty which, but for the preservation of that Gospel, would be very perplexing. It is admitted on all hands that the doctrine of Christ's indwelling, though it may derive some confirmation from, is at least not explicitly taught in, the earlier Gospels. But they contain the institution of the Lord's Supper, which, as implied in the words of institution, and as expounded by St. Paul,[3] is intended to convey the idea of the human nature of Christ affording nourishment to the human soul. Now it is worthy of remark that no kind of surprise is expressed by the disciples at the words of our Lord, unintelligible as they must have appeared without explanation. No questions are asked, no difficulties are propounded, not even for information's sake—all is simple adoring awe and faith. This is en-

[1] Titus iii. 5, 6.
[2] Acts ii. 33, 38. Rom. vi. 3, 4. Col. ii. 12. 1 Pet. iii. 21. This allusion to the connection of Christian baptism with the inherent power of Christ, manifested by His Resurrection and Ascension, is doubtless an expansion of our Lord's discourse to Nicodemus, in which all difficulties are met by the words, "No man hath ascended into heaven but He that came down from heaven." Cf. ch. vi. 62.
[3] 1 Cor. x. 17; xi. 20—29; xii. 13.

The Fourth Gospel and the Epistles. 225

tirely contrary to the picture given of Christ's disciples elsewhere in the Synoptic narratives. They are full of curiosity, incessantly asking questions and seeking information. How, then, is it that they are silent here? What other explanation can be given of the fact, but that whatever difficulties the Saviour's words may have suggested had been met and mastered before, when "many of His disciples went back, and walked no more with Him;" and that they now understood Him to mean that he was Himself the Paschal Lamb, who was not only to be slain for their deliverance, but to be assimilated as the support of their lives, even as St. Paul afterwards expressed it, "Christ our Passover was sacrificed for us, therefore let us keep the Feast"?

We have seen that St. John says but very little concerning the office of the Spirit in his Gospel, and that the writers of the Epistles say a great deal. But there is no fact more noteworthy in the present inquiry than that the great deal is summed up in the very little. There is no one function ascribed to the Spirit in the work of our redemption by St. Peter and St. Paul which may not be traced to the words recorded in St. John. The whole work of redemption is, in the Epistles, ascribed to the Spirit as the efficient cause. If we dwell in Christ, it is through Him. If we partake of Christ, it is by His means. If we grow in grace and in the knowledge of Christ, it is through His instrumentality. Our sanctification is sanctification of the Spirit, though it is the work of Christ. The simple explanation of the mystery is that He is Christ's Spirit, sent by Him from the Father, speaking only what He hears, proclaiming what He has derived from Christ, communicating the new birth, the cleansing and refreshing influences of the Gospel, nay, even the Flesh and Blood of Christ.[1] Nor is this all, but, as we have seen,[2] the Epistle to the Hebrews is needed to explain a very enigmatic sentence in the Fourth Gospel. Christ declares it to be impossible that the Comforter should come until He had gone away. It is hardly conceivable that a sentence so brief, so oracular, so absolutely free from the slightest allusion to the Epistle which suggests the explanation, should be the result of a careful study of that Epistle—an application of principles which are only suggested by deep meditation on its contents. The argument of the Epistle to the Hebrews and the declaration of the Gospel of St. John exactly fit into one another, and with the doctrine suggested by Gen. vi. 3. The completed Sacrifice of the Son, offered in heaven, is the means whereby God's Spirit returns to earth to dwell with men. The passage in Genesis states the fact of the alienation between man and the Spirit. The fourth Gospel asserts that the return of the Spirit can only be consequent upon Christ's Ascension into heaven.[3] The Epistle to the Hebrews most undesignedly explains to us how this moral necessity arose. Is it possible to find a more singular exemplification of the fact that "the whole counsel of God," as unfolded by the Apostles, lies concealed in the deep and pregnant sayings of Christ recorded in the Gospel of St. John? Is it possible to find a more striking instance of the way in which a single sen-

---

[1] St. John vi. 63: "It is the Spirit that giveth Life."
[2] Above, p. 152.
[3] The Acts tell us th t it is He who hath shed forth this Spirit.

The Fourth Gospel and the Epistles. 227

tence contains within itself the guarantee of its own authenticity?

But we may carry this argument one step farther. There is a strong probability that the Apostles are accustomed to quote words of our Lord which the fourth Gospel alone hands down to us. As we have already seen, the expression, "the Lord is the Spirit" bears every mark of being a quotation by St. Paul of words known to be uttered by the Saviour. Nor is it the only one. The expression, "Christ our Life," in the Epistle to the Colossians, can, one would think, only owe its origin to the tradition which had reached the Apostle that Christ proclaimed Himself to be the Life. At least, it is not to be found in any genuine record of our Lord's teaching if St. John's Gospel be not genuine. The declaration that Christians are "light *in the Lord*," and "children of light," can hardly have been made without some warrant from Christ Himself — some knowledge that He had declared Himself to be the Light. Nay, the expression, "they of the way," which we find in the Acts, may not unreasonably be supposed to be an allusion, not, as some have supposed, to the way of salvation, but to Jesus, Himself the Way, according to His word. We need not discuss again the passages already treated of in Part I., in which the Apostles would seem to be indebted for their expressions to words uttered by Christ which were not as yet recorded.[1] Other quotations may be adduced, which are equally significant. "There is therefore no condemnation to them which are in Christ Jesus, who walk

---

[1] pp. 26, 102, 104, 106, 110, 111, 116, 119, 132, 136, 151, 154.

not after the flesh but after the Spirit," is surely a repetition of the Lord's words, " He that believeth not is condemned already, because he hath not believed in the Name of the only begotten Son of God," with an allusion also to the new birth of the Spirit, and the renunciation of the old birth of the flesh, which the same discourse to Nicodemus contains. If this passage be not the result of the teaching of the third chapter of St. John, from whence is it derived? It breathes the very spirit of the discourse there recorded. The antagonism between the Spirit and the flesh, again laid down by Christ in the third and sixth chapters of St. John's Gospel, is the source of the various declarations of St. Paul to the same effect, such as, " Walk in the Spirit, and ye shall not fulfil the lusts of the flesh." " As he that was after the flesh persecuted him that was after the Spirit, even so it is now." " They that are in the flesh do mind ($\phi\rho\nu\nu\hat{\nu}\sigma\iota$—are inclined in their mind to) the things of the flesh, but they that are after the Spirit do mind the things of the Spirit."[1] So in the reference to Christ as the Good Shepherd, as we have before seen, and in the command given to St. Peter to

[1] The proof that St. Paul is quoting St. John, and not St. John St. Paul, may be shown from two considerations: (1) that St. Paul strongly asseverated at all times that he was preaching the Gospel of Jesus Christ, which could hardly be the case, unless he had the authority of Jesus Christ for the leading doctrines of his system; and (2) that when similar ideas occur in two different authors, we are compelled to regard that writer as presenting them in their original form in whose pages they display least traces of the other's influence. Thus we find almost all St. John's words, phrases, and ideas in the Epistles of St. Paul, while many of St. Paul's most characteristic expressions and turns of thought are entirely absent from St. John. It is reasonable to suppose, then, that St. John is reporting discourses actually uttered by Christ, which St. Paul had received and embodied in his teaching.

"feed the sheep" of Christ, we have indisputable proofs not only that the substance of the doctrine of the Epistles, but even the form in which it was delivered, is due to the discourses attributed to Christ in the fourth Gospel.

Nor are we compelled to relinquish our argument here. We may go on to assert that not only were the Apostles in their Epistles indebted for their doctrines to the discourses of Christ, as contained in the fourth Gospel, but that what we may venture with reverence to describe as the *obiter dicta* of Christ, His less important utterances, were carefully circulated among the disciples, were eagerly appropriated by their instructors, and made to serve as the basis of many an exhortation and argument.

We will commence with the practical effect of the Gospel of Christ on man's moral nature. We have before treated of the results of the Incarnation in the restoration of our fallen humanity to purity and perfection. But we shall find, upon examination, that although the fourth Gospel does not enter very fully into the subject, it nevertheless has a definite theory as to the *modus operandi* of Christ in destroying the power of sin. Sin, in fact, holds mankind in bondage. It is this captivity which holds him back from fulfilling the law of his being, and the work of Christ is to set him free. Let him once be detached from the chains of his captivity, and he will at once, with Christ's help, proceed to fulfil the purposes for which he was created. Christ is reported in the fourth Gospel to have said, " If ye continue in My Word, then are ye My disciples indeed, and ye shall know the truth, and the truth shall make you free." This idea was a strange one to the Jews, as we might well imagine, and the scorn with which they received it is a touch of nature which adds to the evidence for the genuineness of the Gospel. "We are Abraham's seed, and were never in bondage to any man: how then sayest thou that we shall become free?" Our Lord replies to them by the remarkable declaration, which it is impossible to help regarding as the source from which St. Paul drew some of his most emphatic teaching. "VERILY, VERILY I SAY UNTO YOU, WHOSOEVER COMMITTETH SIN IS THE SLAVE OF SIN;" and he adds, "if the Son shall make you free, ye shall be free indeed."[1] The strong impression which this utterance made upon the first disciples is not confined to St. Paul. Little as St. James reflects anything beyond the mere ethical portions of his Master's system, we can see that some such declaration as this has taken firm hold of his mind. We are reminded by him that the Gospel is a "law of liberty,"[2] and are recommended to speak and act as men who will be judged by such a law.[3] The fact that no such statement is made or even hinted at[4] by the Synoptists, makes this passage in St. James not a little significant, and its significance is not a little heightened by the discovery that St. Peter's writings are coloured by the same idea. In each of his Epistles he adverts to it. In the first he asserts the freedom of the Christian and qualifies his assertion by the remark that this

[1] St. John viii. 31–36.
[2] The "Authorized" Version translates ἐλευθερία indifferently by "freedom" and "liberty."
[3] St. James ii. 12.
[4] We can hardly regard the passage in St. Luke iv. 18 as containing such a hint, especially if we refer to the original text.

freedom must not be used as a cloak for licence, inasmuch as every Christian is the slave of God.[1] In the second, he reminds those who promise themselves and others the liberty to sin, that by so doing they make themselves the slaves of corruption.[2] Was St. Peter, as well as St. James, under the influence of the Saviour's words when both these passages were penned? or did the writer of the fourth Gospel, with startling power, compress them, together with the similar utterances of St. Paul and St. James, into an apophthegm, and place it in the mouth of Jesus?

St. Paul, too, has been indebted for some of the most striking passages which have flowed from his pen, to a saying which, if we are to admit the spuriousness of the fourth Gospel, had never been uttered. In one of his earliest Epistles he refers to it, and he recurs to it again and again in the later ones. In the Epistle to the Galatians, contending against those who would impose the law of Moses upon the Gentile converts to Christianity, he insists that the law was bondage, typified by Hagar, and the Gospel freedom, typified by Sarah. He thus reverses the proposition of the Jews, that, as Abraham's seed, they were never in bondage to any man; and it is as a Christian, not as a Jew, that he speaks when he winds up his argument with the words, "So then, brethren, we are children, not of the bondwoman, but of the free." This conclusion is made the point of departure of a new argument. "Stand fast," he says, "in the liberty wherewith Christ hath made you free;"[3] while, with St. Peter, he warns his disciples against that spurious liberty which enslaves men to their

[1] 1 Pet. ii. 16. [2] 2 Pet. ii. 19. [3] Gal. iv. 22; v. 1.

own flesh, and insists that the only law to which man is now subject is a law of love.[1] This view is expanded further in the great treatise on Justification. It commences with a powerful description of the bondage in which mankind are held by sin.[2] He draws upon his own personal experience for an illustration of the nature of this bondage, and paints in vivid colours the abject impotence of the human will, the utter impossibility of fulfilling the higher law which man's mind and conscience set before him, the distress and misery consequent upon the struggle between the loftier and baser elements of our nature.[3] And then, with a burst of gratitude, he tells how the "law of the Spirit of life hath set him free from the law of sin and of death."[4] This was but an extension, by a reference to his own inner life, of a truth which he had previously declared. "Sin," he had said, "had no dominion over them who are not under the law, but under grace." Men were the slaves of the power under whose dominion they voluntarily placed themselves, whether of sin unto death or of obedience unto righteousness; and when made free from sin, they were enslaved unto righteousness.[5] To such declarations as these he returns from time to time in his other Epistles. He reminds the slave who has united himself to Christ that he is henceforth "the Lord's freeman."[6] Those who repent are described as having recovered themselves out of the snare of the devil, in which they had been taken captive.[7] And another turn is given to the thought in the Epistle to

---

[1] Gal. v. 13, 14. [2] Rom. i., ii. [3] Ib. vii.
[4] Ib. viii. 2, 15. [5] Ib. vi. 14–18. [6] 1 Cor. vii. 22.
[7] 2 Tim. ii. 26.

The Fourth Gospel and the Epistles. 233

the Hebrews, where the devil is said to have held mankind in bondage through the power of death, until Christ, by His death, delivered them.[1] This idea of Christianity as a translation from bondage to freedom permeates the minds of all the Epistle-writers. No saying of the kind is attributed to Christ in the Synoptic Gospels. Whence, then, does it derive its origin, if not from an authentic discourse of Christ, recorded in the fourth Gospel alone?

In connection with this doctrine of freedom comes that of sanctification. It is once more in St. John, not in the Synoptists, that we find the germ of the doctrine of man's progressive sanctification, through the working of the Divine power implanted in him, which is so obvious a feature of Apostolic teaching. St. Peter addresses his Epistle to those who were elect according to sanctification of spirit,[2] and he urges them to add one Christian grace to another.[3] St. Jude, while copying St. Peter's dedication,[4] desires those whom he addresses to build themselves up upon their most holy faith.[5] The Apostle St. Peter, in each of his Epistles, begs his hearers to "grow" in "the word"[6] and "in grace."[7] St. Paul adopts the same metaphor,[8] and the words "sanctify" and "sanctification" occur continually in his writings.[9] He refers to sanctification both as a past[10] and as a future act.[11] Salvation is to be "worked out," even by those who are already sanctified.[12] He himself can do no more than stretch forward to a perfection he has

[1] Heb. ii. 14, 15. [2] 1 Pet. i. 2. [3] 2 Pet. i. 5.
[4] Ib. v. 1. [5] Jude i. 20. [6] 1 Pet. ii. 2.
[7] 2 Pet. iii. 18. [8] Eph. iv. 16. Col. i. 10; ii. 19.
[9] As for instance, 1 Cor. i. 2, 30. Eph. v. 26, &c.
[10] 1 Cor. vi. 11. [11] 1 Thess. iv. 3, 4.
[12] Phil. ii. 12. They were already saints, ch. i. 1.

not yet reached.¹ Nay, even when this life is ended, there would seem to be still an endless advance towards the same perfection.² But if we turn to the Gospel of St. John, we shall see indeed the source of all these affirmations and exhortations; but it is as usual shrouded in deep and mysterious language. The parable of the Vine and its Branches suggests the idea of a slow and gradual growth; and so, perhaps, do the words, "Sanctify them through Thy Truth."

The doctrine of election, again, may be traced to pages of St. John. The expression "the elect" occurs, it is true, several times in the Synoptists. But it is worthy of remark that the only clear explanation of the term is to be found in the fourth Gospel. It is in the 15th chapter of that Gospel that we find sketched out for us the special relation in which the people of God stand to Him and to the world. "Ye have not chosen Me, but I have chosen you, that ye should bring forth fruit, that whatsoever ye shall ask of the Father in My Name, He may give it you. . . . Because ye are not of the world, but I have chosen you out of the world, therefore the world hateth you." It is of course open to any one to contend that this speech was an after invention, to explain a word which appears as a matter of course in the Synoptic narratives. In that case, it only remains for us to marvel that the explanation should be at once so simple and so exactly accordant with the fuller teaching of the Epistles on this head. And before we quit this subject, it is worthy of a passing remark that, little as St. John says about Predestination and Elec-

---

[1] Phil. iii. 12. Cf. i. 9; 1 Thess. iii. 12.   [2] 2 Cor. iii. 18.

The Fourth Gospel and the Epistles. 235

tion, the Calvinistic doctrine on those points derives as much confirmation from a passage in St. John as from any to be found in St. Paul's Epistles. "No man can come unto Me, except the Father which hath sent Me draw him,"[1] is a passage which may have been misrepresented, but which is at the root of almost every sentence in the Epistles upon which a Calvinistic meaning has been fixed.

It is an additional argument for the authenticity of St. John's Gospel that, though we find abundant assertions that the disciples of Christ were henceforth to enjoy the favour of God, we do not find the technical word grace, afterwards used to express it, except in the Prologue. The same phenomenon is visible in the Gospel of St. Luke as compared with the Acts. Once only in the Gospel do we find the word, and then with reference to the Divine favour as displayed towards the human nature of Jesus Christ.[2] But in the Acts it meets us again and again, as the recognised theological word to express the favour which God displayed towards His Church.[3]

If there be anything which is more closely associated with grace in the minds of the Epistle-writers of the New Testament, it is peace. Peace was prophesied by the father of St. John Baptist: it formed a part of the angels' song at the Nativity, it was the authorized salutation of Christ's messengers before His crucifixion. But it acquires fresh emphasis in the Gospel of St. John. There, for the first time, we find it specially connected with the indwelling of Jesus Christ. It is His

[1] St. John vi. 44.   [2] St. Luke ii. 40.
[3] Acts iv. 33; xi. 23, &c.

peace which he gives to them.[1] He was not merely to give peace on the earth,[2] but this peace was to be "in Him."[3] And it is this view which we find predominant in the Epistles. "Grace, mercy, and peace," are invoked upon the disciples, not only "from God our Father," but "from the Lord Jesus Christ."[4] It is when justified by faith in Him, that we have peace with God.[5] St. Paul goes further, and approaching still more closely to the language recorded by St. John, he declares that Christ Himself is our peace.[6] We may make the same remark regarding the word truth. "The truth,"[7] "the truth of God,"[8] "the truth of Christ,"[9] "the truth of the Gospel,"[10] "the truth as it is in Jesus,"[11]—these are expressions sown broadcast in the Epistles; but it is evident that they derive their stamp from the republication of the Old Testament doctrine of truth which the fourth Gospel, and it alone, contains. Not only does Jesus say to His disciples, "ye shall know the truth and the truth shall make you free,"[12]—not only does He pray, "sanctify them in Thy truth;"[13]—not only does He promise "the Spirit of truth,"[14] but He says,"I am the truth,"[15] thus supplying the necessary authority for the statement of the Apostle quoted above, that it is in Jesus that truth resides.[16]

We need not enlarge upon the agreement between

[1] St. John xiv. 27.   [2] St. Luke ii. 14; xii. 51.   [3] St. John xvi. 33.
[4] Rom. i. 7. Cf. 1 Cor. i. 3, &c.   [5] Ib. v. 1.   [6] Eph. ii. 14.
[7] 2 Thess. ii. 10. 2 Tim. ii. 18; iii. 8; iv. 4. Tit. i. 14. St. James v. 19, &c.   [8] Rom. iii. 7.
[9] 2 Cor. xi. 10.   [10] Gal. ii. 5, 14.
[11] Eph. iv. 21.   [12] St. John viii. 31, 32.   [13] Ib. xvii. 17.
[14] Ib. xiv. 17 ; xv. 26.   [15] Ib. xiv. 6.
[16] "As truth is in Jesus" would be the more accurate translation.

The Fourth Gospel and the Epistles. 237

all the writers of the New Testament in their conception of the κόσμος, beyond the remark that this twofold conception is more marked in St. John than in the Synoptists, and is therefore more likely to contain the genuine utterances of Christ from which the doctrine contained in the Epistles is drawn.[1]

The next question that demands our attention is the relation of the writer of the fourth Gospel towards Judaism. And this is a somewhat important point. It has been laid down, rather more dogmatically than scientifically, that the stand-point of the fourth Gospel was so distinctly alien to what has been termed Judæo-Christianity, that its author could not have been a Jew.[2] If it should turn out that his point of view was precisely the same as that of the other New Testament writers, we shall be led irresistibly to a conclusion directly opposite. And the facts certainly seem to

---

[1] This double conception of the κόσμος, which is common to all the writers in the New Testament, is made a reproach against St. Paul by modern sceptical writers. "St. Paul could not escape from the endless inconsistencies arising from a theological philosophy which controverted the Hebrew Scriptures. Thus, while at one time he describes the devil as the god of this world, he elsewhere asserts that 'the earth is the Lord's and the fulness thereof,'" (Duke of Somerset, 'Christian Theology and Modern Scepticism,' p. 106.) The noble duke is probably unaware of such passages as St. Matt. iv. 8, 9, in which this Jewish writer, who unquestionably believed the statements of his own Scriptures that "the earth is the Lord's and the fulness thereof," nevertheless represents the devil as claiming full liberty to dispose of the kingdoms of the world. See also St. Matt. xiii. 38. St. John, too, bids us not to love the world, lest we should become God's enemies (1 John ii. 15), and yet tells us that "God so loved the world that He gave His only-begotten Son" to redeem it.

[2] Reville, 'Revue des Deux Mondes,' pp. 113, 114. Schenkel 'Sketch of the Character of Jesus,' p. 27 [translation].

point in this direction. The declaration, for instance, that salvation is of the Jews,[1] is a remarkable one to be placed in the mouth of Jesus by a writer whose whole spirit we are told was in opposition to the Jewish tendency displayed by some Christians in his time. But it is in exact accordance with the principles laid down by the great Apostle of the Gentiles, whom none can accuse of too much sympathy with the Judaizing party. "To the Jew first and also to the Gentile," as it was the principle laid down by Christ[2] and acted upon by St. Peter,[3] so it was the theoretical as well as practical basis laid down by St. Paul,[4] who never forgets for a moment that Christ, according to the flesh, was a Jew.[5]

The direct assertion that Moses wrote of Christ,[6] again, is certainly not calculated to sharpen the antagonism between Judaism and Christianity, any more than the remark that the result of searching the Old Testament Scriptures, in consequence of their emphatic testimony to Christ, ought to be to bring men to Christ.[7] In fact, sayings of Christ are scattered broadcast throughout the Gospel which bring into particular prominence the Jewish element in Christ's teaching. He tells the Samaritan woman that the Samaritan worship is founded in ignorance, an ignorance which was not shared by her Jewish neighbours.[8] He does not confine Himself to

---

[1] St. John iv. 22. Yet the author of 'Supernatural Religion' can say, as though the fact admitted of no contradiction, that "the Jews are not once spoken of as the favoured people of God," vol. ii. p. 416.
[2] St. Luke xxiv. 47.   [3] Acts iii. 26; xi. 17, 18.
[4] Ib. xiii. 42, 46; xvii. 2; xix. 8; xxviii. 28. Rom. ii. 9, 10.
[5] Rom. ix. 4, 5. Gal. iii. 16, &c.   [6] St. John v. 46.
[7] Ib. v. 39.   [8] Ib. iv. 22.

the statement that Moses wrote of Him, but goes on to assert that unbelief in Him was the direct result of the want of a firm belief in the principles of the Jewish law.[1] If we compare such statements with the discourse of Christ with the two disciples on their way to Emmaus,[2] or with the exclamation of St. Paul, "King Agrippa, believest thou the prophets? I know that thou believest,"[3] or his previous statement in his own defence that he "was saying none other things than those which Moses in the law, and the prophets did write,"[4] we can find no difference between them. And not only so, but we find in St. John's Gospel the germ of that spiritualizing interpretation of the Old Testament which was so largely adopted by St. Paul. As Christ reminds us in the Synoptic Gospels that the priests on the Sabbath profane the law, and are blameless, so in St. John he tells them how circumcision is performed on the Sabbath in order that the true spirit of the law may not be disobeyed.[5] But we may go farther. The lifting up of the brazen serpent in the wilderness was a type of Christ.[6] So that in the teaching of Jesus Himself we have the authority for the allegorical interpretations in which St. Paul and his school indulged—the view of the Old Testament Scriptures which saw in the Jewish history types of the Christian Sacraments,[7] in the narrative of Sarah and Hagar a foreshadowing of the Jewish and Christian covenants,[8] and in the ritual of the Law a very precise indication of the work of Atonement which was to be

---

[1] St. John. v. 45-47. [2] St. Luke xxiv. 27.
[3] Acts xxvi. 27. [4] Ib. v. 22. Cf. xxiv. 14; xxviii. 23.
[5] St. John vii. 23. [6] Ib. iii. 14. [7] 1 Cor. x. [8] Gal. iv. 21-31.

fulfilled by Christ.[1] So also St. Paul's powerful argument in the Epistle to the Galatians that the original object of circumcision was to place men in a covenant of blessing, not of condemnation,[2] finds its origin in the words "Moses gave you circumcision—not that it was of Moses but of the fathers;"[3] and the whole of the early part of the Epistle to the Romans seems to have grown out of the brief but pregnant utterance, "Did not Moses give you the law, and yet *none of you keepeth the law?*"[4] Another instance of the spiritual interpretation of the law may be found in the saying, "If ye were Abraham's children, ye would do the works of Abraham."[5] This is but a condensed enunciation of St. Paul's principle, "He is not a Jew which is one outwardly, neither is that circumcision which is outward in the flesh; but he is a Jew which is one inwardly, and circumcision is that of the heart:" a principle yet more fully unfolded in the Epistle to the Galatians, where we are told[6] that the true children of Abraham are those who possess a faith like his. Nor is the attitude of Christ towards the Jews in any way different in the fourth Gospel to what we find in the Synoptists. So far, in fact, from the antagonism to Judaism being more, it is really less pronounced in the fourth Gospel than in the other three.[7] We read

[1] Epistle to the Hebrews. [2] Gal. iii. 17, 18.
[3] St. John vii. 22.   [4] Ib. v. 19.   [5] Ib. viii. 39.
[6] Gal. iii. 7.
[7] The author of 'Supernatural Religion' remarks, as a proof of the ante-Judaic character of the fourth Gospel, that in it Jesus calls the Jews the children of the devil (viii. 44). Is this one whit stronger than the words in St. Matt. xxiii. 15, "Ye compass sea and land to make one proselyte, and when he is made, ye make him twofold more the child of hell than ye are yourselves?" Cf. v. 33, "How can yo

there of no woes denounced against the Scribes and Pharisees; no fierce apostrophes such as those which speak of them as a "generation of vipers." Opposition there is, but it is of a calmer kind; so much so, that, since the Gospel of St. John is to be got rid of at all risks, we may expect to see a school arise which rejects it on account of the unnatural tenderness it displays towards Jewish prejudices, its clear and marked Judæo-Christian bias. Schenkel and others[1] have laid great stress upon the opponents of Christ being described as a body as "the Jews," and insist upon this fact bearing witness to a date when the conflict between Judaism and Christianity had developed into a settled hostility. We are not concerned to deny the statement, for there is abundant evidence that this had already taken place before the end of the Apostolic period. It dates, no doubt, from the conversion of Cornelius. Every student of the Acts can perceive that the reception of the Gentiles into the Church excited serious jealousies even among the converts to Christianity, and was the turning point of the relations between Christianity and Judaism. It was the admission of the Gentiles which led to the persistent opposition, the "contradicting and blaspheming" of which we read as the universal result among the Jews of the teaching of St. Paul. It was this opposition which caused the Apostle, in his earliest Epistle, to accept as reasonable the well-

---

escape the judgment of hell?" Gehenna is the word in each case, not Hades. And once again, ch. xii. 34, " O generation of vipers, how can ye, *being evil*, speak good things?"

[1] 'Sketch of the Character of Jesus,' p. 25.

known unpopularity of his nation among the Gentiles.[1] There are several various readings in the later part of the Acts, which ought, it would seem, to be received into the text, in which, as in St. John, the opponents of the Gospel are spoken of as "the Jews."[2] That St. John, therefore, writing at a time when the Jews had finally rejected the mission of Christ, and had received the punishment of their sins in the destruction of their temple and its worship, should have spoken of the opposition to Christ as proceeding from the Jews in general, cannot be held to be in any way surprising. Still less can it be held to imply a strong anti-Jewish tendency. On the contrary, it is a proof of how little there is to justify such a conclusion, when we find so imposing a superstructure built upon so slender a foundation.

The manner in which the conversion of the Gentiles is spoken of is a confirmation of what has been already said. It had been an acknowledged fact, long before Christ came, that He was in some way to bring peace and happiness to the Gentile world. The utterances of the Evangelical prophet are too clear to have allowed any doubt to exist on this point; and the holy Simeon, in the infancy of our Lord, receives Him not only as the Redeemer of Israel, but as the "light" which was "to lighten the Gentiles" also. The fact was admitted:

[1] 1 Thess. ii. 15, 16. Observe here the antithesis already between "the Jews" and the Judæo-Christians.

[2] Acts xxiii. 12, according to A, B, and C. The τῶν in ch. xxvi. 7 is, however, omitted in the best MSS. They are equally divided as to the absence or presence of the article in xxvi. 4 and 21. But surely this is evidence enough that long before St. John's Gospel, if genuine, was composed, "the Jews" was a term applied to the assailants of Christianity, and that by those who were themselves Jews. Cf. ch. xviii. 12.

the only dispute was as to the mode. It was not the admission of the Gentiles into the Church, but their admission to equal privileges with the Jews which gave offence. Is there, then, any difference between the doctrine of St. John and the Synoptists on this point? Does the latter hint with St. Paul at a rejection of the Jews as a whole, and the substitution of the Gentiles in their place? Does he place in the Saviour's mouth any justification of the course which Christianity had taken, any distinct assertion of the right of the Gentiles to equality with the Jews, any prophecy of the future judgments which were to fall on the chosen people in consequence of their refusal to acknowledge Jesus as their Messiah? The very contrary is the case. It is the Synoptists who announce the calamities to fall on the Jews,[1] the approaching destruction of Jerusalem,[2] the pouring upon the head of the present generation the accumulated store of vengeance which the Jewish nation had deserved for their long course of rebellion against God.[3] We read of nothing of this kind in St. John. The destruction of Jerusalem was already a thing of the past; yet he never refers to it, or any of our Lord's prophecies referring to it. The universality of redemption is only hinted at, in the mystical and figurative language which all the Evangelists agree in ascribing to Christ. Whosoever believed on Him, Christ said, should have everlasting life.[4] If He were lifted up, He would draw all men unto Him.[5] And He further hints at this admission of all races of men into His kingdom on equal terms, in the well-known words,

[1] St. Matt. xxi. 41, 43; xxiv. 21.   [2] Ib. xxiii. 38; xxiv. 2, &c.
[3] Ib. xxiii. 35, 36.   [4] St. John iii. 15.   [5] Ib. xii. 32.

"Other sheep I have which are not of this fold : them also I must bring, and they shall hear My voice, and they shall be one flock and one shepherd."[1] Can we imagine a strong opponent of Judæo-Christianity, writing a partially fictitious narrative more than fifty years after the destruction of Jerusalem, and the consequent humiliation of the Jewish party in the Church, making no further allusion to the principles of the triumphant party than these?˙ Does it not strengthen our belief in the authenticity of the narrative, when we find precisely the kind of oracular utterances ascribed to Christ that we know Him to have been in the habit of making, dimly foreshadowing the great revolution He purposed to bring about, but leaving it for his Spirit, in after years, to guide His disciples into the fuller meaning of His words? That they were afterwards grasped in their fulness, not only by St. Paul but by St. Peter, we have sufficient evidence. It was he who said that "God was no respecter of persons, but in every nation he that feared Him, and worked righteousness, was accepted with Him,"[2] and on another occasion affirmed that God put no difference between Jews and Gentiles, purifying the hearts of all by faith.[3] But these, as well as the eager assertion of St. Paul, that there was "no difference" between Jew and Gentile,[4] that God "had made both one,"[5] that the Gentiles were "fellow-heirs," and members of "one body" with the Jews,[6] and the like, are amplifications— it may be said very considerable amplifications—of the statements recorded by St. John. There was one occa-

[1] St. John x. 16. [2] Acts x. 34, 35. [3] Ib. xv. 9.
[4] Rom. iii. 22. [5] Eph. ii. 14. [6] Ib. iii. 6.

sion, moreover, in the narrative when the writer could have given his partialities full play, if he entertained them. When the Greeks came up to Philip and desired to see Jesus, there was an admirable opportunity for placing in His mouth a discourse welcoming them as the first fruits of the Gentiles, and explaining their future equality with, if not superiority to the Jews. But of all this there is not a word. Jesus receives them with the words, "The hour is come that the Son of Man should be glorified," and then proceeds to connect this proclamation with His approaching death.[1] Nay, there is even what the late Professor Blunt would have regarded as an undesigned coincidence between the incident here recorded and the speech of our Lord given by the Synoptists, "I am not sent, but unto the lost sheep of the house of Israel." It is clear that the request of the Greeks was not acceded to by Philip without some hesitation. He did not comply with it until he had first consulted his brother Andrew, and even then they first acquaint Jesus with the fact, instead of at once introducing the Greeks into His presence. It is for the opponents of the authenticity of the Gospel to explain this hesitation. It is intelligible enough in those who had heard the Saviour's emphatic declaration just quoted, who remembered His treatment of the woman of Canaan, and who could scarcely have forgotten the scarcely less remarkable words that salvation had come to the house of Zacchæus, "for so much as he also is a son of Abraham." But on the supposition that the writer of the Gospel was a Christian of strong anti-Jewish proclivities, who invented discourses and events

[1] St. John xii. 20.

just as it suited him, the hesitation here displayed is as inexplicable as is the fact that in this place only are Gentiles represented as being brought to Christ.[1]

There is surely, then, very little authority for the statement so dogmatically insisted on, that while the Apostle St. John appears in the narratives of the other Evangelists as one possessed with strong Jewish prejudices, the author of the fourth Gospel displays prepossessions of an exactly opposite nature. Here, as elsewhere, he would seem to be in exact accordance with his fellow-labourers, keeping within, rather than pressing on beyond, the limits of their statements; precisely at one with them in the task of laying, surely and firmly, the foundations of God's Church.

We will but notice one other point in which the teaching of St. John coincides with what we find elsewhere in Holy Writ. It regards the principles of Divine service. Christ was asked by the woman of Samaria whether Gerizim or Jerusalem ought to be regarded as the centre of the religious life of the people of Palestine. He replies by announcing the near approach of a time when the devotional aspirations of men shall no longer be directed to any particular spot. They shall henceforth worship Him who is Spirit in spirit and in truth; and the true test of the acceptableness of their worship will be, not the place at which, but the disposi-

[1] St. John nowhere makes Christ marvel at a faith exceeding that of any Jew, as St. Matthew does in ch. viii. 10. Nor does St. John ever use any expressions on this subject as strong as those in St. Matt. viii. 11 : "Many shall come from the east and west, and shall sit down with Abraham, and Isaac, and Jacob, in the kingdom of heaven. But the children of the kingdom shall be cast out."

tions with which He is worshipped. Hints are given in the Synoptists that this was Christ's intention ;[1] but it is nowhere explicitly declared. Nor do we hear of it much in the earlier stages of the Church's history. St. Stephen's whole speech, however, proceeds upon the principle laid down in the discourse with the woman of Samaria. He shows, from the history of the Jewish people themselves, that the idea of a local worship, of which the temple at Jerusalem was the centre, forms no essential part of the Jewish economy. It was unknown to Abraham and the patriarchs, to Moses, to Joshua, even to David himself; and he is proceeding to explain how in the nature of things it is destined to pass away, when he breaks out into the words of sharp rebuke which arouse the indignation of his hearers, and goad them to their deed of blood. And after the first Gentile was admitted into the Christian Church, no difficulty whatever is raised about places of worship. Though the temple is still, as a matter of course, regarded by every Jew with the deepest veneration, it is no longer the place to which the thoughts of God's people are directed. Wherever even the smallest body of believers is to be found, there is the Church of God,[2] and there may prayer acceptably be offered. "I will therefore that the men pray everywhere, lifting up holy hands, without wrath and disputation,"[3] says St. Paul; and in these words we have the theory of Christian worship as foreshadowed in the saying, "Woman, believe Me, the hour cometh, when ye shall neither in this mountain,

[1] St. Matt. xviii. 19, 20.
[2] Rom. xvi. 5. "The church that is in their house." Cf. 1 Cor. xvi. 19. Col. iv. 15. Philemon 2.
[3] 1 Tim. ii. 8.

nor yet in Jerusalem, worship the Father; .... the hour cometh, and now is, when the true worshippers shall worship the Father in spirit and in truth."

It would not be uninteresting to follow out the minuter shades of agreement between the fourth Gospel and the rest of the New Testament,[1] and to show how in each case the doctrine of the New Testament may be traced to discourses of the founder of our religion recorded in the fourth Gospel. But it may be doubted whether the interest would not be felt far more keenly by those who are already convinced of the authenticity of this Gospel than by those who are in doubt on the subject. We will therefore bring our inquiry to a close here, merely premising that the subject of the coincidences between the fourth Gospel and the rest of the Gospels and Epistles is far from exhausted, and that to pursue it further would be to confirm the impression which what has been said is calculated to produce, namely, that in the Gospel bearing the name of St. John we have a faithful record of discourses of Christ not elsewhere recorded—discourses which embody the essential principles of Christianity, and which had therefore of necessity sunk deeply into the minds of the Apostles, and had formed the basis of all their subsequent teaching.

[1] Neander remarks on the unity of the doctrine of St. Paul and St. John on the subject of sin. "The new life," he says, "developed by the practical operation of faith, infers a continual mortifying of the sinful principle" in St. Paul's writings. "So likewise in John we find the same relation exhibited between being born of God, and maintaining a conflict between the world and sin." 'Planting and Training,' ii. 47. And St. John's theory of conflict between the world and the disciples of Christ is obviously the reflection of the teaching of Christ in His last discourse with His disciples, and especially of chap. xvii.

CHAPTER IV.

CONCLUSION.

WE have now subjected the doctrine of the fourth Gospel to a minute and searching analysis, and have instituted a rigorous comparison between it and the contents of other writings of the Apostolic period. We proceed to explain the bearing of what has been said upon the question of the genuineness of the Gospel. It has been affirmed that the divergencies between the conceptions of Christ in the fourth Gospel and those presented to us in the other three are so wide as to be absolutely irreconcilable. While the Synoptist writers breathe a spirit of profound reverence for Christ, they are entirely unaware of any claim to Deity on His part; whereas the fourth Gospel reflects the spirit of an era when that reverence and affection had insensibly grown into a desire to impute Divine attributes to its object. And besides this, there are not wanting in this Gospel traces of the influence of writers subsequent to the Apostolic age. Considerations like these have induced critics of admitted ingenuity and ability to pronounce confidently that the Gospel in question was a production of the second century.[1]

[1] "The teaching of Jesus in the Synoptics is almost wholly moral, but, in the fourth Gospel, it is almost wholly dogmatic. If Christianity

We are now in a position to estimate the amount of truth there is in such accusations. We have found, in the first instance, that the discordance between the four Gospels in their conceptions of Christ has been much exaggerated, and that it is more apparent than real. If the doctrine concerning Christ contained in the fourth Gospel be not expressed in the other three, the greater part of it is at least implied, and it is identical in substance, and even to a considerable extent in form, with that of St. Peter and St. Paul. Moreover, St. Mark and St. Luke, the writers of two of these three Gospels, were in constant and familiar intercourse with the two last named Apostles, were well aware of the doctrines they taught, and assisted them in disseminating them. Either, then, they intentionally suppressed in their narratives the deeper features of Christian doctrine, or they designedly lent their aid to the inculcation of doctrines which they knew to be inventions of the Apostles, and to have received no warrant whatever from Christ. On this latter supposition, the fabrication of a Gospel to give some semblance of authority to Apostolic teaching concerning Christ would amount to a necessity. But such a Gospel would surely

---

consist of the doctrines preached in the fourth Gospel, it is not too much to say that the Synoptics do not teach Christianity at all." 'Supernatural Religion,' vol. ii. p. 463. Precisely so. The Synoptists record the great bulk of the moral, the fourth Gospel the great bulk of the dogmatic teaching of Christ. In the Epistles both are found combined. What inference can we draw from this but the genuineness of all the four Gospels? It may be observed that in his notes the author of 'Supernatural Religion' has introduced us to several well-known authors in quite a new character. It is somewhat surprising to find Baur, Bretschneider, Renan and Davidson figuring as *apologists* of the Gospel of St. John. Ib. p. 464.

Conclusion. 251

have borne the name of St. Peter or St. Paul, St. Mark or St. Luke. It would have betrayed its origin by its language, and would not fail to reproduce and put into the mouth of Christ the expressions and turns of thought of the theological school which brought it into being. The Gospel ascribed to St. John, on the contrary, is admitted on all hands to display a remarkable originality of conception and expression. It is entirely free from any trace of Pauline or Petrine influence. Even its strongest opponents have not yet ventured to suggest that it was written for the purpose of bridging the chasm—though most unquestionably it *does* bridge the chasm—between St. Peter, St. Paul, and the earlier biographies of Christ. As to the supposed indications of familiarity with the systems of Valentinus or Basilides, they have disappeared entirely upon examination. Certain words are to be found in each; but these words are of frequent occurrence in the Old Testament Scriptures, and the first indications of their being employed in a new sense are to be found, not in St. John, but in the writings of the Gnostics. In all other respects the writer of the fourth Gospel is totally ignorant of the writings of either Basilides or Valentinus, and emphatically opposed to those adumbrations of their ideas which had existed during the lifetime of St. John.

But the comparison we have instituted has produced further results. Not only is the Gospel free from all signs of Valentinian and Basilidian, Pauline and Petrine influences, but the evidence leads us to precisely the opposite conclusion. Not only Valentinus and Basilides, Ignatius and Justin Martyr, but St. Paul and St. Peter also, are indebted for their theological system to the principles laid down in the Gospel of St. John. Not only do we come continually across passages in their Epistles which we can trace to no other source than discourses of Christ recorded in the fourth Gospel, but all the essential features of their teaching, if it be, as they declare, from Christ, are found in the fourth of the Evangelical narratives, and it alone. It will hardly be contended that the theological system of St. Peter and St. Paul was derived from the Synoptic Gospels, since it is the absence from them of the special doctrines common to those Apostles and St. John which is the sole article in the indictment which has been framed against the Gospel of the latter. If, therefore, what St. John gives us as the discourses of Christ were never uttered, then the whole theological system, not only of the Fathers of the second century, but of St. Peter and St. Paul also, is absolutely unauthorized. There is scarcely a word in their Epistles which is not an invention of their own. For of the purely moral teaching of the Synoptists they knew nothing. There is scarcely a moral precept in their writings which has not a dogmatic basis, and that basis the dogma of the fourth Gospel. On the hypothesis that it is a genuine Gospel, all is natural and reasonable. We trace the doctrine of the Apostles to its source, and that source the words of Christ. Those words have no appearance of being after-thoughts, put into His mouth to explain the bold assertions of His Apostles; for, without the least need of wresting or straining, they present themselves to us as the foundation upon which the Apostolic superstructure was built. But on the opposite hypothesis we are at once plunged into a very ocean of

Conclusion. 253

difficulties. We cannot hold St. Paul to be the inventor of the dogmatic system of Christianity, because we find it in St. Peter also. We cannot say that the fourth Gospel borrowed its theological system from the Epistles of St. Paul and St. Peter; for what instance is there of a doctrinal system ever having been borrowed without its terminology? We cannot contend that the fourth Gospel borrowed its terminology from the writings of St. Peter and St. Paul, because it has been shown that a critical examination of their contents leads us to a precisely opposite conclusion. We cannot account for the fact that St. John's Gospel, if it be indeed of post-Apostolic times, so strangely and markedly avoids the expressions which are familiar to us in the writings of the Apostles and their immediate successors. Nor can we explain either the origin of the theology of St. Peter and St. Paul, or its universal acceptance at once by the Christian Church. To what conclusion, then, are we driven? Once more, that in the fourth Gospel we have a genuine record of the doctrinal teaching of Jesus Christ. If St. John's Gospel were spurious, it might with reason be remarked what a chasm existed between the Christ of history and the Christ of theology. It would be necessary to explain how the one could develop into the other without the violent convulsions such an abnormal development would require. The assumption of two distinct theological schools, which this hypothesis demands, rests, as we observed at the outset, upon no historical basis. It is for those who hold it to explain how one of these schools has vanished from sight, and left not a trace behind, as well as to point out to us the steps of the process by which the man highly gifted, highly favoured by his Father, endowed with many exquisite mental and moral gifts, the inaugurator of a new and improved system of religion and morals, grew into the Word made flesh, the subtle and all-pervading principle which unites each of us to the other, and all to God.

Historical evidence on these points there is none, and we may well hesitate before we substitute for facts the assumptions of the critics. And it is to be observed that they give us nothing but assumptions. They rest their case upon the barest surmises, and there is nothing which amounts even to the shadow of a proof. But we have before observed[1] that nothing but the most unequivocal demonstration would be sufficient to establish their point, in the absence of historical evidence in its favour. In view of the utter failure, therefore, of the attempts to explain the phenomena presented by the fourth Gospel on the hypothesis of its being a forgery, we may reasonably be contented with a simpler explanation, which does violence neither to criticism nor history. That explanation regards St. John's Gospel as an authentic biography of Christ, written by a disciple whom He honoured by a strong and particular affection, and who had retained the main features of His dogmatic teaching with special minuteness. It regards the divergencies between the Evangelists as the result of the way in which the doctrine of Christ was preached to the world. While the earlier Evangelists sought to win men by a portraiture of the human character of Christ and the beauty of His ethical teaching, St. John wished to place on record the main features of His spi-

[1] Above, p. 14.

ritual system—a work which had not been necessary so long as there were those living to whom He had imparted it. St. John's Gospel explains what would otherwise have been inexplicable, namely, the doctrine preached by the Apostles, who certainly were not content with impressing the beauty of Christ's character, nor the perfection of His example, upon their hearers. Such a Gospel is necessary to account for the fact that a system of regeneration, redemption, justification, and a divine indwelling in the soul,[1] taught, beyond a doubt, in the infancy of the Church, rested upon Christ as its sole foundation. Remove the Gospel of St. John, and you strike at the root of the theology of the New Testament; nay, you reduce the whole history of the Christian religion to a chaos. Without the aid of his Gospel it is impossible to trace the origin and development of Christianity. At the same time that Apostles and their disciples are composing biographies of Christ, those very Apostles we find preaching doctrines which, on the supposition that the theology of the fourth Gospel is incompatible with that of the other three, are absolutely and irreconcilably at variance with the narratives to which their *imprimatur* is desired and obtained. No one protests, no one dissents, so far as we have history to guide us; nay, no one even asks the reason for a course so unusual. No difficulties are started, not even by the opponents of the faith, at least during the Apostles' lifetime, nor for long after their death, nor in any single instance are those opponents led by the difficulties they do find to the natural and obvious course of denying the authority of all the New Testament

[1] See above, p. 14.

save the Synoptic Gospels, and perhaps the Epistle of St. James. And what is most incredible of all, not a single Apostle displays even the least anxiety to offer any explanation or apology for the fact, of which he could not but be aware, that he was presenting to the world as Christ's a doctrine which Christ Himself never preached, and which He would never have authorized any one of His disciples to preach. Whatever, then, may be the true explanation of the divergencies between the first three Gospels and the fourth, it seems plain enough that it is not to be found in denying the genuineness of the latter. An honest and careful comparison of its contents with the rest of the New Testament makes such a conclusion an impossibility. No book can be detached from the Canon of Scripture with less safety than the Gospel of St. John. No book is so essential to a proper account of the historical development of Christianity. In fact, the Synoptists and St. John, St. John and St. Paul, St. Paul and St. Peter, St. Peter and St. James, St. James and the Synoptists again, constitute the whole circle of revealed truth. They form links in a chain which can never be dissevered; and if any one of those links be more absolutely necessary to the integrity of the whole than any other, that link is the Gospel according to St. John.

APPENDIX I.

ON GRACE.

I HAVE more than once intimated my conviction that the doctrine of grace, as a kind of assistance rendered by God to man, has somewhat tended to throw the Scriptural doctrine of a Divine indwelling into the background, and that the prominence given to grace owes its origin in some measure to the fact that the Latin theologians were hampered in their expositions of Scripture by their use of a Latin version of the New Testament rather than the original. I do not dispute that St. Augustine, for instance, understood Greek, but it does not seem that he could follow the original with the freedom and accuracy of the Greek Fathers. Hence his theology became insensibly coloured by a mode of conception in some measure alien from the tone of the Scriptures themselves. His theory of grace was unquestionably calculated to introduce a *tertium quid* between man and the Persons of the Holy Trinity, which made the relations of God and man less intimate than they were conceived to be by St. John and St. Paul.[1] This state of things did not originate with him. Tertullian, though he understood Greek, as the fact that three treatises, not now extant, were composed by him in Greek,

[1] Neander ('Hist. of Christian Dogmatics,' Bohn's Trans. p. 359) describes St. Augustine's idea of grace as "a sort of enabling influence of God's power, not closely identified with the communication of the human life of Christ."

proves,[1] laid more stress on grace than did Clement or Origen.[2] But in St. Augustine the doctrine of grace becomes defined. Grace is throughout the book 'De Correptione et Gratiâ' spoken of as the help of God.[3] It is opposed to free-will,[4] and to nature.[5] It is distinguished from law.[6] It is that by which nature is freed and regulated.[7] Faith itself is among its gifts.[8] It not only assists the just, but justifies the impious.[9] In fact, even in the work of justification, instead of bearing its original signification of favour and kindness, as opposed to debt or the claims of human merit, it has become converted into a kind of power enabling a man to receive that favour. Hence we begin to hear of prevenient grace, co-operating grace, and all the theological formulæ which have been so fruitful a source of controversy in later times. Hence in process of time we come to grace *ex congruo*, and *ex condigno*, phrases which have played so conspicuous a part in the disputes as to the relative claims of Divine grace and human merit. For when once God's favour had been formulated into a quality or power, there was no retracing the steps which had been taken. Aquinas taught the accepted doctrine of grace with his usual clearness and ability. It was an infusion of grace

[1] See 'De Virg.,' vol. i. 1; 'De Baptismo,' 15; 'De Coronâ Militum,' 6.

[2] Tertullian ('De Animâ,' 21) gives the first indications of the antithesis between nature and grace, which has since become a theological commonplace.

[3] Adjutorium, or auxilium Dei. Compare also 'Enchirid. ad Laur.,' 28; 'Contr. Julian.,' vi. 15.

[4] "Pelagiani liberum sic asserunt voluntatis arbitrium ut gratiæ Dei non relinquant locum." 'Retract.,' i. 8.

[5] 'De Patientiâ,' *passim*.

[6] "Distinguenda est Lex et Gratia. Lex jubere novit, Gratia juvare." 'Ad Innocent.,' 5.

[7] "Librum ergo quo Pelagio respondi, defendens gratiam, non contra naturam, sed per quem natura liberatur et regitur, de Naturâ et Gratiâ nuncupavi." 'Retract.,' ii. 42.

[8] 'Ad Simpl.,' I. ii. 7.   [9] 'De Pat.,' xx. 4.

by which man was justified,[1] rather than of the Divine nature itself. He divided grace into two kinds, prevenient and co-operating grace, of which the one must be sought for to be liberated from sin and accepted with God, the other in order to acquire perseverance in good works.[2] And so matters went on until the Reformation. Even the opponents of the Thomists did but oppose them with subtleties of their own, not with the true principles of Holy Scripture. But it is surprising to those who know how much influence St. Augustine had over the minds of Luther and the Reformers generally, and upon the whole spirit of theology up to our own time, to observe how seldom the word grace occurs in the Confessions of Faith of the Reformed bodies. In our own Church, as we know, there was an article on grace in the Prayer Book of 1552, but it was withdrawn in 1571.[3] The Helvetic Confession, it is true, in the article on Predestination, speaks of "the grace of predestination and free election." But, though several of the Confessions contain articles on such heads as "how the new obedience of the Christian is pleasing to God," they say but little of "grace" in the received theological acceptation of the term. Was it that the revived study of the New Testament had suggested difficulties to their minds which they were sufficiently enlightened to avoid, but not to discuss? It would seem nearly certain that this was the case. The Würtemberg Confession speaks of the "grace and favour of God."[4] The Saxon Confession, in an *obiter dictum*, explains "under grace" to mean "reconciled and accepted unto grace," *i.e.*, favour. And in the article on good works, not one word is said, as would almost certainly be said in any modern

---

[1] "Ad infusionem gratiæ qua homo justificatur." 'Lect. iii. on Ep. to Rom.,' c. 9.
[2] 'Lect. i. on 2nd Cor.,' c. 6.
[3] It is worthy of remark that in the 42 Articles the ordinary language is corrected. We read of "grace, or the Holy Spirit which is given by it."
[4] 'De Prædestinatione.'

sermon, about their being done "by the grace of God," but they are ascribed to Christ, working by His Holy Spirit, who is called the Spirit of Grace, because what He does in us is done "that we may be in grace."[1] The Scriptures, be it remembered, never define χάρις as assistance, nor is there a single passage in the New Testament where the translation "favour" would be inadmissible. We find much the same phenomenon when we turn to the Greek Fathers. As an instance, let us take St. Cyril's treatise on Worship in Spirit and in Truth, in which he deals with such topics as man's fall, conversion, justification, sanctification, and the like. The word χάρις is seldom used. St. Cyril seems to go out of his way sometimes to use ἡμερότης instead. And when χάρις does occur, it is not in the sense of assistance. His doctrine of redemption and regeneration is that we see the formation afresh of human nature in Christ and its restoration unto its old condition; the metamorphosis, as it were, into what it was in Adam, when it had not lost its sanctity and glory from above.[2] So he speaks of the grace by which we are justified, and the grace of baptism.[3] But he makes very little use of the term, and when he does use it, is accustomed to do so in the sense of a favour conferred by God rather than in the sense assigned to it by the Latin Fathers. St. Chrysostom, too, deals in a similar manner with the word grace. As an instance, we may quote a passage from his 9th Homily on the Epistle to the Romans. Commenting on ch. v. 2, he says, "What grace, tell me? That we should be *esteemed worthy of the knowledge of God*, that we should be freed from error, that we should comprehend the truth, that we should attain to all the blessings which baptism confers ... for *when he says grace, he plainly means all we at present receive.*"

[1] "Quomodo fieri possint bona opera."
[2] 'De Adoratione Spiritu et Veritate,' lib. ii.
[3] In the Commentary on Isaiah, *passim*.

APPENDIX II.

ON JUSTIFICATION.

It is not my intention in this and the previous Appendix to do more than offer some illustrations of the remarks I have made in the text, in order that I may escape the reproach of having made assertions entirely without foundation. It may be mentioned in reference to justification that while its original classical sense is "to make righteous," in the great majority of passages in which the verb δικαιόω appears in the Septuagint it means to declare, or make manifest, a righteousness which already exists. In many of the others, while it possibly may have the forensic sense of acquittal, or reckoning one righteous who is not so, such is not the only possible rendering. In one passage, Is. xlv. 26, it has precisely the same force as in the Epistle to the Romans. In Micah vii. 9, it seems to mean doing justice. We have also to remember that in most cases it is a rendering of the Hebrew word הִצְדִּיק; and, that although this word unquestionably may mean to acquit, as, for instance, in Exod. xxiii. 7, its original signification is clearly "to make righteous." In Gen. xxxviii. 26, δικαιόω is used to translate צָדְקָה מִמֶּנִּי "she is more righteous than I." In xliv. 16, Judah uses the Hebrew word in the sense of "to clear oneself." So in 1 Kings viii. 32, it is used in the sense of pronouncing that holy which is already so, "to declare the righteousness of the righteous, to give him according to his righteousness." Consequently, without making ourselves responsible for the Tridentine exposition of the doctrine of justification,[1] we may contend, with some show of reason, that imparted as well as imputed righteousness forms a part of the Apostolic teaching, and that it is quite as possible that righteousness may be imputed because it is imparted as the converse. The Greek Fathers understood the use of the word perhaps as well as any other set of men, and St. Chrysostom explains it in his Homilies on the Romans as the equivalent of δικαίους ποιεῖν. This is his exposition of the crucial passage in Rom. iii. 24. "What is the manifestation of righteousness?" he asks. It is like a manifestation of wealth: not only that He Himself is rich, but He would make others rich. And of life: not only that He Himself should be alive, but that He should vivify the dead. And of power: not only that He should be powerful, but should give power to the weak. So is the manifestation of righteousness; not merely that He should be righteous, but that others, who were thoroughly corrupt in wickedness, *He should make immediately righteous*" (δικαίους ποιεῖν). After this there can be little doubt what St. Chrysostom's doctrine of justification was. But we may subjoin one or two more passages from his Homilies on the Romans. In Hom. 10, on ch. v. 16, he says that "Righteousness is more than life, for it is the root of life;" and again, "Not only were the sins taken away, *but righteousness also was given.*" Whence Neander (Ch. Hist., vol. iv., sec. 4) tells us that Chrysostom understood by justification " not merely forgiveness of sins, but also the communication of that more exalted dignity and worth which far transcended the powers of the limited finite nature by means of the fellowship of life with Christ." St. Cyril's exposition of the

[1] The definition of Justification by the Council of Trent represents it to be "not only remission of sins, but also sanctification, and the renovation of the inner man by a voluntary reception of grace." And again, "we are not merely reputed, but are just, receiving righteousness (justitia) into ourselves." Conc. Trid. 'De Justificatione,' cap. 7.

Johannean differs little from St. Chrysostom's exposition of the Pauline doctrine of an imparted righteousness. As a specimen of many similar passages we may take his remarks in his 5th book on St. John, c. 2. After citing Eph. iii. 5, he goes on, "If, then, we are all embodied (σύσσωμοι) into each other in Christ, and not merely into each other, but into Him, Who plainly came to be in us through His own flesh, is it not now clear that we all are one thing both in one another and in Christ? For Christ is the bond of unity, being Himself God and man." And a little above he represents Christ as saying, "I made you partakers of the Divine nature, making My Spirit dwell in you; for in you is Christ by the Spirit, converting that which by nature is corruptible into incorruptibility, and translating that which is liable to death into that which has no such liability."

APPENDIX III.

ON THE TRACES OF JOHANNEAN THEOLOGY IN THE SECOND CENTURY.

THE earliest writer after the Apostles, if, indeed, his Epistle was not even of the same date as the Apocalypse, was Clement of Rome. That there should be but few signs of his acquaintance with St. John's Gospel would be by no means surprising, supposing that it had not been published when he wrote. But even in his pages there are not wanting indications that the tradition of Christ's words, recorded in the fourth Gospel, had reached him. The opening words of ch. 49 bear a striking resemblance to those of our Lord recorded by St. John. "He who hath love in Christ let him keep the things proclaimed by Christ;" "through the love which He had to us, Jesus Christ our Lord gave His blood for us; and His flesh for our flesh, and His life for our lives," are expressions which bear at least a singular resemblance to such sayings as "If ye love Me, keep My commandments:" "Greater love hath no man than this, that he lay down his life for his friends;" "My flesh, which I will give for the life of the world;" "I lay down My life for the sheep." I have before intimated my opinion that the disconnected and unfinished compositions which we find in the Syriac could only be regarded as the genuine Epistles of Ignatius by those who desired for some reason to evade the testimony of the shorter Greek version.[1] But of course the testi-

[1] I owe to Professor Lightfoot's papers in the 'Contemporary Review' the knowledge of a confirmation of this opinion in the fact that

mony of that version can only be quoted with the reservation that its authenticity is denied by many critics of ability and learning. Subject to that reservation, however, we may venture to cite some passages from the Greek recension which are, however, but specimens of many more which could be adduced to prove that the doctrine supposed to be peculiar to the fourth Gospel was at least known to Ignatius. Such an instance we have in the 5th chapter of the Epistle to the Ephesians, where they are spoken of as "blended together, as the church is in Jesus Christ, and He in the Father, that all might be harmonious in unity." This can be hardly any other than a quotation from St. John xvii., for if not, it is difficult to assign its doctrinal spirit to any other source. So the declaration in ch. 9, that Christians were θεοφόροι and χριστοφόροι, would seem to imply a similar reference. In ch. 10 we have a plain allusion to the words, "Abide in Me and I in you;" where the disciples are exhorted to abide (μένειν) in Jesus Christ. The words "only let us be found in Jesus Christ that we may live the true (ἀληθινός) life" (ch. 11), are again highly suggestive of the influence of the fourth Gospel. When Jesus Christ is called the ἀρχὴ ζωῆς in ch. 14 again suggests Johannean ideas. And if the reference to the Lord "dwelling in us," in ch. 15, be claimed as the heritage left to the church by St. Paul, at least let us remember first that it disposes of the theory that the doctrine was invented by the author of the fourth Gospel; and next, that it only removes the difficulty a step farther, and requires us to discover whence St. Paul derived it. We might also ask where St. Ignatius obtained the expression ἄρχων τοῦ αἰῶνος τούτου in ch. xix. from,[1] and this question is the more important inasmuch as this passage is found

an Armenian version of these Epistles has been brought to light which is in substantial accordance with the Greek version.

[1] The same expression is found in the Epistles to the Romans and Philadelphians.

in the Syriac, and its genuineness will therefore not be contested. The expression is used by St. Paul of the human rulers of this world; by St. John, only with the substitution of κόσμος for αἰών, as referring to the devil. The Epistle to the Magnesians again speaks of union "in the flesh and blood of Jesus Christ our continual life," which is Johannean theology, and no other. Jesus Christ is said to "have pleased Him who sent Him in all things"—a manifest quotation of St. John viii. 29. Nor is there any need, with Lardner, to suppose the passage which speaks of Christ as the λόγος ἀΐδιος to be an interpolation.[1] The remarkable passage in the Epistle to the Romans, cap. 7, must not be omitted, where Ignatius unmistakably refers to St. John vi. I should, perhaps, add that it is not so much the verbal and historical as the theological evidence that I would lay stress upon. The theology is Johannean pure and simple, the phraseology a mixture of St. John and St. Paul. Ignatius writes, "I desire the bread of God, the heavenly bread, the bread of life, which is the flesh of our Lord Jesus Christ who came in the last times of the seed of David and Abraham; and I desire the drink of God, His blood, which is love uncorrupted and endless life."[2] To make the reference more

---

[1] See the whole question discussed by Cotelerius and Vossius *in loc*.
[2] It will not surprise us to find that the author of 'Supernatural Religion,' with Scholten, finds that "nothing can be proved" by this "analogy," because St. John says πόσις and Ignatius πόμα, St. John αἰώνιος and Ignatius ἀέννιος ; and because there is a reference to Jesus "being born of the seed of David and Abraham." It might be sufficient to reply to the last argument, if it can be called one, that Ignatius was not aware of any reason why he should not combine passages from St. John and St. Paul, any more than any Christian of modern times. And if slight divergences in phraseology are to have any weight, they must be allowed to have weight on both sides of the question. Thus the argument that the passage refers to the institution of the Lord's Supper as recorded by the Synoptists, and to the eating bread and drinking wine in the kingdom of God is inadmissible on the writer's own principles. In the Synoptists, Christ says "body" and not "flesh," He speaks of "eating bread and drinking wine."

pointed, Ignatius uses just before the expression "living water" (ὕδωρ ζῶν), which occurs in the fourth chapter of the same gospel. In the Epistle to the Philadelphians Christ is spoken of as the door (ch. 9), and there is a manifest quotation of St. John iii. 8, " the spirit (translated " wind " in our version) bloweth where it listeth and thou hearest the sound thereof, but canst not tell whence it cometh and whither it goeth."[1] Even the short Epistle of Polycarp yields us at least one quotation from St. John's Epistle: " Whosoever confesseth not that Jesus Christ is come in the flesh, is anti-Christ."[2] But we are told that this Epistle, too, is not genuine. It must be confessed that it is somewhat difficult to establish the genuineness of any book whatever, if the genuineness of every book which makes the slightest allusion to it is questioned, down to the time to which it is desired to assign it. Father Hardouin, we know, contended that Virgil, Lucretius, Livy, and even Aristotle, were the productions of

(οὐ μὴ πίω; ὅταν αὐτὸ πίνω), and He mentions the kingdom of God. Ignatius uses the word πόμα, and says nothing about the kingdom of God. Consequently, on the writer's own showing, Ignatius had never seen the Synoptic narratives, and knew nothing about them, while the obvious quotations "Bread of God," "Bread of Life," "Flesh of Christ," and the allusion to the bread which came down from heaven, stamp the passage as derived from St. John. We may also be allowed to notice the calm assumption in regard to a much controverted question, by which the author speaks of the above passage as occurring in "the pseudo-Ignatius." And he seems quite unaware of the fact that the most important portions of the passage are found in the Syriac. It may be remarked that Ignatius, "chained to ten leopards" (Ept. Rom. c. 5), was not very likely to have access to a library. His citations from memory are therefore the more easily explained. In fact the cumbrous nature of the books of those days, and the difficulty of their multiplication, may often have compelled the earliest Fathers to trust to their memories.

[1] Ch. vii. " The Spirit is not deceived, being from God, for it knoweth whence it cometh and whither it goeth, and proveth the secret things." In this last passage, as the Greek shows, there is also a reference to St. John xvi. 8.

[2] Ch. vii.

the monks of the Middle Ages; and by such a method as this his position would have been quite unassailable.

The Epistle to Diognetus, long ascribed to Justin Martyr, but containing allusions to the condition of Christians which would lead us to place it at the beginning of the second century, contains manifest quotations from St. John. He says that "God fixed the truth and His holy and incomprehensible Word in man and confirmed Him in their hearts:" and he adds that this was "no angel nor Archon, but the architect and framer of every thing, by whom He created the heavens and shut up the sea in its own boundaries."[1] He sent Him "not as a judge, but as one who loved mankind."[2] And the author speaks of Christians as being "in the world, but not of it."[3]

I pass over the Shepherd of Hermas, because it can hardly be regarded as having been published earlier than the middle of the second century. I proceed, therefore, to Justin Martyr. This writer, who was martyred about the same time as Polycarp, that is to say, about the year 166, not only speaks continually of Christ as the Word, but quotes the declaration of Christ recorded by St. John, "Except ye be born again, ye shall not enter the kingdom of heaven."[4] Now if St. John's Gospel be not earlier than the middle of the century, Justin must have become a convert before it appeared, for he was a voluminous writer, and required some little time to mature his many productions. It must be admitted, therefore, that the discourse to Nicodemus, with its specially Johannean theology, was one of the "authentic traditions" to which the writer of the fourth Gospel had access. Again, he tells us that Christ "became flesh," "had flesh and blood for our salvation," "and that by His flesh and blood ours are nourished."[5] And that we were taught that we thus became the flesh and blood of Christ. Therefore the

[1] Ch. vii. [2] Ib. vii. [3] Ib. vi.
[4] 1st Apology, c. 61. [5] Ib. c. 66.

peculiarly Johannean doctrine of chapter vi. was an accepted Christian tradition before the fourth Gospel was written, if we are to accept the theory of its spuriousness. But then this very doctrine is the ground on which it is pronounced spurious. Reasoning like this, it must be confessed, has all the signs which belong to the well-known "vicious circle." It may be further remarked that Justin at least would hardly be inclined to look with favour upon a biography of Christ which was composed to mediate between Gnosticism and the Church. In his dialogue with Trypho he calls the Valentinians and Basilidians, with others, "blasphemers, atheists, impious, unrighteous, and sinful,"[1] and remarks on the fact that each of them were called, not after Christ, but after the originator of their doctrines. Further information on this subject will be found in Lardner, Westcott on the Canon, and Tischendorf on the date of the Gospels. I have here only noted down what has occurred to me on this point in the course of my own reading.

Since writing the above, I have made acquaintance with the treatise bearing the title 'Supernatural Religion,' and have admired the remarkable passage in which its writer deals with Justin Martyr's quotations from St. John. He makes but a feeble attempt to deny the substantial identity of the doctrine contained in Justin's first Apology with that of St. John iii. 5. He does not discuss the source of the doctrine of regeneration, which does not appear in any other extant record of the words of Christ. But he resorts to verbal quibbles of the minutest kind, as though it were not the universal custom of the earlier Fathers to quote from memory. Justin, forsooth, *omits the* "*Verily, verily.*" He has ἂν μὴ ἀναγεννηθῆτε instead of ἐὰν μή τις γεννηθῇ ἄνωθεν. He has βασιλεία τῶν οὐρανῶν instead of τοῦ θεοῦ, and the like. We must perforce, again, accept the reading of the Codex Sinaiticus because

[1] C. 35.

it uses the word which Justin and the other MSS. do *not* use. ἄνωθεν cannot, our author decides *ex cathedrâ*, be translated "again," though Tischendorf (and not a few others) declare that it can, for has not the Peshito Syriac, which could hardly, by the way, furnish its readers with *both* renderings, even if it conceived them both to be admissible, decided on the former? It might have been imagined that to be born from above was in some sense a second birth; and there is some evidence in the words of Nicodemus that he regarded it as such. But no; Justin says ἀναγεννηθῆτε, and St. John does not; and there are sundry other differences of expression, all, it is true, presenting precisely the same ideas to the mind. But the author of 'Supernatural Religion' is resolved that Justin Martyr shall never have seen St. John's Gospel, and St. John's Gospel, therefore, he never did see. "Justin speaks simply of regeneration by baptism; the fourth Gospel" (which for about 1800, or at least 1700, years has been supposed to do the same) "indicates a later development of the doctrine by spiritualising the idea."[1] It might be asked what regeneration by baptism was, apart from its spiritual idea, or who ever believed in "regeneration through the water" without a birth "from above and of the Spirit." But it would be useless to pursue further an argument with a writer who deals with his authorities, like a barrister with opposing testimony in a court of justice, and with equal probability of convincing an impartial jury. Thus he argues that Justin says that Christ became ἄνθρωπος, not σάρξ, though the

[1] Dr. Keim is of precisely the opposite opinion. Justin, he thinks, as a writer of no eloquence, and of moderate mental power, could not have been in any way the source of the ideas contained in the fourth Gospel; and it is, moreover, impossible to dispute the signs of a far more advanced development in his writings: 'Jesus of Nazareth,' vol. i. p. 187. Before the fourth Gospel succumbs to the assaults of its adversaries, it will be necessary for them to be a little more of one mind. Weizsäcker, moreover, in the opinion of Dr. Keim, has shown that Justin Martyr has derived his ideas from the fourth Gospel.

Nicene Creed does the same; and that when he does say that Christ became flesh he does not say σὰρξ ἐγένετο, but σαρκοποιηθείς. See 'Supernatural Religion,' vol. ii., pt. 3 ch. i. This is but a specimen of the author's whole method of dealing with external evidence. His analysis of the Clementines is marked by the same ingenious hair-splitting, which would be profoundly interesting and amusing in a case of Nisi Prius, but which may, perhaps, be a little out of place when dealing with questions which affect the deepest convictions of millions of his fellow-creatures. The climax of the audacity of this intrepid writer is when, in spite of what he finds or ought to have found in Justin, Irenæus, Hippolytus, and a host of others, he identifies the Simon of the Clementines with St. Paul, regardless, too, of the fact that St. Paul is honoured with separate mention, not altogether complimentary, in that singular romance.[1] It is, perhaps, not altogether needless to remark that the above observations were penned before Canon Lightfoot's masterly papers in the 'Contemporary Review' had reached the writer. Several almost verbal coincidences occur between them and these observations. I may, perhaps, be allowed to conclude this brief notice of the external testimony with the words of Canon Rawlinson in 'Aids to Faith' on the subject. He remarks (pp. 241, 242), "Authorship generally is mere matter of notoriety, and usually the best evidence we have for it beyond common repute is the declaration of some writer, later by two or three centuries, that the person to whom a given work is assigned, composed a book answering in its subject and general character to the one which we find passing under his name." So that the canons of criticism laid down with regard to the New Testament, would, if applied generally, entirely deprive us of the materials of history.

[1] 'Recognitions,' i. 70.

APPENDIX IV.

ON THE CONNECTION BETWEEN ST. JOHN'S GOSPEL AND THE OLD TESTAMENT.

IT is admitted on all hands that our Lord in His teaching fully exemplified His own description of "the scribe which is instructed unto the kingdom of heaven," who, like "a man that is an householder, bringeth out of his treasure things new and old." The Lord's Prayer, we are told, is a *cento* of Rabbinical petitions, yet so combined by Infinite Wisdom as to present us with the perfection of all possible prayer, embracing every kind of petition which man could possibly desire to offer, and in precisely the order which should serve best to teach us our relations to God, to one another, and to our own needs. The same character is displayed in the discourses of Jesus recorded by St. John. They convey the new wine to us in the old bottles—the ideas of the new revelation in the phraseology of the old —not in the sense in which Jesus repudiated such a policy in St. Matt. ix. 17, but in the spirit of His saying, "A new commandment give I unto you, that ye love one another"—new in its extent and intensity,[1] but, as His Apostle reminds us, old in fact and form.[2] The Synoptic Gospels are said to be those which display the Jewish spirit most clearly. The very reverse is the fact. No Gospel is so strongly interpenetrated by Jewish ideas as that of St. John. He who "was not sent but unto the lost sheep of the house of Israel," who always suited His dis-

---
[1] St. John xiii. 34.   [2] Levit. xix. 18. 1 John ii. 7; iii. 11.

courses to the temper of those to whom they were addressed, adopts the imagery of the Old Testament when he desires to impart His doctrine. We proceed to give some instances of this fact. We have seen that Life, Light, Grace, Truth, Peace, Righteousness, Pleroma, and the like are said to be Gnostic ideas. We will now endeavour to show of how completely Hebrew an origin they are.

1. *God is Life* (the Gnostic *Zoe*).—This is not only attributed to God when He created the world, and breathed the breath of Life into man's nostrils, nor when He keeps the tree of Life under His care, but it is a phrase of continual occurrence in the Prophets and Psalms. Thus we read, "Thou wilt show me the path of Life," Ps. xvi. 11. "In His favour is Life," xxx. 5. "With Thee is the fountain of Life, and in Thy Light shall we see light," xxxvi. 9. God "promises His blessing and Life for evermore," Ps. cxxxiii. 3. So in the book of Job, "Thou hast granted me Life and mercy," Job x. 12. Wisdom (in Prov. iii. 18) is "a tree of Life to them that lay hold of her," and wisdom and discretion are "Life to the soul and Grace to the neck," Ib. ver. 22. "The commandment is a lamp (λύχνος, LXX.), the law is Light, and reproofs are the way of Life," Ib. vi. 23. Cf. St. John v. 35; xiv. 6. He who "findeth Wisdom findeth Life, and shall obtain favour of the Lord," Ib. viii. 35. "The mouth of the righteous is a fountain (πηγή, LXX.) of Life," Ib. x. 11, St. John iv. 14. "The fruit of the righteous is a tree of Life," Ib. xi. 30. Cf. St. John xv. "In the way of Righteousness is Life," Ib. xii. 28. "The fear of the Lord is a fountain of Life," Ib. xiv. 27. "He that followeth after Righteousness and mercy shall find Life, Righteousness and glory," Ib. xxi. 21. "Thus saith the Lord, I set before you the way of Life," Jer. xxi. 8. See also Prov. iv. 22; xiii. 12; xv. 24: xxii. 4.

2. *Light.*—Beside the passages above cited, where Life and Light are combined, we find such phrases as the "Light

of Thy countenance," Ps. iv. 6; xliv. 3; lxxxix. 15; xc. 8. The last but one of these passages is remarkable for its combination of "Johannean"—may we not say Gnostic —ideas. "Righteousness and judgment are the habitation of Thy throne, mercy and Truth go before Thy face. How blessed are the people who know the joyous cry; in the Light of Thy countenance, O Lord, shall they walk." We read in Job xxxiii. 28, "My life shall see the Light," or "with the Light;" and again in v. 30, of being "enlightened with the Light of the living." The whole passage is very suggestive of the theology of the fourth Gospel. In it Elihu speaks of a Messenger to show man his uprightness (cf. St. John xvi. 8, 14, 15), of deliverance from destruction (cf. St. John iii. 16), of the "grace" God shows to the Messenger, of his righteousness which returns to man, of the return of man to the days of his youth, when his flesh shall ·be fresher than a child's (cf. St. John iii. 3–5), and of the joy with which man shall see God's face (cf. St. John xvi. 22). So God is "Light and Salvation," Ps. xxvii. 1. "His Word is Light to our paths," Ps. cxix. 105. See also Ps. lvi. 13; cxviii. 27; cxix. 130. Isaiah expresses himself in precisely the language of St. John. "The people that walked in darkness saw a great light, and they who dwelt in the land of the shadow of death, upon them hath the Light shined," Is. ix. 2. Judgment is to be "a light of the people," Ib. li. 4. He calls the people to arise, "for their light is come;" and the imagery of darkness and light is continued throughout the passage, Ib. lx. 1, 2, 3, 19, 20. Nor should we omit to notice the correspondence of v. 21 with many passages in St. John's Gospel: "Thy people also *shall be all righteous*: they shall inherit the land for ever, a *branch* of my planting, a *work* of my hands, that I may be *glorified*," (or that they may be glorified.) See also v. 20; Dan. ii. 22; Hos. vi. 5; Mic. vii. 9.

3. *Truth* (the Gnostic *Aletheia*).—God is asked to "send out His Light and His Truth," Ps. xliii. 3. God did not

deprive Abraham "of His mercy and Truth," Gen. xxiv. 27. Jacob is unworthy of the "least of all the mercies and of the Truth which God had shewed him," Ib. xxxii. 10. God proclaims Himself to be "abundant in goodness and Truth," Ex. xxxiv. 6, as well as merciful and gracious. Cf. "Thou hast redeemed me, O Lord, thou God of Truth," Ps. xxxi. 5; "God shall send forth His mercy and Truth," Ps. lvii. 3; "Thou, O Lord, art a compassionate and gracious God, slow to anger, and great in goodness and Truth," Ps. lxxxvi. 15;[1] "Truth shall spring up as a plant from the earth, and righteousness from heaven hath looked forth," Ib. lxxxv. 11. Cf. St. John iii. 3, and Rom. iii. 21-25; and Ps. xxv. 10; xlv. 4; lxi. 7; xci. 4; cxix. 151; cxlvi. 6.

4. *Peace* (the Gnostic *Eirene*).—It is not only proclaimed innumerable times to Israel and Jerusalem, as in Ps. cxxii. 6; cxxv. 5; cxxviii. 6; but one of the Psalms (Ps. xxix.) which speaks most of the power of God ends with the promise that "God will bless His people with peace." It would be unnecessary and tedious to give all the passages in which this word occurs. The Prophets and the Psalms literally teem with it; but we may perhaps select a few. Of these the most important is the passage in which the future Messiah is spoken of by Isaiah as "the Prince of Peace"—a passage which, even if it be held to have no Messianic bearing, is at least decisive against the Gnostic origin of the ideas connected with the word Eirene. Ps. lxxii., again, either written by Solomon or dedicated to him, speaks of the peace which the mountains and hills afford God's people by means of righteousness (ver. 3), and tells how, in the reign of the heaven-sent King, the righteous shall flourish, and that there shall be abundance of peace as long as the moon endureth (ver. 7). In Ps. lxxxv. not only do we hear of righteousness and peace having kissed each other (cf. Rom. v. 1, remembering that

---

[1] A quotation of Exod. xxxiv. 6.

276 *The Doctrinal System of St. John.* [APP.

the verb δικαιόω signifies to make or account righteous), but in the whole passage we have Righteousness, Truth, and Peace, all mentioned in connection with a Divine work upon earth, in a manner quite in keeping with Pauline and Johannean ideas. God is to speak peace to His people, and to those who have received mercy from Him, and so they will "not turn again to folly" (ver. 8). Salvation (v. 9) is nigh, and glory. (Cf. St. Paul *passim*, and St. John viii. 50; xi. 4, 40; xii. 28; xiii. 32; xvii.) It is difficult to conceive a closer connection of ideas than that which exists between this passage and the discourses of Christ recorded in the fourth Gospel, or to find any passage which more effectually refutes the notion that its sphere of ideas is anti-Judaistic. We may, however, venture to append references to a few out of the many passages in which Moses, the Psalmist, and the Prophets, had they lived a few centuries later, would have been accused of borrowing from the Gnostics their Æon Eirene. Numb. vi. 26; xxv. 12; 1 Chron. xxii. 9; Ps. iv. 8; xxxvii. 11, 37; cxxii. 7; cxlvii. 14.; Prov. iii. 17. (In this passage wisdom is a tree of Life, and her paths peace.) Is. xxvi. 3 (here the gates are to be opened; the righteous nation which keepeth truth is to enter in, and the firm of purpose is to be kept in perfect peace. The Hebrew word for truth here means that on which we can rely; but the LXX..renders it ἀλήθεια); liv. 10, 13; lxvi. 12; Dan. x. 19; Hag. ii. 9.

5. *Righteousness* (the Gnostic *Dikaiosune*).—Here, again, it is impossible to cite a tithe of the passages which prove the Jewish origin of the idea. The words " righteous " and " righteousness " are, as it were, the backbone of the law. The revelation of a Righteous God was its one main principle, just as the main principle of the Gospel was the unfolding of a means whereby this righteousness of God could be imparted.to man. Righteousness, or justice, for the same Hebrew word is rendered indifferently by the two English ones, is predicated of God in every book of

the Old Testament. God commends the righteousness of His servants, Gen. vii. 1; xv. 6. Pharaoh is compelled to acknowledge this, Exod. ix. 27. "A God of truth and without iniquity, just and right is He," Deut. xxxii. 4. (or righteous and upright), "The righteous Lord loveth righteousness," Ps. xi. 7. Cf. Ps. xxiv. 5; xxxiii. 5; xlv. 7; xlviii. 10; lxxii. 2; lxxxv. 13, &c.; Is. xxxiii. 5; xlv. 19; liv. 17; Jer. xii. 1. " Righteous art Thou, O Lord." Cf. ix. 42; xxiii. 6; xxxiii. 16; Dan. ix. 7, 16; Micah vi. 5, &c. &c.

6. *Grace* (the Gnostic *Charis*).—Grace is poured on the lips of God's favoured one, Ps. xlv. 3. " God is a sun and a shield: He will give grace and glory," Ps. lxxxiv. 11. Wisdom is " life to the soul, and grace to the neck," Prov. iii. 22. God "giveth grace to the lowly," Ib. *v.* 34 (quoted by St. James iv. 6). Cries of " Grace, grace to it " were to accompany the bringing forth of the head or top stone by Zerubbabel in Zech. iv. 7. A spirit of grace and prayer was to be poured out upon Jerusalem, Zech. xii. 10.

7. *Fulness* (the Gnostic *Pleroma*).—" Let the sea roar and the fulness thereof," Ps. xcvi. 11; xcviii. 7; 1 Chron. xvi. 32. " The earth is the Lord's and the fulness thereof," Ps. xxiv. 1; l. 12; lxxxix. 11. We may compare also such expressions as " The Lord loveth righteousness and judgment, the earth is full of His mercy," Ps. xxxiii. 5. " The earth is full of Thy possessions," Ps. civ. 24. " The earth is full of Thy mercy," Ps. cxix. 64. " The earth is full of the knowledge of the Lord as the waters which cover the sea," Is. xi. 9. " The earth is full of His praise," Hab. iii. 3. " I," says the prophet Micah, " am filled with strength, and judgment, and power, by the Spirit of Jehovah," chap. iii. 8.[1]

Nor is the evidence of familiarity with Jewish ideas confined to the phraseology so absurdly supposed to be of Gnostic origin. It may be traced throughout the Gospel. The idea of the new birth was, we are told by the opponents of the authenticity of the Gospel, so familiar to the

---

[1] The Hebrew construction seems to imply that the Spirit of God is Himself strength, wisdom, and power. Cf. Isa. xi. 2.

Rabbins, that it is quite incredible that Nicodemus could have been so ignorant of it as the narrative in chap. iii. represents him to be. As usual, the argument is overstated. There is a considerable difference between the passage, e.g. cited by Lightfoot from the Talmud, that a proselyte is *like* a child new born, and the announcement which caused such surprise to Nicodemus; nor is there any proof that this description of a proselyte was a common one, or that it was used as early as the time of our Lord. Even if it were, Lightfoot, in his Rabbinical exercitations on the Gospel of St. John, tells us that the Rabbins never thought of applying it to Jews, and that it was the entirely unheard of idea of applying it to Jews that excited Nicodemus' surprise. But if we admit that the idea was essentially Rabbinical, it is at least clear that the contents of the fourth Gospel display a familiarity with Jewish ideas which quite forbids us to assume as a matter of course that its writer was not a Jew.

In the fourth and seventh chapters, again, Old Testament phraseology is freely used. Jesus speaks to the Samaritan woman, and to the Jews at the feast, of living water, and this of course in a spiritual sense. What language could be more redolent of the spirit of the ancient prophets? We find the idea in the prophecy of Balaam, who sees in a vision the tents of Jacob and the tabernacles of Israel spread forth as the valleys, as gardens by the riverside, as the trees of lign aloes which the Lord hath planted, as cedar trees beside the waters. " Israel shall pour the water out of his buckets, and his seed shall be in many waters " (Numb. xxiv. 5, 6, 7). The Psalmist tells us of those who, passing through the vale of weeping, make it a well, the pools of which are filled with water (Ps. lxxxiv. 6). Such a passage as this entitles us to attach a spiritual meaning to Ps. cvii. 35, " He turneth the wilderness into a standing water, and dry ground into watersprings." And there is a passage yet more apposite in Ps. xlii. 1. " As the hart panteth after the water brooks, so panteth my soul after thee, O God." In all the spiritual allusions to water in the New Testament there may be detected the Jewish idea of gratitude to Him "Who turned the rock into a standing water, and the flint into a fountain of waters," Ps. cxiv. 8. No Jew could possibly forget the outburst of praise in the prophecy of Isaiah, one of the noblest pieces of poetry to be found in any language, which has inspired our translators with a vigour rare even in their work; wherein, after describing the wilderness blossoming as the rose under the returning favour of God, and urging the faint-hearted and fearful to be of good courage, the prophet proceeds: "For in the wilderness shall waters break out and streams in the desert. And the parched ground shall become a pool, and the thirsty land springs of water," Is. xxxv. 6, 7. (With this we may compare Ps. lxiii., "My soul thirsteth for Thee, my flesh longeth for Thee in a land dry and faint, without water." And perhaps Ps. cxliii. 6; but the Hebrew word translated "thirsty," is the same as that which I have translated "faint" above, and does not seem necessarily to imply thirst; while the verb "thirsteth" is arbitrarily introduced by our translators, in the place of the verb in the former part of the sentence, which, no doubt, should be understood here.) If any further evidence be wanted of the Jewish complexion of the ideas employed by our Lord in the passages above referred to, it may be found that the very phrase "living water," which He uses, is a Hebraism for clear, springing water, and is employed in the very spiritual sense in which He employs it in more than one passage of Holy Writ. See Jer. ii. 13, "My people have committed two evils; they have forsaken Me, the fountain of living waters, and have hewed them out cisterns, broken cisterns, which can hold no water." The same idea is repeated in ch. xvii. 13, and a similar one may be found in Zech. xiv. 8. For the use of living in the sense of running water, cf. also Gen. xxvi. 19; Levit. xiv. 5, 6, 50, 51, 52; Cant. iv. 15. It is not surprising, therefore, that we find the train of thought in St. Paul's writings, as in 1 Cor. x. 4.

The idea of a spiritual meaning attached to the bread given by God from heaven is also a Jewish one. The idea is suggested in Deut. viii. 3, and was adopted by Christ in His answer to the tempter recorded by the Synoptists: "Man shall not live by bread alone, but by every word that proceedeth out of the mouth of God." The shew-bread, too, may not improbably have conveyed to the mind of a Jew his nation enjoying the favour of God and nourished with the bread of heaven, and thus compacted into the twelve loaves which, as symbolical of the twelve tribes, were offered with sweet incense before the Lord continually. And if this idea is spiritualised in Philo as it is in St. John's Gospel,[1] and the Word is repeatedly called the bread of heaven, by which God's people are fed, it does not necessarily lead to the conclusion which the author of 'Supernatural Religion' would draw from it, that St. John borrowed the idea from Philo. "This thing," says St. Paul to Agrippa, of the ministry of Christ, "was not done in a corner." Not only were the great events of the Passover and Pentecost of the year 30 A.D. enacted in the face of a multitude of Jews drawn from all parts of the civilised world, but the Apostles continued for twelve years to challenge the fullest investigation of their doctrines and statements of fact, and there is abundant evidence that they attracted no slight amount of attention.[2] And if the coincidence of phraseology between Philo and St. John regarding the Bread of Life might suggest that the latter borrowed from the former,

---

[1] "Bread is very frequently used in the Jewish writers for doctrine." —Lightfoot, 'Hebrew and Rabbinical Exercitations on St. John,' ch. vi. He gives an instance: "Feed him with bread; that is, make him take pains in the warfare of the law."

[2] "In the nature of the case, John's Gospel was published from the time of the Resurrection and Ascension, and known as far as the Christian Church extended."—Hengstenberg, 'Commentary on St. John,' Concluding Observations.

it must be remembered that he does not stop there. He goes on to say that this Bread of Life was the Flesh and Blood of Jesus, an idea which would have been, to use M. de Pressensé's expression, "appalling blasphemy" to Philo. It is, at all events, quite as possible that Philo borrowed his ideas from Jesus Christ, as that St. John borrowed his from Philo. Of course those who prefer to accept the former alternative—to *believe*, in fact, the former *doctrine*—are at liberty to do so, but they cannot present their conjectures to the world as verified facts without a great deal more evidence than as yet they have been enabled to produce.

Two more instances of the strongly-marked Jewish character of this Gospel, which impressed itself upon so unprejudiced and qualified a critic as the late Professor Ewald, will conclude these remarks. The first is the description of Christ as the Good Shepherd, which is not only especially characteristic of St. John, as the repetition of the figure in the twenty-first chapter reminds us, but of the Old Testament also. Few of us can have forgotten the exquisite passage in Isaiah, the deep and touching tenderness of which inspired Handel with one of his sweetest melodies: "He shall feed His flock like a shepherd. He shall gather the lambs with His arms and carry them in His bosom, and shall gently lead those that are with young." Nor is the equally touching Ps. xxiii. one whit more likely to be forgotten: "The Lord is my shepherd; I shall not want: He shall feed me in a green pasture, and lead me forth beside the waters of comfort." The same idea is repeated in Jeremiah xxxi. 10. But the evidence of a Jewish turn of thought in this passage is made yet stronger by the fact that in the announcement "I am the Good Shepherd," Jesus is declaring the fulfilment of a prophecy. Ezekiel twice—in ch. xxxiv. 23, and in ch. xxxvii. 24—foretells the coming of Christ as David, the servant of God, the "one shepherd" who shall feed the sheep, and also be a prince and a king amongst them. The words "there shall be one flock and one shepherd," are an actual quotation from these chapters, from which the whole tone and colouring of the discourse of our Lord of which we are speaking are derived. Had the writer of the fourth Gospel been either slightly acquainted with, or decidedly hostile to, the views and writings of the Jews, he would either have avoided such a coincidence of thought altogether, or have called special attention to the prophecy to which he was alluding. The passage suits best with the ordinary belief that St. John's Gospel is a faithful record of the words of One who, Himself " of the seed of David according to the flesh," is speaking to men thoroughly acquainted with the Jewish Scriptures, and using language familiar from infancy to their minds.

No other conclusion can be drawn from the parable of the vine and the branches. It is entirely Hebraistic in spirit. The vine that was " brought out of Egypt," and planted in a new land whence the heathen had been cast out, was the well-known description by Asaph of the Jewish Church, and its continual recitation formed a part of the worship of the chosen people. Consequently, the same figure recurs frequently in the writings of the prophets. The fifth chapter of the prophecy of Isaiah invests the old theme with beauties all his own, as he pathetically laments that when it should have brought forth grapes it brought forth wild grapes. Jeremiah again (ch. ii. 21) gives the figure a new turn when he puts the complaint into the mouth of Jehovah that He had planted Israel a noble vine, but it had degenerated and become strange to Him. Ezekiel (ch. xvii.) less poetically, but with an individuality strongly marked, treats the same idea with the same application ; while in Hosea we meet with an inversion of the conception approximating yet more closely to the passage in St. John's Gospel : " Israel is an empty vine, he bringeth forth fruit unto himself " (Hosea x. 1). The idea of a man's actions being regarded as fruit acceptable or unacceptable to God is essentially Jewish. The Synoptic Gospels introduced it in the cursing of the barren fig-tree, in the parable of the vineyard, and in many other passages. It perpetually comes before us in the Epistles. And the prominent place which it occupies in the fourth Gospel is only an additional proof how strongly that Gospel is permeated with Jewish ideas. A few instances from the Old Testament may suffice—the more familiar the better. Every one knows the description of the good man in the first Psalm, that "he shall be like a tree that is planted by the water-side, that bringeth forth his fruit in due season." Jeremiah's vision (ch. xxiv.) of the good and bad figs will at once occur to the mind of every habitual reader of the Scriptures. Isaiah prophesies that "Israel shall blossom and bud and fill the face of the world with fruit." Hosea tells how Israel shall "grow as the lily and cast forth his roots like Lebanon;" how "his branches shall spread, and his beauty be as the olive tree;" how he shall "revive as the corn, and grow as the vine;" while Amos laments that "judgment is turned into gall and the fruit of righteousness into hemlock;" and Micah bewails a land which is desolate "for the fruit of her doings." And to meet these abundant evidences of the Jewish cast of thought so predominant in the fourth Gospel, we are treated to a few instances where it is said that its author displayed his ignorance of Jewish customs and names, though it appears extremely doubtful whether the ignorance be not that of the objector,[1]

[1] 'Supernatural Religion,' vol. ii., pp. 417–431. The most remarkable part of this passage is that in which the author corrects St. John's derivation of Siloam. It really means, we are told, "a spring, a fountain, a flow of water." But the author omits to add, what is known to every tyro in the Hebrew language, that it comes to have this signification by being derived from the word שלח, *he sent*, inasmuch as waters are sent forth from their source. The best authorities, ancient and modern, agree in this derivation, the only dispute being whether the word can have a passive signification or not. It cannot therefore be set aside on the *ipse dixit* of a writer who seems to have studied in a school, not of genuine criticism, but of foregone conclusions.

and are told that no Jew, writing for Gentiles in a distant country, would speak of the Passover as a feast of the Jews, or of a dispute between John's disciples and an objector as one between a Jew and the followers of the Baptist.[1] Is it *quite* certain that a Hindoo, writing in English for the benefit of Englishmen, would not speak of Suttee as a Hindoo custom, or refer to a controversy between the adherents of the Brahma Samâj and their opponents of the older faith of Hindostan as a dispute between the disciples of Keshub Chunder Sen and a Hindoo?

[1] Mr. M. Arnold in the 'Contemporary Review' for May 1875. Mr. Arnold somewhat unfairly suppresses the fact that there is a various reading, "Jews" for "a Jew," which is not altogether unsupported.

APPENDIX V.

ON THE LAST SUPPER.

WHILE these sheets were passing through the press, my attention was attracted by an assertion in a letter in the *Guardian* relative to Jewish customs, to the effect that the Jews had a practice, since their dispersion, of adding an alternative day to the ordinary one of the Paschal celebration, lest by any misreckoning the dispersed Jews should be disturbed by scruples on account of having kept the Passover in an irregular manner. I find from Jewish authorities that this statement is substantially correct. The custom arose shortly before the destruction of the second temple, when the Sanhedrim, fearing that the Jews might, in consequence of their distance from Palestine, keep the feasts a day too early or too late, added a second day on which they might be kept. This arrangement, however, did not extend to the fasts. In earlier times fire-beacons were used to flash from hill to hill the news that the Paschal moon had risen.

It is obvious that this fact will serve to explain the apparent discrepancy between St. John and the Synoptists concerning the Paschal Supper. If the idea of an alternative day for the celebration of the Passover were familiar to the Jews of our Lord's time, the keeping of an anticipatory Passover by our Lord would have been fully understood by the disciples, who were already well aware that circumstances were to be expected which might prevent the day itself from being observed by Christ in their company. This custom of an alternative day for the Paschal celebration disposes of the argument of Dean Alford, in which he dismisses such a supposition as "wholly unprecedented and irregular, in a matter so strictly laid down by the law." ('Commentary on St. Matt.,' ch. xxvi.)

This custom seems to be very little known, at least among Christians. The author of the article on the Passover in Smith's 'Dictionary of the Bible' is obviously unaware of it. I can find no allusion to it in the Mischna, nor in the Commentary of Surenhusius. Basnage, in his elaborate history of the Jews, does not mention it: nor is it to be found in the pages of Lightfoot, who entirely rejects the explanation that our Lord ate a passover by anticipation, on the authority of Maimonides. An account of it may, however, be found in Jost, 'Geschichte des Judenthums,' part 3, pp. 188, 189, and it is a well-known fact among the Jews.

This mode of accounting for the discrepancy between the Evangelists does not, however, tell us whether the alternative day could properly be observed by Jews when in Jerusalem, nor does it clear up the difficulty about the slaying of the lamb, which, according to tradition, must be slain in the Temple. See Lightfoot, Surenhusius, Basnage, &c.

APPENDIX VI.

SUPPLEMENTARY OBSERVATIONS.

I FIND that I have omitted to notice the recognition of Christ's Godhead by St. Thomas contained in the twentieth chapter of St. John. The omission does not affect the argument much, except that it might be said that I have intentionally attempted to extenuate the testimony of St. John to our Lord's Divinity, in order to place his doctrine more on a level with that of the other Evangelists. On the other hand, I might have observed how absolute is the claim of Jesus Christ to forgive sins in St. Luke vii. 40, *sqq.* He had forgiven the sins of the penitent, therefore she loved Him much, and displayed a love to His person far exceeding that of those who presumed that in their case He had little or nothing to forgive. There is no hint of any delegated authority, nor is there any instance in Scripture where Jesus makes so direct a claim to the power of remitting sins on His own sole authority, as in this one. Yet that this was a Divine attribute is fully recognized by the Jews, who naturally ask, " Who can forgive sins but God alone ?" See St. Mark ii. 7, and St. Luke v. 21. I might also have strengthened my argument in part ii. chap. iii., by remarking how purely elementary the teaching of the fourth Gospel is on the subject of the death of Christ. There is no hint there of its being a propitiatory Sacrifice, such as we find in the Epistles of St. John, St. Peter, and St. Paul, nor of its effecting a ransom, as in the Gospel of St. Matthew. The vague, detached hints of the "lifting up" of the Son of Man, of its "drawing all men unto Him," of its being in some mysterious manner a source of healing, as was the lifting up of the serpent in the wilderness, of His laying down His Life for His friends—are all we find, and they surely fit in better with the hypothesis that they are the spoken words of Jesus Christ, than that they were invented and ascribed to Him after the theory of Propitiation had been taught in the Apostolic Church, and had obtained a full expression in the elaborate treatise on that subject addressed to the Hebrews.

www.ingramcontent.com/pod-product-compliance
Lightning Source LLC
Chambersburg PA
CBHW030817230426
43667CB00008B/1258